C000076394

MATTHEW'S MESSIAH

MATTHEW'S Messiah

A
Guide to
Matthew's
Gospel

A.W. Wilson

JOHN RITCHIE LTD
CHRISTIAN PUBLICATIONS

40 Beansburn, Kilmarnock, Scotland

ISBN 1 904064 08 6

First published, 2000. Second Revised Edition, 2002
Copyright © A.W. Wilson, 2000

Apart from the author's own occasional translations and the occasional
use of the KJV, all other Scripture quotations are from the New King
James Version, copyright 1979, 1980, 1982, 1992, by Thomas Nelson,
Inc. Publishers.

All rights reserved. No part of this publication may be reproduced, stored in a retrievable
system, or transmitted in any form or by any other means – electronic, mechanical,
photocopy, recording or otherwise – without prior permission of the copyright owner.

Typeset by John Ritchie Ltd., Kilmarnock
Printed by Bell & Bain Ltd., Glasgow

Acknowledgements

*A*mongst the many who have specially helped in the writing of this book, I particularly mention Mr. Sam Jennings, Mr. John Riddle, and my father, Dr. Raymond Wilson. Their helpful suggestions, considered criticism and, most of all, their Christ-like encouragement (Matthew 12:20) have all made an enormous difference in the final form of the book. To the past and present members of the Bible Class in my local Church, to whom I promised nearly ten years ago that I would write an essay on a book in the New Testament along with them, I offer my overdue contribution. Lastly, I thank my wife, Gillian, for her love, support, help and prayers during the entire process of publishing this book.

Contents

Foreword   9

Introduction   A Puzzling Genealogy   11

Chapter 1   Matthew and His Gospel   26
              (Outline of Matthew's Gospel)   50

Chapter 2   Christ's Beginnings   (1:1 - 4:25)   55

Chapter 3   Excursus: The Kingdom of Heaven   64

Chapter 4   Christ's Teachings   (5:1 - 7:29)   84

Chapter 5   Christ's Miracles   (8:1 - 9:34)   97

Chapter 6   Christ's Preaching   (9:35 - 12:50)   108

Chapter 7   Christ's Parables   (13:1 - 13:52)   118

Chapter 8   Christ's Kingdom and Israel   (13:53 - 16:12)   126

Chapter 9   Christ's Secrets   (16:13 - 18:35)   139

Chapter 10   Christ and Life   (19:1 - 21:11)   153

Chapter 11   Christ and Religion   (21:12 - 23:39)   166

Chapter 12   Christ and the Future   (24:1 - 25:46)   182

Chapter 13   Christ's Betrayal   (26:1 - 26:75)   217

Chapter 14   Christ's Death and Resurrection (27:1 - 28:20)   226

Appendix   Matthew's Messianic Prophecies   236

Foreword

*B*elievers throughout the Christian era have always been attracted to the Gospels, especially those who derive their pleasure from the pursuit of Holy Scripture. To read and meditate upon the Unique and Beloved Son of God manifested in wondrous grace and wisdom is certainly the food of the Lord's people. This is truly partaking of the Manna and eating the Old Corn of the Land.

All such believers are indebted to whoever it was in perusal of the Gospel records discovered the delightful four-fold portrayal of the Lord as presented in each Gospel. J.N. Darby is credited with this illumination, but whether this is so or not, at least he was instrumental in the hands of the Spirit to develop this helpful line of teaching. Matthew is seen as the Gospel of the King while Mark depicts the Lowly Servant. Luke sets before us the Perfect Man and John develops the Son of God.

Many are the books that are written on the Gospels and most if not all will weave the different portraits of Christ into their pages. Books and commentaries on the Gospels, while numerous, still leave room for more. Therefore a new book with a fresh approach to the Gospels is always welcomed by the Lord's people.

Now by the goodness of our God another book on the Gospel of Matthew is in our hands. Andrew Wilson has put much labour and thought into the preparation of *Matthew's Messiah* and how glorious that another presentation of the King is given to us in these days of the King's rejection. Andrew, while aware of the usual divisions of Matthew's Gospel, has departed from these. His unique division takes in every discourse of the Lord, every miracle and every narrative and he weaves them all together in a most interesting and instructive way. Any saint who loves the Lord will be thrilled with the harmonious presentation of the King in these pages. This is not a simple record but in places most profound, however simple delightful passages occur throughout that will thrill even the youngest of believers.

This is a book worthy of a place on your bookshelf and to be often used in study. Again, much profit is to be obtained by just carefully reading it through. It is bound to do you good.

Samuel W. Jennings

Introduction - A Puzzling Genealogy

O ne of the most pleasant memories of my childhood is of holidays to Ireland. We had to catch a Jumbo Jet, visit lots of nice people and eat lots of lovely cakes. However, nothing about a trip to Ireland annoyed my brothers, sister and I as much as having to stop at some country churchyard while Dad wandered through the headstones searching for the graves of our ancestors. Children denied decent weather and cooped up in the back of a small rented car could not understand what an older generation found so fascinating about a family tree – let alone a graveyard on a drizzly day.

Older people seem to develop an interest in the past. For many younger people, however, the past is of little importance. The world is changing so rapidly that society almost scorns people who are always looking back and refuse to get up to speed with a changing future.

And so I suppose some readers might at this point be feeling rather tempted to skip this introductory chapter about the Genealogy of Christ in Matthew's Gospel. In fact, I suspect that most Christians would probably admit to having been tempted at some time in their usual reading of the Bible to just skip Matthew's Genealogy. After all, it is just a list of names, most of which we find rather hard to pronounce quickly (if at all) and many of which mean nothing to us. We might not say it out loud, but perhaps in our hearts we don't really think that God has anything much to say to us from Matthew's Genealogy.

And that is where we make our mistake. Matthew's Genealogy deserves careful reading. It is no coincidence that God has placed it at the very doorway to the Gospel. The key to unlock the whole book hangs right here. Let us take a closer look at it for a moment.

A Strange Genealogy

First of all, we must notice that it is *not* just a list of names. Christ's Genealogy in Luke 3 is just a list of names. Matthew, however, adds little bits of information every now and again. For example, in verse

2 we read 'Abraham begot Isaac, Isaac begot Jacob, and Jacob begot Judah *and his brothers*'. Now, why is there this little note added about Judah's brothers? Why wasn't Esau mentioned if Matthew was interested in telling us all about which of Christ's ancestors had brothers? Then again, in v6 we read 'and Jesse begot David *the King*'. There are plenty of Kings in this genealogy. Why is only David called 'the King'? Then again, in v11 we read 'Josiah begot Jeconiah *and his brothers about the time they were carried away to Babylon*'. Why does Matthew add this little rider about the carrying away to Babylon here? Why is this important?

Even more significantly, why does Matthew specially mention certain women in this list of names? He mentions five in all if we include Mary. No doubt there are some women who might feel aggrieved that more of Christ's female ancestors were not mentioned. After all, they played no small part in Christ's descent. Why does Matthew only mention these five? And why does he not mention women like Sarah and Rebecca – women of faith – instead of a woman like Tamar who stooped to prostitution?

Then, even stranger than the occasional little note that Matthew throws in are the omissions. If we compare the genealogy with Luke's again, we find that Luke's has about fourteen more names in the genealogy from Abraham to Christ than does Matthew. Matthew has left out four of the Kings and about ten of Christ's ancestors after the Babylonian captivity. Is not the overriding requirement of any Genealogy absolute accuracy?

Matthew's Genealogy has some strange and puzzling features. Why does it emphasise certain people and incidents in the long history of Christ's ancestors but pass over other names that we count more important without the slightest comment? And why does he omit some ancestors altogether?

Some Method in Matthew's Madness

I suggest the reasons for these seemingly strange features in the Genealogy can only be understood once we stand back a little and look at a slightly bigger picture. That is, we have to notice the incidents that follow on straight after the Genealogy. Now let us look very briefly at what I am going to call the first great section of Matthew's Gospel. It consists of

1. The Genealogy: 1:1 - 1:17
2. Christ's Birth: 1:18 - 1:25
3. The Visit of the Wise Men: 2:1 - 2:12
4. The Flight to Egypt: 2:13 - 2:15
5. The Slaughter of the Infants: 2:16 - 2:18
6. The Return to Nazareth: 2:19 - 2:23
7. John's Baptism: 3:1 - 3:12
8. Christ's Baptism: 3:13 - 3:17
9. Christ's Temptation: 4:1 - 4:11
10. The Commencement of Christ's Ministry in Capernaum: 4:12-4:17
11. The Call of the four Fishermen: 4:18 - 4:22
12. Christ's Galilean Ministry: 4:22 - 4:25

Now this first section of Matthew's Gospel deals with one general theme, the theme of "Beginnings". It concentrates on the details of Christ's birth and the beginnings of His ministry. We shall look at it in more detail later on in the book. For the moment, though, we shall concern ourselves with the part that the Genealogy plays in this section. It obviously has an important part to play in any consideration of Christ's beginnings – it tells us where he came from ancestrally.

The Four Women

Without a doubt the most prominent feature that stands out in the Genealogy is the four women it mentions, excluding Mary for now. They are Tamar, Rahab, Ruth and Bathsheba. Now what do these women have in common? These women are linked together by the part they played in the Old Testament by their marital (and extra-marital) activities. Three of them are notorious for either being prostitutes or for their adultery. The other one, Ruth, is famous because of how she got married.

The Genealogy thus subtly reminds us of the sins of Judah with Tamar (Matthew 1:3) and then of David with 'her who had been the wife of Uriah' (1:6). What more sickening incidents in all of Scripture could we be reminded of? They make us shudder and wince when we have to read them. We would nearly prefer to skip over the chapters concerning those events. Why did Matthew have to remind us of them in His Genealogy? Why couldn't he have reminded us of some of the more positive qualities of men like David?

He could have mentioned some of the more faithful and loving relationships in the Genealogy – like Isaac and Rebekah. Instead he took us back to these incidents.

The reason is not far away. We only have to keep reading the rest of Matthew Chapter 1 and we are again brought up against a matter that is both moral and marital. What is the very first story in Matthew's Gospel all about? It is the story of the birth of Christ. What is the central point Matthew is trying to bring out in that story? Precisely the fact that there was **no moral or marital sin** involved in it.

It is as though the Genealogy of Christ is the background in a large painting. The subject in the centre of the canvas that the artist wishes us to focus our eyes upon is the birth of Christ. He wants us to notice that there was no fornication or extra-marital sin in the birth of Christ. He tells us that Joseph thought that Mary's child was born of fornication and he was about to divorce her. However, the angel of the Lord appeared to him in a dream and said that there was no sin involved in the birth – 'that which is conceived in her is of the Holy Spirit'. So how does Matthew highlight the holiness of Christ's birth? By painting it on an extremely dark and dirty background. As our eyes scan the background we notice all these little figures (mentioned in the Genealogy) in the distance. Looking more carefully, we pick out in the darkness David and Bathsheba and Judah and Tamar and, with a nearly nauseating revulsion our eyes move from the darkness of the background to the light and beauty of the principal subject – Christ. Matthew in the Genealogy is trying to heighten our sensitivity to sexual immorality so that when we come to Christ's birth immediately after the Genealogy we will have consciences ready to make a contrast. Matthew is using the Genealogy to contrast the sinlessness of Christ's birth with the stain His ancestors left upon the page of Scripture.

Matthew is also hinting that early Jewish Christians were acutely aware of the reality of immorality and did not accept the Virgin Birth out of some primitive, superstitious ignorance but, like Joseph, after careful thought.

But then in the background of the painting we notice the two other female figures alongside their husbands in the distance. They are Rahab and Ruth (1:5). Why does Matthew emphasise their forms in the backdrop? Well, remember that both of these two women were foreigners. Rahab was a

Canaanite (and a harlot as well) and Ruth was a Moabite. Yet they both chose to leave their own people behind to live amongst God's people. This was a very serious decision to make. How would they handle living amongst the most xenophobic race on earth? Who would marry them? How would they survive as single women? And now we notice alongside them in the background two noble men – Salmon and Boaz, descendants of the most famous family in the tribe of Judah. And what did their nobility chiefly consist in? It consisted in these two men being prepared to marry foreigners – women who were of low reputation in the eyes of men (although in God's sight these were no ordinary women).

So why does Matthew emphasise these two couples – Salmon with Rahab and Boaz with Ruth? Because as we turn our eyes back to the main subject again, we not only notice Mary's innocence of any immoral behaviour, but we also notice the part Joseph played in Christ's birth. Matthew, in fact, focuses more attention on Joseph's behaviour than Mary's in the narrative of Christ's birth. He shows Joseph's moral integrity in being initially prepared to put away Mary. Joseph was not the sort to tolerate immorality. But then he also shows Joseph's nobility in marrying Mary although she was with child not by him and knowing he would have to cope thereafter with the slur of fornication. In taking this noble step he was rewarded by God with the honour of being the legal father, guardian and protector of the Messiah. But it must have cost him his reputation. What a man! Thus, Matthew uses the reminder of these two noble men from Christ's ancestry to highlight Joseph's nobility.

The Omissions

Just as Matthew has drawn our attention to four women in Christ's ancestry, so too we must notice that four Kings are conspicuous by their absence. Why does Matthew omit Ahaziah, Joash, Amaziah and Jehoiakim? If we have noticed that the women are emphasised for their marital activities, we would expect Kings to be emphasised for their political activities. And Chapter 2 of Matthew's Gospel majors on the political intrigues that surrounded Christ's birth. There Matthew introduces to us another King – Herod.

Now, Herod shares some important characteristics with these kings that Matthew omits from the Genealogy. Firstly, we must concentrate on the first three kings: Ahaziah, Joash and Amaziah. How are they related to Herod?

By another slightly more obscure woman, *Athaliah*, herself another *omitted Monarch* over Judah. Look at the family tree below:

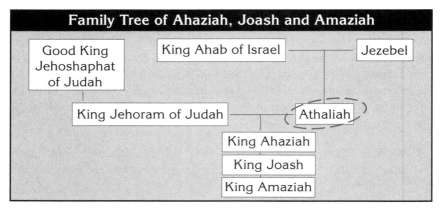

These three Kings were the son, grandson and great-grandson of the wicked queen Athaliah (circled above). King Jehoshaphat erred greatly when he married his son Jehoram (Joram in Matthew 1) into the family of Ahab and Jezebel. Their daughter Athaliah turned out as despicable a woman as Jezebel her mother. Look what she did as Queen.

First of all, her husband Jehoram killed all his brothers once he became King to remove any possible political threat from them. Athaliah's influence seems to have been behind this (see 2 Chronicles 21:6). God seems to have punished Jehoram and Athaliah for this by having all their children except the youngest (Ahaziah) slaughtered by invading Arabians (2 Chronicles 21:16-17 and 22:1). After her husband's death, Athaliah seems to have had great influence over her son Ahaziah. Three times we are told that he followed the counsel of his mother and the house of Ahab (2 Chronicles 22:2-5). After Ahaziah's death, Athaliah tried to exterminate the royal seed of the house of David – even though they were her own grandchildren! She killed all of Ahaziah's children except the youngest (Joash) who was hidden from her. Athaliah, having this second time tried to remove all political opponents, then assumed power herself and ruled for six years.

Now, does this pattern of bloodthirsty political purges of any opposition remind you of anyone in Matthew's Gospel's opening pages? Does a foreign impostor on the throne remind you of anyone in Matthew Chapter 2? The similarities to Herod are too overwhelming to escape comparison. Herod was not a Jew – he was an Edomite. He should never have been on the throne of Judah. Moses' Law forbade the taking of a foreign King. When Jesus, the Messiah and true King of the Jews, was born, lo and behold, there was already someone on His throne, a foreign impostor! How like Athaliah. And like Athaliah, Herod tried to destroy the royal seed and exterminate all political opposition. And as in the case of Joash, God intervened to protect the infant Jesus from the intentions of King Herod.

But why does Matthew omit the son, grandson and great-grandson of this woman? Surely they were not accountable for her evils. Let us first notice that God had cursed Ahab's descendants to complete destruction through Elijah in 1 Kings 21:17-29, just as God promised the utter destruction of the Edomites, Herod's nation, in the prophecy of Obadiah. God declares that He visits the iniquity of the fathers upon the children to the ***third and fourth generations*** of those who hate Him (Exodus 20:5, Exodus 34:7, Numbers 14:18 and Deuteronomy 5:9). Eventually each of these three Kings were assassinated. God would not forget their evil ancestors. It was going to take a while to flush Athaliah's influence out of the line of the Kings. Notice that Amaziah tried to conquer Israel, possibly thinking that as a descendant of Ahab he had the right to the thrones of both Israel and Judah (2 Chronicles 25). There was still some Athaliah in him! It is not until the fourth generation that God allows another King to be listed in Matthew's Genealogy. Athaliah, the ***sixth woman*** of Matthew's Genealogy, is omitted along with her three descendants because she should never have sat on David's throne. Nor should her three descendants, ideally. Nor should the dynasty of a Herod have ruled in Israel.

Jehoiakim the son of Josiah, the fourth King omitted from the Genealogy, shares a different characteristic with Herod. He is the king who called for Jeremiah's scroll to be brought before him, and then as it was read out to him he cut it with his penknife and threw its pages into the fire (see Jeremiah 36). Herod had a similar attitude to God's word. He called for it to be consulted (pretending, like Jehoiakim, to be God-fearing) but his real aim was (like Jehoiakim) to destroy anything that might undermine his throne. God does not allow such an attitude to His Word to go unnoticed. He deliberately omits the name of such a man of the list of the kings. It hardly needs stating what God's attitude was to Herod. There is maybe a lesson in that, too, for those who would approach the Gospel of Matthew with a similar intention of abusing it.

Thus Matthew sees fit to omit these four kings on the grounds that they descended from murderous foreigners who ruled over the land and because of their attitude to God's Word.

One more omission remains. Why does Matthew omit the names of ten of Christ's ancestors after the Babylonian captivity? Permit a suggestion. When we come to the end of Matthew 2 we find a great jump in the record. We learn nothing about Christ (in Matthew's Gospel, anyway) from His early childhood escape from Herod until nearly thirty years later when, in Chapter 3, John the Baptist comes onto the scene. Many people have wondered about those silent years. Some have even invented stories about the child Jesus. But God has shone little light upon those quiet years.

Do those years not remind you of any period of Israel's history? Do they not remind you of those 400 years in between the Old and New Testaments in which God was silent? He sent no prophets. There were no books of the Bible written. There were no great Biblical heroes. The names in this period in Matthew's list mean nothing to us. We do not know these men – although God does. And the ten or more names that Matthew must have omitted seem to correspond to God's veiling in obscurity not only these years Biblically but also the years of Christ's development toward manhood. The inter-testamental years were a period of waiting until the Messiah would come. And so it was in the silent years of Christ's youth.

The Carrying-Away

Finally, what shall we make of the emphasis that Matthew places upon the carrying away to Babylon in v11? Here we need to consult the Greek to establish exactly the term that Matthew uses. When he says 'they were carried away' he is literally in the Greek saying 'they moved (house)'. This again rings bells in our minds. For this is exactly what happened to Christ as a child. He moved to Egypt and then to Nazareth – so Matthew tells us as he proceeds through the rest of this first section. In fact, Matthew spends a good part of the first great section of the Gospel telling us of the moves that Christ made – first to Egypt, then to Nazareth, then from Galilee to John at the Jordan and then later back to Galilee to Capernaum. Why does Matthew tell us of all of Christ's childhood 'moves'?

The reason is obvious once we put ourselves in the position of a Jew living at the time of Christ. The Jews were on the tiptoe of expectancy for God to send the Messiah to deliver them. How would they know Him? Easy, first of all, He would have to come from Bethlehem. Well, Jesus came from Bethlehem, didn't He? Most people living in Christ's day would have said that He was Jesus of Nazareth, not Jesus of Bethlehem. They would have considered Jesus a fraud. No good thing – let alone a Messiah – came out of Nazareth. Actually, says Matthew, Christ *was* from Bethlehem. However, His family moved a number of times during childhood, eventually settling in Nazareth.

Moreover, the 'moves' that Christ made were very similar to some of the 'moves' that some of Christ's ancestors made. Remind yourself, for a moment, of the circumstances under which Jeconiah and his brothers 'moved' to Babylon. You will no doubt remember that Jeconiah was the second last king of Judah – Zedekiah was the last. Zedekiah came to a rather unhappy end – all his sons were slain before his eyes after the fall of Jerusalem, then his eyes were put out and he was sent to Babylon. But before Jerusalem was destroyed, God saw fit to have the second-last king, Jeconiah, taken captive to Babylon where his life was preserved and the royal line was able to continue. What had seemed bad for Jeconiah turned out in the end to be for the preservation and salvation of the royal house of David. So it is in Matthew's Gospel. Before Herod destroyed the infants of Bethlehem God directed Joseph to move to Egypt with the Child and His mother where His life was preserved[1].

---

[1] This is the reason, by the way, for the little note that Matthew adds in Chapter 2:18 about the prophecy of Jeremiah (Jeremiah 31:15). Matthew quotes Jeremiah's description of 'Rachel weeping for her children' as being fulfilled in the slaughter of these infants. Now, at first this little quote from Jeremiah (if you look him up and observe the context) seems to have absolutely nothing to do with a prophecy about Christ. It makes Matthew look slightly mad! Jeremiah does not seem to be prophesying about Christ at all. But when we realise the background of Jeremiah's quote we quickly see a connection. Jeremiah was the prophet who wrote at the time of the Babylonian captivity. In chapters 30 and 31 he writes of the trauma of God's punishment upon the nation (and graphically describes it by speaking of Rachel, who was buried near Bethlehem, weeping over all her slain children). But he also speaks in these chapters of the certainty of the return of her children. In the very next verses (Jeremiah 31:16-17) we read 'refrain your voice from weeping, and your eyes from tears; for your work shall be rewarded, says the Lord, and they shall come back from the land of the enemy. There is hope in your future, says the Lord, that your children shall come back to their own border'. Why was there hope? Because God had 'moved' Jeconiah away before the end and one day his seed would come back. So too, God preserved Christ by moving him to Egypt and he too would return.

This, I suggest, is the reason for the little note about Judah and his brothers too. Doesn't the expression 'Judah and his brothers' ring some bells in your mind? If you have been reading in the book of Genesis lately it should (see Genesis 37:26 & 44:14). The expression 'Judah and his brothers' only occurs elsewhere in the Bible in the story of Joseph's 'move' to Egypt and the subsequent preservation that God effected through it. Judah was the prime mover in that bad business and he was the one who had to fix it up in the end as well. Remember how Joseph responded to the brothers' plea for mercy at the end of Genesis, thinking that Jacob being dead, Joseph might try to get some revenge on them. Joseph said 'you meant evil against me but God meant it for good, in order to bring it about as it is this day, to save many people alive' (Genesis 50:20). Joseph saw in his 'move' to Egypt (by being sold as a slave by his brothers) God's plan for the survival of his family. Christ's 'move' to Egypt was exactly the same.

You see, to the ordinary Jew of Christ's time it was bad enough to hear that the Messiah came from Nazareth, but to hear that the Messiah had come from Egypt was almost heresy. So Matthew goes to great lengths to justify Christ's move to Egypt by reminding us (in the Genealogy) that God had preserved the nation of Israel by 'moving' them to Egypt and Babylon too. So here again we see another clear connection between the Genealogy and the narratives that follow it.

We have thus seen that a connection between the Genealogy and the rest of the first section of the Gospel provides an acceptable reason for many of the special features we observe in the Genealogy. Let us conclude this chapter by noticing two lessons that the Genealogy teaches us about Matthew's Gospel as a whole.

Matthew is Selective

Firstly, in his Genealogy Matthew is deliberately being very selective in who and what he makes little notes about. And it is just the same in his Gospel as a whole. Matthew in his Gospel does not tell us **everything** that he knows about Christ's life. Instead Matthew carefully selects and emphasises certain incidents in Christ's life so that we learn important lessons from them. In the process, he also has to omit much that is not essential to his purpose.

John, at the end of his gospel makes precisely this point about having been very selective about what he has told us. He says 'there are also many other things that Jesus did which if they were written one by one, I suppose that even the world itself could not contain the books that would be written'. In other words, John is stating that he has had to carefully select just a few incidents for inclusion in his gospel. All of the Gospels are like this. They emphasise what is important and omit what is unnecessary to the point they are making.

Matthew is Arranged in Groups of Incidents

Matthew has another reason for the omission of names from the Genealogy. Notice what Matthew says after his genealogy in verse 17. He says 'So all the generations from Abraham to David are fourteen generations, from David until the captivity in Babylon are fourteen generations and from the captivity in Babylon until the Christ are fourteen generations'. Matthew is calling our attention to what seems to him a very important (and maybe the most important) thing in the Genealogy. He is giving us a clue as to why he has made his omissions. It is in order, so he tells us, that the genealogy might fit into an arrangement, a pattern – *three groups* of fourteen names. He has had to do some editing to make it fit this pattern and he makes sure to tell us so at the end of it. Why?

The reason is of great importance. I suggest it is because Matthew is again giving us a hint as to how he is going to write his Gospel. Matthew's whole Gospel is arranged very carefully, just like the names in this Genealogy. Matthew's Gospel might at first appear a long unbroken narrative. However, it is not. Rather, it consists of lots of little incidents all strung together one after another – narratives of miracles, important events, sermons and conversations. Even in the most narrative-like sections of the gospel (for example, the accounts of the betrayal, trial, crucifixion and resurrection of Christ) we do not get a detailed, minute-by-minute account of *everything* that happened. Rather, certain little events are picked out and emphasised.

For example, of the seven sayings of Christ from the Cross, John mentions only three, Luke mentions only three (and they are completely different ones) while Matthew and Mark both mention only one. Again, Matthew and Mark's saying is not found in either Luke or John. Different gospel writers therefore focus on different sayings of Christ upon the Cross. And so it is throughout the Gospels as a whole. The writers pick out and emphasise the different little incidents which suit their purpose. They do not all report exactly the same events.

Matthew's Gospel is a collection of incidents from Christ's life. How then are these incidents arranged? Firstly, bear in mind that the original writers did not put our chapters and verses there. Chapter divisions were included in the Bible after AD 1205 and verses after AD 1551. God did not put chapters and verses there. These are simply artificial divisions added to help us find things quickly in our Bibles.

I suggest that the incidents we find in Matthew's Gospel are arranged in *groups*. We have seen this from the way Matthew has 'grouped' the Genealogy with the Birth Narratives in Matthew Chapters 1 to 4. Most of the incidents in a given group occurred at about the same stage in the life of Christ. However, this is not the main reason they are all put in the same group.

Matthew's Gospel is not arranged chronologically, although that is perhaps the way we would initially expect it to be written. Sometimes some of the other gospels depart from a chronological order of events, too. We shall verify this in the next chapter. The reason why we have different events next to each other in the Gospels is not simply because one event happened the day after the first – as if there were no other connection between the two events. The reason certain incidents are grouped together is that they have certain things in common with each other – for example, they teach us a similar truth about Christ or about how we should follow Him.

Luke also in his Gospel specially mentions the fact that he has taken care to arrange the events in his Gospel very carefully. In his prologue in Luke 1:1-4 he twice uses the idea encapsulated in the word '*order*'. He says: 'Inasmuch as many have taken in hand to *set in order* a narrative of those things which are fully believed among us, just as those who from the beginning were eyewitnesses and ministers of the word delivered them to us, it seemed good to me also, having had perfect understanding of all things from the very first, to write to you *an orderly account*, most excellent Theophilus, that you may know the certainty of those things in which you were instructed'.

Why Should We Pay Attention to Arrangement in Matthew's Gospel?

Why should Matthew's Gospel show order in its arrangement (assuming for the moment that it does)? Because it is from God. Just as God intends us to see His handiwork in the perfection of Creation (as the first half of Psalm 19 tells us), so He also wants us to see the traces of His genius in Scripture (as the second half of Psalm 19 tells us). We see that He is the Author of Scripture, says the Psalmist, because 'the law of the Lord is *perfect*' (Psalm 19:7). He is the God of Order. Matthew's Gospel is not a higgledy-piggledy hotchpotch written by some Mr. Muddle (if you remember your Enid Blyton days). Sadly, that is what you will read a lot of modern books saying about Matthew's Gospel – and the other Gospels too (in much more professional academic language, of course). No, we shall see that Matthew's Gospel is a literary masterpiece of such monumental proportions that it is worthy only of the genius of God.

But someone will say, Even if there is this arrangement that can be seen in the Gospel, isn't it more important that we spend our time simply reading, believing and obeying the message of the Gospel rather than analysing it as literature? The answer to that question is, Of course it is. But that does not remove the question: Why then has God put all this careful arrangement into Matthew's Gospel? The answer to that question is that God has arranged the gospel in this way so that we will understand all the more quickly the lessons that we are being taught from it.

The Parable of the Candle

For example, let us take the very common parable of our Lord's – that of putting a candle under a bushel. Now this parable occurs in Matthew, Mark and Luke's Gospels. However, quite surprisingly, this parable is used in three different ways in each of the Gospels.

In Matthew 5:15, the candle pictures the Christian. The Lord uses the parable to encourage a Christian to do good works. He says, 'Let your light so shine before men that they may see your good works and glorify your Father in Heaven' (verse 16).

In Mark 4, however, the parable is used in a completely different way. The Lord has just told the parable of the Sower. The disciples then expressed their perplexity at the meaning of the parable and even at the Lord's use of parables altogether (as obviously, no one in the crowds had understood what Christ was teaching). So, having explained the meaning of the parable to His disciples, the Lord tells the further parable of the candle under the bushel. The Lord here, I suggest, is using the parable of the candle as a 'parable about parables'. He is teaching that, just as no one brings out a candle to put it under a bushel or a bed, so too he has not told the parable of the sower to keep its meaning a secret. He is assuring His disciples that He is telling His parables to enlighten rather than to perplex. He says in the verse after the parable of the candle, 'For there is nothing hidden which will not be revealed, nor has anything been kept secret but that it should come to light.'

When we come to Luke, the parable about the candle is again used in a completely different way. In Luke 11:14, the Lord has cast out a demon from a dumb man who now speaks. The crowds are amazed, but some blindly ascribe Christ's power to Beelzebub and some others obstinately seek another sign from heaven from Him. Christ in turn addresses each of these three responses to His miracle over the next twenty verses. Then, in v33, Christ tells the parable of the candle, after which he tells the parable of the evil eye. Christ is using the parable of the candle here to picture His miracle. His miracle bears witness to who Christ is. It is like a candle set upon a candlestick so that all may see the light. However, if we (like some of Christ's critics) have an evil eye, it does not really matter how much light there is. It will not matter how many miracles Christ performs. The blind will still fail to see.

Now, my point is this. We might read the parable of the candle in Mark's or Luke's Gospels and, perhaps not understanding what we are being taught by it, fall back on the lesson that we learned from Matthew's Gospel that we must be good-living Christians so that others might see our lives and become Christians too. This might give us warm feelings inside as with renewed resolve to be good Christians we feel the Lord has spoken to us from His Word and reminded us of our shortcomings in this department. However, it might not have been the Lord saying this to us. It might have just been the case that we were in a bit of a hurry this particular morning and, not having time to give due consideration to God's Word, we tried to reheat some stale manna gathered on a previous occasion. In the process we completely missed what the Lord was trying to teach us from Mark's or Luke's version of the parable.

If we desire to correctly understand what God is trying to teach us from some incident in one of the Gospels, we must not look at the incident in isolation. We must observe the surrounding incidents to see its relation to them. This will help us to understand the particular point that the writer is making. Incidents that are grouped together help to explain each other. In short, the grouping of incidents is a powerful God-ordained tool to help us understand the lessons of the individual incidents.

The Scope and Purpose of this book

This simply is our purpose in this book then – to study Matthew's Gospel in the arrangement that God has given it to us in. This is not going to be an attempt at a commentary. This is going to be an attempt at an introductory analysis. Doubtless it is wrong in some degree – all analyses of Scripture are subjective and different people look at things in different ways. God made us all different, for which the majority of us give God thanks. Nevertheless, because God is not the God of disorder, there must be some order and structure to His Word. It is therefore quite possible that we may observe it if we search for it. When we find it we may be sure it will be so self-evidently correct that it will admit no opposition. On the other hand, any obvious flaws in this analysis should only prompt readers to search all the more keenly for the correct answer.

Like the Gospel writers themselves, much that is not to our purpose will have to be passed over. There will be the occasional use of the analysis to attempt to answer a knotty question or two. But really this book is not intended to deal with every little question that we could ask about Matthew's Gospel. That would spoil Bible study, a good part of which consists in answering questions as they present themselves in reading the Word of God. In fact, allow me here to say that I would be very disappointed if this book caused readers to depend upon *books* on the Bible for answers to their questions instead of simply studying the Bible for themselves. This book is intended to be a tonic to further Bible study rather than a substitute for it. May God bless it so that it might in some small way cause readers to love, study and live their Bibles all the more.

Chapter 1 - Matthew and His Gospel

part from the title 'Matthew's Gospel', we are not told anywhere in the Bible who wrote Matthew's Gospel. However, early church tradition confirms that Matthew wrote the first Gospel. Early Christian writers in the first few centuries of the Christian era universally attest to the Apostle Matthew's authorship. For example, Origen (AD 185-254) wrote: 'As I have learned by tradition concerning the Four Gospels, which alone are received without dispute by the Church of God under heaven: the first was written by St. Matthew, once a tax-gatherer, afterwards an apostle of Jesus Christ, who published it for the benefit of the Jewish converts, composed in the Hebrew language'. Perhaps just as importantly as the early Church tradition, Matthew's authorship is affirmed by *all* of the manuscript copies we possess of Matthew's Gospel from earliest times. Apart from flimsy conspiracy theories, there is just no other contender for the title.

In addition to this overwhelming, unanimous direct testimony to Matthew's authorship, Matthew's Gospel itself provides considerable internal evidence that Matthew wrote the first Gospel. That is, there is such a line-up of indirect clues about the man behind Matthew's Gospel from within its own pages that the author's profile matches perfectly someone with the same background influences, perspectives, character, temperament and training as the Apostle Matthew.

In this Chapter we are therefore going to explore some of the characteristics of Matthew's Gospel where Matthew's personality comes out. In doing so we shall also embark upon our primary task in this book and start to examine the way Matthew's Gospel is arranged. The masterly way that Matthew's Gospel presents and arranges the life of Christ not only provides further evidence of Matthew's authorship, but also helps us to understand the important messages that God is teaching us through it.

Matthew the Apostle

What we know about Matthew himself is pretty limited. We are all probably familiar with his conversion. Matthew left his tax-collecting to follow Christ, amazed and overjoyed that Christ should call him – a sinner. Shortly thereafter he put on a great feast in his house for Christ and His disciples as well as his old tax-collecting cronies. However, after this, apart from finding him amongst the lists of the twelve apostles, we hear nothing more. Matthew seems to have been one of the quieter, less public apostles.

Matthew may have come from a godly Jewish family, at least if names are anything to go on. He is called Levi in Mark and Luke's Gospels. He also had a brother and fellow-apostle named James, the NT equivalent of Jacob (compare Matthew 9:9-13 with Mark 2:14-17 and 3:17). It seems that Matthew's parents had a love for Israel's ancient heritage and had hopes for godly sons from Levi and Jacob. Yet their plans for Matthew's life seem to have gone sadly wrong. Matthew turned his back on the faith of his people and nation and became a tax-collector.

Matthew, in becoming a tax-collector, committed three crimes. Firstly, he committed a political crime. He betrayed his nation to serve the Romans. There is no nation as patriotic as the Jews. Matthew seems to have taken the non-conformist anti-patriotic alternative. Secondly, he committed a religious crime. In dishonouring his nation, he had denied his nation's God-given place, and thus forsaken Israel's God. And thirdly, he had embraced a lifestyle that was highly immoral. Tax-collectors were so well known for their materialistic, live-it-up-while-you-can attitude, their greed and extortion that they were placed on the same level as 'sinners', prostitutes and Gentiles by their fellow-Jews.

And yet, amazingly, Matthew left this life at Christ's call. A tremendous change took place in his life – morally and religiously. Above all, in being sent out by Christ as an apostle to his own people and nation, his antagonistic attitude towards them had to undergo a huge transformation.

Matthew's Gospel reflects some of the perspectives that fit precisely those of a man in Matthew's unusual position. That is, Matthew's Gospel's style and themes make us turn and look in the direction of a man like Matthew.

Matthew's Gospel is a very Jewish Gospel

It was written by a Jew for Jews. Consider the following:

* Matthew presents Christ as the 'son of Abraham' (1:1) and only traces Christ's ancestry back to Abraham, whereas Luke traces it to Adam.

* Matthew's Gospel does not stop to explain Jewish customs – as do Mark, Luke and John. Notice how Mark explains Jewish customs in Mark 7:3-4 (but Matthew does not in Matthew 15). Notice how Luke explains Jewish customs in Luke 2:23-24 and John does in John 4:9.

* The author highlights fulfilled Old Testament prophecies about Christ far more than the other Gospel writers. In fact, Matthew interrupts his narrative twelve times to draw our attention to fulfilled prophecies[2].

* Notice the words in Matthew 1:21: 'you shall call His name Jesus, for He will save His people from their sins'. 'His people' here refers to the Jewish nation. Of course, this does not mean that God's salvation is limited to Jews only, but simply shows an implicit Jewishness.

* Only Matthew's Gospel focuses upon the official Jewish reaction to Christ's Resurrection, relating the setting and the report of the guards.

Matthew's Gospel is the most Politically-Sensitive of the Gospels

Matthew's Gospel presents Jesus as the Christ, the Son of David (1:1) – that is, the Messiah, the King of the Jews, which incidentally is why David is called 'David the King' in the Genealogy. Matthew's Gospel mentions the Kingdom of Christ more than any of the other gospels. And yet Matthew emphasises the fact that Christ's Kingdom was not quite the sort that the Jews of his day hoped for. Christ's message about His Kingdom surprised, bewildered and stumbled most patriotic Jews of Christ's time. Christ – the King of Israel – had not come to reign. He had come to die.

It took a special sort of Jew to write a gospel for the Jews showing that Jesus

2 1:22-23, 2:5-6, 2:15, 2:17-18, 2:23, 3:3, 4:14-16, 8:17, 12:18-21, 13:35, 21:4-5, 27:9-10 (27.35 is omitted by virtually all the manuscripts of the Greek New Testament). By contrast, Mark's Gospel has only two instances (1:2-3, concerning John the Baptist and 15:28, concerning Christ's death), Luke's Gospel only one (3:4-6, concerning John the Baptist) and John's Gospel has seven editorial comments about the Scriptures being fulfilled, in addition to the Lord's own comments (12:15, 12:38, 12:39-40, 19:24, 19:28, 19:36, 19:37).

was the Messiah. It took someone with strange political views. Virtually all Jews were passionately patriotic and had great difficulty in accepting a Messiah devoid of immediate political ambitions like Jesus. It took a non-patriotic Jew like Matthew the Roman tax-collector, free of any narrow Jewish nationalism, yet also now repentant of the almost anti-Jewishness that characterised his tax-collecting days, to realise that Jesus was the Messiah his nation had been waiting for. Matthew was thus able to embrace Christ's radical announcements about the Kingdom and was perfectly suited to present that message in his gospel to his fellow-Jews.

Matthew's Gospel is a very Moral Gospel

Matthew's Gospel presents Christ's radical moral teachings in great detail. Matthew contrasts Christ's moral teachings with the stuffy, superficial, severe, legalistic and hypocritical morality of the Pharisees. Christ's denunciation of the Pharisees in Chapters 5, 6, 12, 15, 16 and particularly 23 shows just how hot Christ's (and Matthew's) righteous anger at the hypocrisy of the Pharisees was.

Matthew the tax-collector had earlier rejected the pompous and phoney showmanship of the Pharisees. His hunger for true morality had been satisfied in Christ's teachings. In the Sermon on the Mount in Chs.5-7 we see Matthew's delight in recording in detail the perfection of Christ's moral outlook. Matthew, of all the Evangelists, lays most emphasis upon the very high standards of personal righteousness that Christ set for a follower.

Matthew's Gospel also places enormous emphasis upon Discipleship. In Christ's Great Commission with which the Gospel ends, Christ did not send His apostles out to make converts or even simply believers. Christ said, 'All authority has been given to me in heaven and on earth. Go therefore and make *disciples*'. He wanted them to make men who heard and obeyed His teachings. In Matthew's Gospel, Christ is not interested in half-hearted, Sunday-only 'followers' or even people who *said* they believed in Him. Christ says we must be disciples. Matthew was a man who had – even in his unconverted days – learnt to turn his back on the expectations of other people, to turn a deaf ear to his family's wishes, to renounce his past. Then he had to go through the whole process again when he left all to commit himself entirely to follow Christ. No one knew what it was to turn his back on his past and be a disciple better than Matthew.

Matthew also gives far more space than any of the other Gospels to Christ's teachings about how believers should receive others of God's children. He had felt the pain of being rejected and ostracised by his own people and the joy of being received by Christ. Christ, of course, was (and still is) famous for stooping to receive those who had been barred from society. Matthew, understanding better than most how close to Christ's heart this matter was, majors on this. For example, Luke takes only 7 verses (9:46-48 and 17:1-4) to give us Christ's teachings on how we should accept other disciples, whilst Matthew records Christ's teaching on these same subjects over 35 verses in Chapter 18 of his gospel.

Matthew's Gospel is the most Financial Gospel

Another feature of Matthew's Gospel is the way that it shows more awareness of financial matters than any of the other Gospels. Matthew's Gospel mentions 10 different sorts of coins or amounts of money: from the small coins, the kodrantes, the assarius, to the denarius for a days work, the didrachma the temple tribute money, the stater, right through to the large amount of the talent, as well as reference to gold, silver and copper coins and the general term 'money'. By contrast, Luke mentions only 6 sorts of coins or amounts in his Gospel, Mark mentions only 4 and John mentions only 1. Matthew makes 38 references to these coins and amounts in his Gospel in 12 separate incidents whilst Luke's Gospel comes nearest to this with 21 references to coins in 10 incidents. Matthew's Gospel is the most financially literate Gospel.

Luke's Gospel, by contrast, mentions riches or rich men 14 times compared to Matthew only mentioning riches or rich men 4 times. This is because Luke's Gospel looks at riches, not from a financial point of view, but from a social perspective. Luke's Gospel alone mentions the stories of the rich fool, the rich man in Hell and Zaccheus ('and he was rich') which specially emphasise the evil and the danger of the love of riches.

Matthew's Gospel's Brevity Indicates it was written by a Professional Note-taker

Another feature of Matthew's gospel is the way that it avoids interesting details, preferring brevity. For example,

• Matthew chooses not to tell us the most interesting part of the story of the paralysed man brought to Christ in Matthew 9 – the fact that the paralysed man was lowered through the roof. There is no way Matthew did not know about this. He deliberately omitted it.

• Matthew also condenses stories such as the healing of the Centurion's servant, the raising of Jairus' daughter and the healing of the woman with the issue of blood in chapters 8 and 9. Notice the difference in the length of the accounts of these miracles: Matthew takes 9 verses to tell us about the raising of Jairus' daughter and the healing of the woman with the issue whilst Mark takes 23 verses. Compare these stories point-by-point with Mark's Gospel (Mark 5:21-43 for Jairus' daughter and the woman with the issue of blood) and Luke's Gospel (for the Centurion's servant, Luke 7) and you will see surprising differences. In both of Mark's and Luke's accounts of these miracles, there were *two messages* sent from the homes of Jairus and the Centurion whereas Matthew has *only one combined message* in both cases. Matthew abbreviates and abridges stories. He avoids going into all the fine details of what transpired. He wants us to get the gist and the moral of it all. He is not contradicting the other Gospel's versions of events – he is condensing them. Matthew was a note-taker – not a narrator; a record-keeper – not a Hansard reporter. He gives only the outline, the skeleton.

• Matthew condenses the story of the argument amongst the disciples (Ch18 – cf. Mark 9:33-37). Mark's Gospel tells us that the disciples squabbled with each other on the road as to which of them was going to be the greatest. Christ later inquired politely into what they had been disputing over as they walked. The disciples kept an ashamed silence and the Lord, drawing a little child to Him explained that the servant of all and the least of all is really the greatest. However, Matthew, at the beginning of Ch18 represents the whole matter slightly differently. We read 'At that time the disciples came to Jesus, saying, 'Who then is greatest in the Kingdom of Heaven?' And we read, 'Then Jesus called a little child to Him, set him in the midst of them'. Some might try to argue that we have two different incidents here, but the subsequent verses in both gospels cut off this well-intentioned attempt to separate the two accounts. Matthew is more intent on presenting Christ's teachings than the circumstances that prompted it (he devotes the rest of Ch18 to Christ's response). He thus condenses the background build-up into a single question.

• Matthew condenses the story of the cleansing of the Temple and the cursing of the fig tree (Ch21, cf. Mark 11). Again, Mark gives us a detailed description of what happened. Mark's order of events is as follows:

(a) Christ enters Jerusalem and surveys the Temple;

(b) the next day, on the way to the Temple from Bethany he sees the fruitless fig tree and curses it;

(c) Christ then proceeds to the Temple and cleanses it;

(d) the next day on the way to the Temple again, he comes across the now withered fig tree and Peter expresses his amazement.

Matthew's version is as follows:

(a-c) Christ enters Jerusalem and the Temple and cleanses it;

(b-d) the next morning as He goes to the Temple from Bethany He curses the fig tree and immediately it withers, causing the disciples to express their amazement.

What Matthew has done is basically pass over some of the journeys and details that took place. If you want to be a gnat-strainer you could say there was a contradiction between Matthew and Mark, however that would simply be to misunderstand Matthew. Matthew the note-taker just gives us a contracted summary of what happened.

Thus, Matthew repeatedly condenses incidents. It is his systematic policy. Matthew's motto is that a little simplification saves tonnes of explanation. He is a professional record-keeper, not an on-the-spot reporter like Mark or a human-interest biographer like Luke. His intention in writing is to be comprehensive whilst concise, and to present the content of Christ's teachings rather than to catalogue the chronology of events that led to their delivery. He therefore cuts down on interesting but less important details.

Matthew's Gospel's Arrangement is the sort we would expect from a Careful Record-Keeper

That the author of Matthew's Gospel is a record keeper is seen from the very first line of the Gospel. Matthew 1:1 reads 'The book of the generation of Jesus Christ ... '. The word 'generation' is used here in the same way as it is in the book of Genesis (e.g. Gen. 2:4, 37:2, etc.) where the Hebrew word 'toledoth' means 'record' or 'history'. Matthew's Gospel is the book of the *record* of Jesus Christ.

However, we are going to see that the way that Matthew records his account of Christ's Life is quite different to the way we would naturally expect. Matthew's Gospel does not conform to any of the four ways that people commonly *split up* the Gospel: what I shall call the Chronological, the Paragraph, the Chapter and Verse and the Geographical approaches.

Approach 1: The Chronological Approach: A first possible approach treats the Gospel as simply a *time-based* record of Christ's life. It treats the Gospel as a tale being told. Tales sometimes tend to have a life of their own and like real life which they report, can be interrupted with unplanned additions and surprises. They can just roll along in an unpremeditated way. Accordingly, this approach deliberately avoids looking for any organisation in the Gospel. The Gospel is treated as a living unity without any planning.

Now, of course, there is a story line to Matthew's Gospel. It is history and biography. It reports real life. We can hardly miss the moving story line as we read the Gospel. But it is not necessarily true that all tales have to be impromptu, unplanned, off-the-cuff speeches. It is possible to plan how to tell a tale. Most people writing books or preaching sermons plan before writing or speaking.

When Matthew's Gospel is studied it becomes apparent that Matthew's Gospel is not arranged in chronological order. For a simple proof of this, let us compare Matthew's, Mark's and Luke's Gospels' order of five of Christ's most famous miracles: the healing of Peter's mother-in-law, the cleansing of the leper, the healing of the paralysed man lowered through the roof, the healing of the Centurion's servant and the stilling of the storm. Notice that the gospels arrange these miracles in a different order.

Matthew has the miracles in the following order: Leper cleansed (**L**) 8:1-4; Centurion's servant healed (**C**) 8:5-13; Peter's mother-in-law healed (**M**) 8:14-15; Storm stilled (**S**) 8:23-27; and the Paralytic raised (**P**) 9:1-8. Compare this order with the order in Mark and Luke. We shall look at Luke's Gospel first because Mark does not have one of the miracles. Luke's Gospel's order is: **M** (4:38-39), **L** (5:12-16), **P** (5:17-26), **C** (7:1-10) and **S** (8:22-25). Mark's order is **M** (1:29-30), **L** (1:40-45), **P** (2:1-12) and **S** (4:35-41). Notice the comparison between Mark's and Luke's order of these miracles with Matthew's order:

Thus Matthew's order is radically different. Notice furthermore that Mark's and Luke's miracles are spread out over a number of chapters whereas Matthew's are crammed into two chapters. What Matthew has done is to string together a number of miracles. Their order is not particularly based on *when* they happened. In fact, they happened over quite a period of time, as Mark and Luke give us to understand. Matthew instead has grouped the miracles into a section of his Gospel[3].

Another simple proof that Matthew's Gospel is not written chronologically is found in Ch.26. In verses 1&2 Christ tells the disciples that it is *two days* until the Passover when He will be crucified. Following this, Matthew tells us about the incident in Bethany when Christ was anointed with the costly ointment. Matthew does not tell us (but John does – 12:1) that the anointing in Bethany actually happened *six days* before the Passover. Matthew has not got his events out of order. Rather, it is a case of Matthew not being concerned about when particular events happened. He is more interested in helping us to compare and contrast the lessons that can be learned from different events.

Now, this leads to a very important point. If the Gospel is not primarily arranged chronologically, but on occasions is right out of chronological order, there must be some organisation being done for other reasons. Someone who tells a tale and deliberately puts elements in the tale out of order has another agenda. Matthew's Gospel is not chronological, and therefore it must have a definite plan. *Matthew's Gospel is arranged thematically and topically*. He places certain events next to each other in his gospel so that we will compare and contrast the lessons we are learning.

---

[3] Mind you, it can be similarly shown from other incidents in Mark's and Luke's Gospels that they are not always concerned with when events occur chronologically but rather with the significance of the events. For example, notice that Christ's return to Nazareth and His rejection there occurs in Matthew's and Mark's Gospels *after* all these miracles (Matthew 13:54-58, Mark 6:1-6), but in Luke's Gospel it occurs *before* all these miracles (Luke 4:16-30). Luke's account is fuller, but it is the same event. There was only one return to Nazareth – not two. If there were two visits, why would the townsfolk express so much surprise at Christ's wonderful teaching on a second visit (in Matthew and Mark), having already heard Him when He came earlier and they tried to throw Him off a cliff? Compare also Mt 13:57, Mk 6:4 & Lk 4:24. Different Gospel writers place the visit in different parts of their gospels because they want to *relate* its significance to differing events. Significance of events is what determined the order of events in the gospels – not chronology.

Approach 2: The Paragraph Approach: Another way we could approach the Gospel might be the way we might treat the Epistles – in paragraphs. The Gospel is split up into self-contained paragraphs and a catchy title is put on them. This sort of Commentary on the gospel reads like a series of sermons, except that they are based on paragraphs instead of single texts. The Outline of the Gospel's contents becomes an interminably long and quite unstructured listing of all the paragraphs. The paragraphs may occasionally (almost coincidentally) be grouped together into some sets, but there is no real structure in the business. Again, what is being implicitly stated is that there is no overall purpose in the arrangement of the writer's material. The Gospel's author has simply fed us in a willy-nilly way a lot of little interesting incidents in Christ's life – miracles, sermons, narratives, etc.

Now, it is quite true that there are definite paragraph divisions in the Gospel. Paragraph divisions are quite legitimate. However, the point is that it is possible to treat the paragraphs as unrelated little incidents without looking to see how they all fall into their own place in the whole book. Instead, Matthew's Gospel shows evidence of some very careful organisation of the paragraphs.

Approach 3: The Chapter and Verse Approach: Another approach (based on a roughly chronological view of the Gospel) ploughs through using the Chapter and Verse divisions to break it down into manageable bite-sized pieces. The Contents page of such a Commentary would simply list where you might go to find comments upon a certain Chapter. The serious problem with this approach is that the Chapter and Verse divisions in our Bible are not original or inspired. Unlike the paragraph divisions, they are late and artificial additions. They have their uses, but as God did not put them in, we must try to look at the Bible the way God intended us to look at it. God gave us the Bible in books, and we must endeavour to treat a Book as a whole and get a feel for it as a whole. The underlying premise behind a Chapter and Verse Approach is again that the Gospel has little or no organisation or structure. But this cannot be right. If God has given us a great big volume of a Gospel which we cannot read comfortably at one sitting, He probably expects us to make careful judgements about useful divisions into which the Gospel can be split up.

Approach 4: The Geographical Approach: One final approach is to arrange the Gospel according to the Geographical areas that events happened in. Now, there is no doubt that there are geographical notes thrown in by the Gospel's author every now and then, but this approach has serious drawbacks. Firstly, in the vast majority of cases *what* happened in an incident is much more important than *where* it happened. The importance of some events is closely tied to where they happened, of course – but not all events fall into this category. In many events the location is quite irrelevant. And so, such a division of a book can be extremely superficial.

Matthew's Gospel is Arranged Topically

Now, if Matthew's gospel was not arranged chronologically, how was it arranged? There must have been some method in its arrangement. It cannot have been a case of 'toss-it-all-in-however-it-comes'. We are going to see that Matthew's Gospel is a masterpiece in its construction and arrangement. As we shall see, the genius of its arrangement suggests that not only was a professional record keeper with an eye for order behind the Gospel – like Matthew – but behind him we trace the hand of the supreme record-keeper, God Himself.

It is commonly observed that Matthew's Gospel is built around five great Discourses or Sermons. If you possess one of those Bibles that has the words of Christ in red you will notice that Matthew's Gospel has whole chapters and pages of (virtually) unbroken red. They are:

Chapters 5-7:	The Sermon on the Mount
Chapter 10:	The Evangelistic Instructions for the Apostles
Chapter 13:	The Parables of the Kingdom
Chapter 18:	Instructions for Fellowship among disciples
Chapters 24-25:	The Olivet Discourse about the future

These five 'sermons' also have similar comments after each of them:
- Ch 7:28: 'when Jesus had ended these sayings'
- Ch 11:1: 'when Jesus had finished commanding His twelve disciples'
- Ch 13:53: 'when Jesus had finished these parables'
- Ch 19:1: 'when Jesus had finished these sayings'
- Ch 26:1: 'when Jesus had finished all these sayings'

Matthew is an Organiser

We must also notice that these long unbroken 'sermons' in Matthew actually incorporated teachings given on different occasions by Christ. For example, the material in Christ's Sermon on the Mount in Matthew chapters 5-7 was originally spoken on three or more separate occasions as related in Luke chapters 6, 11 and 12. The Lord's Prayer in Matthew 6 forms part of Christ's 'Sermon on the Mount', however when we look at Luke 11, we find that Christ taught His disciples this prayer in private. It would seem very strange if the disciples had to ask Christ how to pray if He had already been teaching the crowds publicly in exactly the same words. It thus appears that Christ actually taught His disciples in private as Luke tells us but that Matthew has incorporated this teaching into Christ's Sermon on the Mount. Likewise, the evangelistic instructions in Matthew 10 combine Christ's instructions before the *two* 'missions' of His disciples (Luke 9 and 10) with some other teachings from Luke 12. The teachings about the future in Matthew are found in no less than three speeches in Luke 12, 17 and 21. Matthew therefore consistently applies this policy of incorporating teachings on one general subject into one large 'sermon' compartment. Notice the somewhat simplified table below:

TEACHING	MATT.	LUKE
Semon on Mount	Chs5-7	6:20-49; 11:1-13; 12:22-34, 57-59
Evangelistic Teaching	Ch10	9:3-5; 10:2-16; 12:1-12
Parables of Kingdom	Ch13	8:4-15; 13:18-21
Fellowship Discourse	Ch18	9:46-48; 17:1-4
Olivet Discourse	Chs24-25	12:39-40,42-48; 17:22-37; 21:5-33

The alternative suggestion that Christ gave these teachings (e.g. on prayer) on more than one occasion in different settings does not seem to ring true to real life. It is quite true that Christ used some proverbial sayings and parables on a number of occasions in different contexts, like the parable about the candle. It is probable, too, that the Lord repeated some parables – like the Talents/Pounds and Great Supper/Marriage – on different occasions with variations, because we see these variations in the two different accounts in Matthew and Luke. Also, there is nothing improbable about Christ repeating public sermons on public occasions. However, it would seem very strange if Christ were to repeat lengthy public speeches word for word in response to private questions, especially if these people had already heard the public sermons. Different circumstances require appropriate replies suitable to the situation, not exact replicas of previous sermons. The fact that the words in the different Gospels are virtually identical indicates that we have recorded for us the same speech.

Luke thus gives us the settings and the circumstances that prompted Christ to say certain things. He is not inventing these settings to add some colour to the story. It actually happened that way. Luke's is thus the more natural arrangement of the material. Matthew, on the other hand, has written his Gospel in a different way to Luke. He omits the background altogether, incorporating all that Christ said on a given subject into one 'sermon'. Matthew has deliberately structured his gospel into sections in which he has brought together all of the relevant incidents relating to a particular aspect of Christ's life. We only need to look at a section like the one dealing with Christ's miracles (Chapters 8 and 9) or Christ's evangelism (Chapters 10-12) to see this happening. However, the important point that needs to be made here is that Matthew also does it with Christ's teachings. Matthew is a collator. He has been a tax-collector and has been used to ruling up columns and putting things in nice, neat, orderly sections like a good book-keeper. This is the way he writes his gospel. Matthew's Gospel is a concise and orderly, topical and thematic, compartmental record of Christ's Life.

Matthew's gospel thus appears at first to be formed of a number of chapters of narratives broken up at regular intervals by between one to three chapters of sayings or teachings of the Lord. The five main 'sermons' of Matthew's Gospel have often been viewed as building blocks for the Gospel. Thus, this leaves us with 11 sections in the Gospel, alternating between Narratives and Discourses.

	CHAPTERS	SECTIONS
1.	Chapters 1-4	Birth Narratives, John Baptist's ministry
2.	Chapters 5-7	Sermon on the Mount
3.	Chapters 8-9	Miracle Narratives
4.	Chapter 10	Evangelism Discourse
5.	Chapters 11-12	Galilee Ministry Narratives
6.	Chapter 13	Parables of the Kingdom
7.	Chapters 14-17	Later Galilean Narratives
8.	Chapters 18	Teaching in the House
9.	Chapters 19-23	Journey to Jerusalem Narratives
10.	Chapters 24-25	Olivet Discourse on Future Events
11.	Chapters 26-28	Narratives about Death and Resurrection

The Two Main Messages of Matthew's Gospel

In addition to Matthew's main message of who Jesus was and what His mission achieved, these 'sermons' teach us of Matthew's other main lesson for us in his Gospel. In the major sermons of Matthew's Gospel we learn of Christ's expectations of a follower – a disciple.

Christ in Matthew's Gospel is not looking for people who claim that they believe in Him. Christ is only interested in true disciples – those for whom Christ is everything. The Gospel concludes with Christ's words 'Go therefore and make *disciples*' – not converts, Christians or even believers. Christ wants the true-hearted and the whole-hearted only. Christ's great commission in the last verses of the Gospel sums up Christ's discipleship-training programme throughout the Gospel:

'make disciples' – referring to the sermon on the mount in Matthew 5-7. Christ expects His follower to be a disciple, someone learning to be Christ-like.

'Go therefore' – referring back to the evangelistic sermon in Matthew 10. Christ expects His disciple to be a soul-winner.

'teaching them' – referring to the parables of the Kingdom in Matthew 13. Christ wants us to understand God's Kingdom's purposes.

'lo, I am with you always' – referring back to the fellowship discourse in Matthew 18, in which Christ said 'Where two or three are gathered together, **there am I in the midst of them'**. Christ's disciple is to take his place in the Church, enjoying the fellowship of Christ and His people.

'even to the end of the age' – enlarged upon in Matthew 24-25.

Matthew's Gospel is thus characteristically **Comprehensive** and this teaches us a lesson. Christ wants us to be all-round Christians, neither ignoring those teachings of Christ we do not care for nor changing the order of Christ's teachings around to elevate our pet subject a place or two. Their order is very significant.

Some Structural Cracks Start Appearing

However, this oft-suggested structure built around the five 'sermon' pillars does not really fully explain Matthew's Gospel's arrangement. For a start, what shall we make of Chapter 23? Chapter 23 is really a sixth 'sermon'.

It is an entirely red chapter – a chapter of Christ's teachings. Furthermore it has the same trademark characteristic of Matthew's other 'sermons' in that it is a 'compilation sermon'. If we look through Luke's Gospel for cross-references, we find the same denunciations of the Pharisees in Matthew 23 occurring in Luke chapters 20, 11 and 13 respectively. Many commentators choose not to include Ch23 as one of Matthew's 'sermons', but this is papering over the cracks. Nor does Matthew 23 form part of the sermon in chapters 24 and 25 where Christ foretells the future, as some commentators try to pass it off. Its subject is entirely different. It therefore completely interrupts the nice, neat pattern of alternating discourses and narratives.

A far more serious misgiving about this structure is that it is dependent upon a policy of largely ignoring the contents of the narrative sections. The narratives in between the 'sermons' are all lumped into the same baskets without even considering the contents. They are just 'in-between' sections. For example, the chapters between Chapters 13 and 18 present a problem. They seem to fall into two separate sections. Nearly all of the stories in Chapters 14, 15 and the first bit of 16 seem to be about feasting or eating bread. We have the stories there of

- the feeding of the 5000 and the feeding of the 4000,

- Jesus being criticised for not washing His hands before eating bread,

- the Canaanite woman's request for her daughter's healing to which the Lord replied, 'It is not good to take the children's ***bread*** and throw it to the little dogs',

- the disciples forgetting to take bread on a journey across the lake,

- the Lord warning the disciples to beware of the leaven (that is, yeast, an ingredient of bread) of the Pharisees and the Sadducees.

These passages are so full of mentions of bread that it must be more than a coincidence. Now, as we shall see later on, these references to bread and feasting are used as metaphors of the Great Eternal Feast of Christ's Kingdom. Thus, these chapters, following on from Ch13 with its parables of the Kingdom, teach us more about Christ's Kingdom.

However, after Matthew 16:12 this imagery of bread and feasting abruptly stops. These chapters instead are all about new revelations that Christ opens up to His disciples – Peter's confession of Him as the Christ, Christ's revelation of His coming death, His Church, His glory on the Mount of Transfiguration and His Coming again. It is no wonder that some Bible scholars split Matthew's Gospel in two right here at 16:13. One commentator rightly referred to Peter's confession of Christ here in 16:16 as the 'watershed', the great dividing point, of Matthew's Gospel. Up until this point Christ had been ministering in and around Galilee. Now, with the announcement of His death, He turns for Jerusalem. Thus we read in 16:21 'From that time Jesus began to show to His disciples that He must go to Jerusalem and suffer many things ... and be killed and be raised the third day'. This is the great turning point of Matthew's Gospel. Thus there seem to be two quite different narrative sections in between chapters 13 and 18, each with a different message. They cannot be just lumped together. This is another weakness of this structure best not advertised.

Overall, this structure seems a little superficial. It adopts an approach to the study of the Gospel based on what colour the writing in our Bible is. It therefore focuses primarily on the teachings of Christ whilst the narrative sections are somewhat ignored and downgraded to the level of simply being in-between sections. Also, someone with a Bible with Christ's words in red will quickly point out that plenty of the narrative chapters have large amounts of red ink too. Finally, to arrange the gospel in eleven sections seems nearly a contradiction in terms. Eleven suggests untidiness.

A Suggested Structure of Matthew's Gospel

It is not until we take into account the fact that the Genealogy in Chapter 1 is an integral part of the Birth narratives following it that we get a helpful clue as to Matthew's structure. The unity of the genealogy and birth narratives shows that narrative sections need *not* always be viewed in isolation. Some of the narrative stretches in between the teaching blocks are definitely linked to the teaching 'sermons' before or after the narratives.

Example 1. Whilst in Chapter 10 the Lord gave His disciples instructions about evangelism, the narratives in Chapters 11 and 12 show the Lord in evangelistic action Himself. Matthew illustrates Christ's teaching in Chapter 10 on evangelism from incidents in Christ's own experience in evangelism in Chapters 11 and 12. Ch11:1 reads 'Now it came to pass when Jesus finished commanding His twelve disciples, *that He departed from there to teach and to preach in their cities'*. Thus it is in Chapter 11 that we find Christ's great gospel invitation: 'Come to me'. We find Christ's warnings of judgement because of the Galileans' lack of repentance and faith in Him in these chapters. We find numerous points of correspondence between the teaching about evangelism in Chapter 10 and the experience of the Lord in evangelism in Chapters 11 and 12. The incidents in Chapters 11-12 form a mirror image of the instructions Christ gave in Ch10. Chapters 10, 11 and 12 comprise one section. We must not separate them.

Example 2. Likewise, Chapter 23 clearly follows on from the brewing religious conflict between Christ and the Jewish religious leaders that began with Christ cleansing the Temple in Chapter 21. Chapter 23 thus contains teachings of Christ just as the other 'sermons' do, but it does not stand alone or belong to Chapters 24 and 25. It forms part of the section from Chapters 21-23. Furthermore, to make Chapters 19 to 23 one big section of the Gospel is to make one big mistake. Chapters 19 to 21 are very different to Chapters 21 to 23. Chapters 19 to 21 are about different matters discussed on the journey up to Jerusalem. Chapters 21 to 23 are about the conflict of Christ with the religious authorities in Jerusalem.

Example 3. Matthew 18, in which Christ speaks about the Church, also follows on from Chapters 16 and 17. In Ch16 Christ gave the first advance notice of His Church. Notice how Matthew repeats Christ's puzzling words in 16:19 about 'binding and loosing' in His Church when we come to 18:18. It is only in Ch18 that these words are explained as Christ talks of discipline in the Church. Matthew 18 seems linked to Matthew 16.

Matthew cannot be split up by the simple sermon/narrative formula. Its contents must be carefully studied and split up according to their subject matter and the lessons they teach. For example, we must not treat Chapters 26 to 28 as one block or section just because, on a very simplistic, superficial level, they are narrating events at the end of the Lord's life. Chapter 26 teaches lessons that are entirely unique and unconnected to those presented in Chapters 27 and 28 that follow. The following table shows what I suggest are the great divisions of Matthew's Gospel, based on the way different incidents in Matthew's Gospel stand together to present Matthew's main themes from Christ's life and teachings.

SECTIONS	CHAPTERS	SUBJECTS
1.	Chs1-4	Christ's Beginnings
2.	Chs5-7	Christ's Teachings
3.	Chs8-9:34	Christ's Miracles
4.	Chs9:35-12	Christ's Preaching
5.	Ch13:1-52	Christ's Parables
6.	Chs13:53-16:12	Christ's Kingdom and Israel
7.	Chs16:13-18	Christ's Secrets
8.	Chs19-21:11	Christ and Life
9.	Chs21:12-23	Christ and Religion
10.	Chs24-25	Christ and the Future
11.	Ch26	Christ's Betrayal
12.	Chs27-28	Christ's Death and Resurrection

The Number 12

Matthew's Gospel was not only written by a careful record-keeper. The author of Matthew's Gospel was also someone who was careful with his counting, as we saw in the numbering of people in the Genealogy. Matthew's Gospel is structured around the number Twelve, a number associated historically with *Israel*, particularly in its *Government*. Matthew presents his History of the Great *Governor* (2:6) in twelve main sections, each of which are carefully divided up into twelve further sub-divisions.

Take for example Matthew 8 and 9 that deal mainly with Christ's miracles. These two chapters seem to constitute a definite section quite unconnected with the Sermon on the Mount preceding them and the teaching on Evangelism that follows. Within them Matthew carefully sets out a number of incidents, mostly miracles, but also other stories about Jesus' *authority*.

There appear to be twelve parts to this section, with four sets of three incidents each teaching a particular lesson from Christ's miracles. We learn firstly the obvious lesson about His sheer *Power and Authority*. Secondly, we learn lessons about *Following* Him from His miracles. Thirdly we learn that the disease which Christ is primarily interested in healing us of is *Sin*. Then finally we learn some lessons about our *Faith* from Christ's miracles.

I do not want to insist too dogmatically on it, but we shall see that it is not too hard to split up each of Matthew's Gospel's main sections into twelve smaller parts. The main sections are not always split up into the four by three pattern – sometimes it is two sets of six parts, six lots of two parts, seven parts and five parts and sometimes there are other combinations. All I say is that the Gospel seems to fall into this pattern of twelve main sections of twelve parts without too much trouble. If this is true – and as soon as this chapter is finished you become the judge – Matthew's progressive presentation of the story line of Christ's life and His teachings amounts to a monumental literary masterpiece.

PART	VERSES	INCIDENTS	LESSONS TAUGHT
1.	8:2-4	Healing of leper	Christ's miracles
2.	8:5-13	Healing of centurion's servant	Show His Divine
3.	8:14-17	Healing of M-in-law and others	*power* and *authority*
4.	8:16-22	The two would-be followers	Christ's authority
5.	8:23-27	The storm on the lake	deals with problems
6.	8:28-34	The two demoniacs	as we *follow Him*
7.	9:1-8	The raising of the paralytic	Christ has authority
8.	9:9	The call of Matthew	to heal us of
9.	9:10-17	The two questions	our *sin*
10.	9:18-26	Jairus' daughter and the woman	People respond to
11.	9:27-31	The two blind men	Christ's miracles in
12.	9:32-34	The deaf and dumb demoniac	*faith* and *unbelief*

Why should Matthew's Gospel not be arranged into twelve main sections each composed of twelve sub-sections? Why should it be thought unlikely for God to arrange an account of His Son in a way that is so numerically precise? God does it elsewhere in Scripture. The book of Genesis, the first book of the Bible, is composed of twelve main sections alternating between Genealogy and Narrative. Why should we be surprised if the first book of the New Testament - which in many respects echoes some of the themes and terms of the book of Genesis (e.g. 'generations', Matthew 1:1) should be as carefully arranged as Genesis? Why should we not be surprised if God should put even more marks of careful arrangement into an inspired account of His Son? Why should we be surprised if God were thus to imprint His own signature upon the work of His servant Matthew?

Some might object that it might be possible to just squeeze a Gospel into whatever scheme one wanted. There is a degree of subjectivity and flexibility involved, however, it is just *not* possible to force a Gospel to fit whatever pattern one likes. To prove this for yourself, try squeezing Matthew into fourteen parts each of fourteen sub-sections or ten parts of ten sub-parts or try squeezing Mark, Luke or John into twelve sections with twelve parts. You will very quickly find out how difficult it really is.

For the Technically Inclined: The Historical Setting of Matthew's Gospel

Most Commentaries on books of the New Testament devote much space to the causes that led to the writing of the books (e.g. Philippians or 1 or 2 Corinthians). They explore the author's background and motivation for writing his book and then the recipients' need for the book or the historical circumstances that prompted it to be written.

However, rarely is there much said about the historical setting of Matthew's Gospel. And this is very strange because most Biblical scholars love to write about the most trivial details of the historical settings behind Biblical books. The reason for this silence is that, in spite of all the evidence we have seen for Matthew's authorship of Matthew's Gospel, modern critical Biblical scholarship casts frowning doubts over the traditional origin of Matthew's Gospel. The problem is, as shocking as it first must sound to an ordinary Christian, that many Biblical scholars consider Matthew's Gospel to have been largely copied off Mark's Gospel. Many scholars have therefore downgraded Matthew's Gospel over the last century to a secondary and less important Gospel. If Matthew, an eye-witness, had to copy off a second-hand reporter like Mark, he must have lacked personality or creative spark, it is feared. His Gospel is thus seen as a bit soulless and faceless by critical scholars. Some radical scholars have even tried to suggest other authors were responsible for the First Gospel, arguing that if the person who wrote the First Gospel copied Mark's Gospel then it need not have been Matthew at all. After all, any old anybody can copy another Gospel. So, the Biblical scholars are unnaturally quite reserved when commenting on the historical setting of Matthew's Gospel. However, I suggest that now that we have examined some of the prominent features of Matthew's Gospel we are in a good position to make some suggestions about the historical circumstances that led to Matthew's Gospel being written and the scholarly arguments over the whole issue.

Firstly: The combination of (a) the unanimous testimony of early Christian authorities, (b) the manuscript evidence and (c) many pieces of indirect, incidental, internal evidence all align to point to Matthew as the author of the Gospel beyond the contradiction of any Conspiracy Theory.

Secondly: There definitely are strong similarities between the first three Gospels, especially in their wording and sequencing of incidents in Christ's life. For example, Mark and Luke are very similar in the way they word and sequence the events of the early Galilean ministry of Christ (compare Mark 1:21-3:19 with Luke 4:31-6:17 and Mark 4:1-6:14 to Luke 8:1-9:17), the later Galilean ministry (compare Mark 8:31-9:40 with Luke 9:18-50), the final week in Jerusalem (compare Mark 11:1-13:37 with Luke 19:28-21:38) and to a lesser degree the narratives of the Last Supper, Betrayal, Death and Resurrection. Even more striking, however, is the way that Matthew and Mark follow nearly the exact same sequence of events from Matthew Chapters 14-28:8 and Mark Chapters 6:14 - 16:9. This is an enormous amount of both Gospels in which, apart from Mark's omission of the sermons and parables of Christ, the two Gospels are so little different that the possibility of copying cannot be ignored or lightly dismissed. We would expect Christ's ***words*** in separate Gospels to be very similar but there is no reason why ***narratives*** have to be worded so closely, unless there was some use of one Gospel by another. If two schoolboys presented 14 pages of nearly identical composition, their teacher would be within his rights to suspect copying. The similarities between the first three Gospels point to two conclusions.

Firstly, the ***general*** conclusion that must be drawn from the similarity of Matthew, Mark and Luke over certain stretches of their Gospels is that their common narratives must have been so standard, authoritative and universally accepted that they must have come from the Apostles themselves. That is, these narratives were not the product of one lone Apostle, like John's account in his uniquely personal gospel. Rather, these narratives derive from the collective witness of the whole Apostolic group. Luke's introduction points to this fact when it says that the source of its information was the teaching of the eyewitnesses (plural).

But secondly, more ***specifically***, these similarities point to a strong connection between Matthew and Mark, a slightly weaker bond between Mark and Luke and an even weaker, indirect link between Matthew and Luke via Mark. It seems that:

(a) one of Matthew or Mark have copied the other to a degree,

(b) one of Mark or Luke have copied the other to a smaller degree, and

(c) Matthew and Luke have not copied each other directly, but that they share some similarities that can only be explained by both of them being connected in some way to (or through) Mark.

Let us remember that Luke in his introduction assures us of the trustworthiness of his material by advertising the fact that he received it from eye-witness sources. So we need not dismiss the idea of one Gospel using another straight away, although it would seem strange (if not plain unnecessary) for God to give us three Gospels if they were just copying each other.

Yet, let us not jump to hasty conclusions, for this is precisely how mistakes have been made in the past. Many Biblical scholars over the last hundred years have asserted that the only possible explanation for the similarities between Matthew, Mark and Luke is that Matthew and Luke have used Mark as a source. However, this is incorrect. It is a logical falsehood. There are actually *three* equally possible logical options to explain the similarities - not just one. In addition to Matthew and Luke both using Mark, Mark could have used Matthew and Luke used Mark or the very reverse of this could have happened: Mark could have copied Luke and Matthew copied Mark. We could represent the three options as follows:

1. **Matthew→Mark →Luke**   (Luke used Mark who used Matthew)
2. **Matthew←Mark →Luke**   (Matthew and Luke both used Mark)
3. **Matthew←Mark ←Luke**   (Matthew used Mark who used Luke)

However, we can rule out the last of these options as unlikely based upon Luke's own direct admission that he used Apostles as sources for his Gospel. Therefore the big question is whether Matthew used Mark or whether it was the other way round[4].

Thirdly: Having established that Matthew the Apostle wrote the First Gospel and having observed some of the characteristic features of Matthew's Gospel, we can draw four conclusions:

1. We would expect that *Matthew's natural training and background* as a

---

[4] There is, of course, a fourth option – that Mark used both Matthew and Luke. However, this option can be immediately ruled out by the fact that Matthew and Luke are not *independent* of each other, like John is. All *three* synoptic gospels are inter-connected with each other to some degree. The weaker, secondary link between Matthew and Luke disproves the idea that they were completely independent, unrelated sources of information that Mark drew upon.

record-keeper would have fitted him more ideally for the job of being the first record-keeper of the life of Christ rather than Peter, a former fisherman and busy, front-line preacher. Thus, even though Peter's influence is seen in Mark's Gospel, it is more likely that Peter used Matthew's written sources rather than vice versa. Furthermore, we would hardly expect Matthew, an eye-witness to the most momentous events in the history of the world (as an Apostle would have viewed them), to need to use a second-hand source (like Mark) for information or words to express himself.

2. In cases of copying it is often hard to tell who copied who. However, Mark's Gospel has give-away evidence of copying. Mark's Gospel is *vivid* and *chronological*, especially in Christ's early Galilean ministry. Matthew's Gospel, on the other hand, uses *brevity* and is *thematic* throughout. These features tell the two Gospels apart. *Yet Mark copies Matthew's abbreviated, thematic style in five places*:

1. the call of the four fisherman (Matthew 4:18-22, Mark 1:16-20),

2. the return to Nazareth (Matthew 13:54-58, Mark 6:1-6),

3. the anointing in Bethany (Matthew 26:6-13, Mark 14:3-9),

4. the scourging and mockery of the soldiers (Mt 27:27-31, Mk 15:15-20), and

5. the events involved in the Crucifixion (Mt 27:33-56, Mk 15:22-41).

In these sections, comparison with Luke's or John's Gospels show that Mark is not only *out of chronological order* but is also giving an *abbreviated* version of events in Matthew's style, where Luke or John instead give a fuller account (cf. 1. Luke 5:1-11, 2. Luke 4:16-30, 3. John 12:1-8, 4. John 19:1-5 and 5. Luke 23:33-44).

3. Matthew's Gospel's characteristic *brevity of detail* and its *thematic, compartmental and comprehensive* arrangement of the life of Christ suggests that it originated as a *Source Book* for the apostles in their preaching early on in the apostolic period. Matthew's records of Christ's life and ministry take the form of an easy-to-locate, subject-based, ready-reference record. Matthew's Gospel was deliberately created as a skeleton-gospel, short on details because the apostles could add their own eye-witness touches from memory. Mark's Gospel, which drew largely on Peter's influence, therefore

seems to have added many little eye-witness touches. It would seem improbable that Matthew used Mark's Gospel but deliberately edited out as many interesting eye-witness touches as he could. That would only diminish his finished product. Matthew's records focussed primarily on the *words of Christ*, not just in the major teaching blocks, but also in the miracle stories and other narrative incidents where Christ's many memorable replies and proverbial statements are recorded.

4. I suggest the history of the Gospels was as follows. Matthew's Gospel was *initially* produced in the mid to late AD 30's in collaboration with the other apostles. It was probably first produced in Hebrew (Aramaic) *solely* for the use of the apostles as their spheres of ministry diverged in Palestine. This initial form of Matthew's Gospel was re-arranged by Peter so that the early Galilean ministry was more chronological. Peter's records were possibly copied by Paul (in about AD 37, three years after his conversion, Galatians 1:18) and then made use of by Luke in his Gospel, or alternatively Luke copied them later directly from Peter himself. Luke's Gospel (written in early 60's), which drew on other sources as well as 'deconstructing' Christ's 'sermons' in Peter's records into their separate parts, thus used Matthew's Gospel indirectly. Peter's records were published by Mark after Peter's decease (1 Peter 5:13, 2 Peter 1:15) in the mid 60's, with Peter's many added eye-witness touches, but excluding the long sections of Christ's teachings because of its primarily *evangelistic* purpose (Mark 1:1). Matthew published an expanded, *final version* of his records in Greek (our Matthew's Gospel), with birth narratives and fulfilled prophecies added, for the Jewish Christian public to counter the shift to legalism amongst Jewish Christians (Acts 21:20) in the late 50's or 60's.

Conclusion

Our Lord thus deliberately picked a professional record-keeper to write what is probably the primary, comprehensive record of Christ's life and the basis for the other two Synoptic Gospels. Matthew's Gospel was placed first in the New Testament because early Christians considered it the most important Gospel. They quoted from it more than any of the others. Some have even called Matthew's Gospel the most important book ever written. I am inclined to agree. Maybe you will, too.

Outline of Matthew's Gospel

1   Christ's Beginnings : 1:1 - 4:25

1.	Christ's Genealogy	(1:1 – 1:17)
2.	Christ's Birth	(1:18 – 1:25)
3.	The Visit of the Wise Men	(2:1 – 2:12)
4.	The Flight to Egypt	(2:13 – 2:15)
5.	The Slaughter of the Infants	(2:16 – 2:18)
6.	The Return to Nazareth	(2:19 – 2:23)
7.	John's Baptism	(3:1 – 3:12)
8.	Jesus' Baptism	(3:13 – 3:17)
9.	Jesus' Temptation	(4:1 – 4:11)
10.	Commencement of Galilean Ministry	(4:12 – 4:17)
11.	The Call of the Fishermen	(4:18 – 4:22)
12.	Features of the Galilean Ministry	(4:23 – 4:25)

2   Christ's Teachings : 5:1 - 7:29

1.	The Beatitudes	(5:1 – 5:16)
2.	The Fulfilment of the Law	(5:17 – 5:48)
3.	Righteousness before God	(6:1 – 6:18)
4.	Riches	(6:19 – 6:24)
5.	Cares	(6:25 – 6:34)
6.	Judging Others	(7:1 – 7:5)
7.	The Dogs and the Swine	(7:6)
8.	Asking, Seeking and Knocking	(7:7 – 7:11)
9.	The Golden Rule	(7:12)
10.	The Two Gates and Paths	(7:13 – 7:14)
11.	The Two Trees and Fruit	(7:15 – 7:23)
12.	The Two Men and their Houses	(7:24 – 7:27)

3   Christ's Miracles : 8:1 - 9:34

1.	The Leper	(8:1 – 8:4)
2.	The Centurion's Servant	(8:5 – 8:13)
3.	Healing of Peter's Mother in Law and Others	(8:14 – 8:17)
4.	The Two Followers	(8:18 – 8:22)
5.	The Storm on the Lake	(8:23 – 8:27)
6.	The Gadarene Demoniac	(8:28 – 8:34)

7.	The Paralytic	(9:1 – 9:8)
8.	Matthew's Call	(9:9)
9.	The Two Questions	(9:10 – 9:17)
10.	Jairus' Daughter and the Woman with the Issue	(9:18 – 9:26)
11.	The Two Blind Men	(9:27 – 9:31)
12.	The Dumb Demoniac	(9:32 – 9:34)

4

Christ's Preaching : 9:35 - 12:50

1.	Christ's Call of the Twelve	(9:35 – 10:4)
2.	Christ's Commissioning of the Twelve	(10:5 – 10:42)
3.	John's Question	(11:1 –11:6)
4.	Jesus and John	(11:7–11:19)
5.	Jesus Rebukes the Cities	(11:20–11:24)
6.	Jesus' Thanksgiving and Invitation	(11:25–11:30)
7.	Plucking Grain on the Sabbath	(12:1 – 12:8)
8.	Healing on the Sabbath	(12:9 – 12:14)
9.	Jesus' Withdrawal	(12:15–12:21)
10.	The Unforgivable Sin	(12:22–12:37)
11.	A Sign Requested	(12:38–12:45)
12.	Jesus' Family	(12:46–12:50)

5

Christ's Parables : 13:1 - 13:52

1.	The Parable of the Sower	(13:1 – 9)
2.	The Disciples' Perplexity	(13:10 – 17)
3.	The Interpretation of the Parable	(13:18 – 23)
4.	The Parable of the Wheat and the Tares	(13:24 – 30)
5.	The Parable of the Mustard Seed	(13:31 – 32)
6.	The Parable of the Leaven	(13:33)
7.	The Fulfilment of the Prophecy	(13:34 – 35)
8.	The Interpretation of the Second Parable	(13:36 – 43)
9.	The Parable of the Treasure in the Field	(13:44)
10.	The Parable of the Pearl of Great Price	(13:45 – 46)
11.	The Parable of the Net	(13:47 – 50)
12.	The Parable of the Householder	(13:51 – 52)

6

Christ's Kingdom and Israel : 13:53 - 16:12

1.	Rejection in Nazareth	(13:54 – 58)
2.	Herod's Opinion	(14:1 – 2)

3. John's Beheading .... (14:3 – 12)
4. Feeding the Five Thousand .... (14:13 – 21)
5. Walking on the Water .... (14:22 – 33)
6. Healing in Genesaret .... (14:34 – 36)
7. Eating with Unwashed Hands .... (15:1 – 9)
8. True Defilement .... (15:10 – 20)
9. The Canaanite Woman's Daughter .... (15:21 – 28)
10. Feeding the Four Thousand .... (15:29 – 39)
11. Pharisees and Sadducees Desire a Sign .... (16:1 – 4)
12. Disciples Forget to Take Bread .... (16:5 – 12)

7

Christ's Secrets : 16:13 - 18:35
1. The Question in Caesarea Philippi .... (16:13 – 20)
2. The Announcement of Christ's Sufferings .. (16:21 – 23)
3. The Requirements of Discipleship .... (16:24 – 28)
4. The Transfiguration .... (17:1 – 8)
5. The Disciples' Question about Elijah .... (17:9 – 13)
6. The Healing of the Demoniac Boy .... (17:14 – 21)
7. Further Announcement of Sufferings ...... (17:22 – 23)
8. On Paying Tax .... (17:24 – 27)
9. Christ's Teaching on Little Children .... (18:1 – 11)
10. Christ's Parable of the Lost Sheep ...... (18:12 – 14)
11. Christ's Teaching on Brothers .... (18:15 – 20)
12. Christ's Parable about Forgiveness ...... (18:21 – 35)

8

Christ and Life : 19:1 - 21:11
1. Question Concerning Divorce .... (19:1 – 9)
2. Christ on Celibacy .... (19:10 – 12)
3. Christ Prays for the Little Children .... (19:13 – 15)
4. The Rich Young Man .... (19:16 – 22)
5. Christ on Riches .... (19:23 – 26)
6. Peter's Question concerning Reward ...... (19:27 – 30)
7. Parable of the First and Last .... (20:1 – 16)
8. Announcement of Sufferings in Jerusalem . (20:17 – 19)
9. Mother of Zebedee's Children's Request .. (20:20 – 28)
10. The Two Blind Men .... (20:29 – 34)
11. Two Sent to Fetch the Colt .... (21:1 – 6)
12. The Entry into Jerusalem .... (21:7 – 11)

9

Christ and Religion : 21:12 - 23:39

1.	Cleansing of the Temple	(21:12 – 17)
2.	Cursing of the Fig Tree	(21:18 – 22)
3.	Christ Questioned concerning Authority	(21:23 – 27)
4.	Parable of the Two Sons	(21:28 – 32)
5.	Parable of the Vineyard	(21:33 – 46)
6.	Parable of the Wedding	(22:1 – 14)
7.	The Pharisees' Question	(22:15 – 22)
8.	The Sadducees' Question	(22:23 – 33)
9.	The Lawyer's Question	(22:34 – 40)
10.	Christ's Question	(22:41 – 46)
11.	Christ Warns of the Scribes and Pharisees	(23:1 – 12)
12.	The Woes upon the Scribes and Pharisees	(23:13 – 39)

10

Christ and the Future : 24:1 - 25:46

1.	Christ's Prophecy & Disciples' Question about the Temple's Destruction, etc	(24:1 – 2)
2.	Warning about False-Signs of the End	(24:3 – 14)
3.	The Great Tribulation	(24:15 – 28)
4.	The Coming of the Son of Man	(24:29 – 31)
5.	The Fig Tree	(24:32 – 36)
6.	As in the Days of Noah	(24:37 – 39)
7.	Two in the Field and at the Mill	(24:40 – 42)
8.	The Thief in the Night	(24:43 – 44)
9.	The Faithful and Wise Servant	(24:45 – 51)
10.	The Parable of the Ten Virgins	(25:1 – 13)
11.	The Parable of the Talents	(25:14 – 30)
12.	The Sheep and the Goats	(25:31 – 46)

11

Christ's Betrayal : 26:1 - 26:75

1.	Christ Foretells and Council Plots the Betrayal	(26:1 – 5)
2.	In Bethany	(26:6 – 13)
3.	Judas' Pact	(26:14 – 16)
4.	Passover Preparations	(26:17 – 19)
5.	Betrayal Announced	(26:20 – 25)
6.	The Supper Instituted	(26:26 – 30)
7.	Disciples' Failure Announced	(26:31 – 35)
8.	Gethsemane	(26:36 – 46)

9.	Judas' Betrayal	(26:47 – 50)
10.	The Disciples' Failure	(26:51 – 58)
11.	Christ's Trial	(26:59 – 68)
12.	Peter's Denial	(26:69 – 75)

12

Christ's Death and Resurrection : 27:1 - 28:20

1.	Delivery to Pilate	(27:1 – 2)
2.	Judas' Hanging	(27:3 – 10)
3.	Christ's Trial	(27:11 – 26)
4.	The Soldiers' Mockery	(27:27 – 31)
5.	The Crucifixion	(27:32 – 44)
6.	Christ's Cry	(27:45 – 49)
7.	Christ's Death	(27:50 – 56)
8.	Christ's Burial	(27:57 – 61)
9.	The Guard Set	(27:62 – 66)
10.	The Women Meet the Risen Lord	(28:1 – 10)
11.	The Bribery of the Guards	(28:11 – 15)
12.	Christ Commissions the Eleven	(28:16 – 20)

Chapter 2 - Christ's Beginnings: 1:1-4:25

1. Christ's Genealogy (1:1 - 1:17)
2. Christ's Birth (1:18 - 1:25)
3. The Visit of the Wise Men (2:1 - 2:12)
4. The Flight to Egypt (2:13 - 2:15)
5. The Slaughter of the Infants (2:16 - 2:18)
6. The Return to Nazareth (2:19 - 2:23)
7. John's Baptism (3:1 - 3:12)
8. Jesus' Baptism (3:13 - 3:17)
9. Jesus' Temptation (4:1 - 4:11)
10. Commencement of Galilean Ministry (4:12 - 4:17)
11. The Call of the Fishermen (4:18 - 4:22)
12. Features of the Galilean Ministry (4:23 - 4:25)

e have already looked briefly at this first section noticing the relationship of the Genealogy to some other parts of the section. We shall now look at what lessons Matthew is trying to bring out of this first section of his Gospel.

In this section we learn of a number of Beginnings. Firstly, there is the Genealogy that traces Christ's ancestral origins, or beginnings. Then there is the account of Christ's birth – His beginning in an earthly sense. Then we have four narratives dealing with the reaction of Herod to Christ's birth. We shall see shortly that what Matthew is particularly interested in emphasising in these narratives is Christ's birthplace – His origin in a geographical sense – which is of no little importance. Then, in the second half of this opening section, we learn about the beginnings of Christ's ministry. Firstly, we read of John – the one sent before Christ to prepare the way. Then we read of Christ's own preparation for His ministry – in His baptism and temptation. Then finally we read of the beginnings of Christ's ministry in the last three parts of this section – the move to Capernaum and the message He preached, the call of followers and the general synopsis of His early Galilean ministry. We shall firstly pay some attention to four themes that feature in this section. Then, finally, we shall draw the different threads together to see the main point that Matthew makes here in the first section of his Gospel.

Miracles

We shall start off by looking at what, for some people, is a problem that puts them off the story of Jesus' birth entirely. It is the problem of the miraculous in Jesus' birth. Jesus was born of a virgin. A virgin birth contravenes natural laws and modern people are not going to believe such things. We are told that it might have been possible to get away with stories of miracles in the First Century (or even the 18th) but modern science has worked out how things like birth happen and superstitious and primitive explanations must now be discarded. Men and women of the First Century, so it is claimed, were so ignorant of the scientific explanation for childbirth that it was possible to make up the story of the virgin birth to cover Christ's illegitimacy.

Mind you, the story of Christ's birth contains more than one miracle. We have angels, dreams and guiding stars in the story too. The whole thing is miraculous. Furthermore, the miracles did not end with Christ's birth. The whole story of Christ's life is full of miracles. So we might as well face up to the question of miracles before we proceed any further with the Gospel. If miracles cannot happen then the whole story is just a superstitious fabrication.

The dismissal of miracles as primitive superstition and myth by many modern people is not as intelligent as it is presented to be. There is a serious problem with the sceptical dismissal of miracles. Miracles are obviously presented to us in the Bible as the work of an All-Powerful God intervening in our world's (His world's!) affairs to fulfil His plans for it. A sceptic will of course at this point interrupt to ask how we can know that such a God exists. Granted that if such a God existed He could perform miracles – but what evidence have we got for His existence in the first place? This is a fair question. We should not believe in an unseen God without good reasons. How shall we test whether there is a Supernatural Person who rules over our Universe? The sceptic demands proof. What sort of proof will satisfy him or her, then? Presumably the only sort of proof that could ever impress a sceptic of the reality of God is a supernatural event – something that contravenes the known, reliable and unbreakable laws of nature – in other words, a miracle. Yet when the sceptic is presented with miracles like the ones recorded in the Bible we immediately get a strange answer. They reply that miracles are impossible.

In other words, they pretend to be honest sceptics awaiting miraculous proof of God's existence. Yet miracles are immediately ruled out of court as evidence for God's existence. There is something suspiciously insincere about this sort of scepticism. A true miracle, that is, a contravention of natural laws by a higher power, must be the last thing a sincere sceptic will rule out of court. This is precisely the proof he must demand. He or she should, upon being presented with claims of miracles, then commence a simple investigation to determine whether the miracle really happened.

It is therefore high time to explode the myth of the honest or open-minded atheist. We should be considering the question, not of whether God exists, but whether honest atheists exist. They rule out the possibility of miracles and then demand proof of God's existence. They 'bid the gelding be fruitful'. That is a funny way to start a quest for truth! Maybe their mind was already made up before they started.

So, how must the honest enquirer proceed to determine whether the miracles reported in the Bible occurred or not? People today usually ask for scientific proof for anything before they will accept it. However, they forget that there are many things that scientific experiments cannot prove. Try proving the existence of Napoleon by scientific experiments. Scientific experiments will never be able to prove the existence of Napoleon for the reason that scientific experiments only prove that something is a fact by repeating the experiment time and time again. However we cannot make Captain Cook come back and sail to Australia again to prove it happened.

Scientific proof has its limits. The legal system uses a different sort of proof to determine whether historical events happened. The main method of determining how any historical event – from a murder to a car accident – happened is to examine the witnesses or witness statements. The sort of legal evidence that modern courts (like ancient courts before them) need to confirm whether an event was historical or not is the testimony of witnesses. Some people are so cynical and sceptical they cannot believe that sometimes other people can tell the truth. However, this is the way historical evidence is weighed. The witnesses must be examined to see whether they confirm or contradict the story. If all the witnesses agree, the case is usually 'open and shut', as they say.

Now, for some of the miracles in the Bible, there are very few enquiries that someone can make about whether a miracle happened or not. There are few witnesses to cross-examine. However, the important miracles of the Bible – like the history of the life of Christ – are recorded and reported in the Bible in a way that is precisely designed to be investigated by honest enquirers. There are eyewitnesses to check and compare. There are historical checks for an honest sceptic to make.

The proof of the central miracle of the Bible – the resurrection of Christ – is seen in two facts. Firstly, the fact that all the witnesses tell us the same story. Then secondly and almost as significantly, the fact that Christ's enemies, instead of providing the sort of evidence which would immediately silence the claims of Christ's followers, reached for their swords for nearly three hundred years to try to quash the evidence. Had contrary evidence existed, why was it not produced?

The atheist who asks God for immediate proof of His existence by sending lightning to zap him within the next minute is not being honest, either. Christ was once asked (see Matthew 12) for a sign from Heaven – a lightning bolt or something similar – to prove He was God's Son. This was despite the fact that He had just healed a blind and dumb man. One miracle didn't seem to be enough for these people. They were still not satisfied. Christ said No. The only sign they would get would be the sign of His resurrection. Christ's rising from the dead was to be the ultimate proof of His power and His claims. What more could a modern sceptic ask for from God? What greater natural law to overcome than the irreversibility of death? The fact that the modern atheist still asks for God to thunderbolt him despite God having already provided the ultimate miracle is proof of the insincerity of his enquiry.

The fact that the story of Christ is so full of miracles – miracles that really happened – is the watertight proof we need to be satisfied that God was indeed intervening in our world's history in a way that had not hitherto nor ever again will be witnessed. God was acting out the central scene of the Great Drama of Earth's History. The only explanation for the unparalleled profusion of miracles accompanying Christ's life is found in Matthew 1:23: 'they shall call His name Immanuel, which is translated, *God* with us'.

The Problem with a Messiah

Turning back to Matthew's Gospel now, we cannot avoid noticing the importance that is placed upon Christ's relation to His ancestors – both as ancient as Abraham and David and as immediate as Joseph and Mary. The Genealogy makes the point before it starts that its purpose is to demonstrate that Christ is 'the Son of David, the Son of Abraham' – 1:1. Whereas Luke in his Genealogy traces Christ's ancestry back to Adam to stress the common humanity He shares with all of us, Matthew traces Christ's genealogy in the opposite direction – from Abraham through David to Christ – to teach that Christ is the fulfilment of God's promises to them. In short, Matthew is intent on proving that Jesus is the Messiah. He calls Him so in his first verse – 'Jesus *Christ*' (which means Messiah). To do so he traces His genealogy through the line of the kings to Joseph, who is addressed by the angel as 'Joseph, son of David'.

However, for the Messiah to be a descendant of David creates a dilemma – a dilemma that threatens to impale any prospective Messiah upon one of its two horns. The dilemma is as follows. How can any Messiah who is merely a human descendent of David and his line, whose moral failures have been so carefully emphasised in the Genealogy, be anything other than a failure like they were? On the other hand, if God were to send a sinless Messiah into the world – by a virgin birth – how could He be a true descendant of David like God promised the Messiah would be?

Matthew goes into some detail to show how this little problem was overcome in the history of Christ's birth. He firstly plainly states that Mary 'was found with child of the Holy Spirit' (1:18) by a virgin birth. But then Matthew goes on to show the important part that Joseph had to play in the piece. Joseph, although he was not the natural father of the child, was not only told by the angel in a dream to marry Mary but most importantly to *himself* name the child Jesus (notice carefully verses 21&25). Thus, in marrying Mary and in naming the child (which only a parent has the right to do), Joseph was legally adopting the child as his own. Thus Jesus legally became the heir to the throne. He became a son of David legally without becoming a son of David morally.

The Problem of Christ's Birthplace

A third thing that Matthew emphasises very heavily in this section is Christ's birthplace – Bethlehem. He not only states that Christ was born in Bethlehem quite forthrightly when telling us about the visit of the wise men but he also uses the fourth, fifth and sixth stories to reinforce this point. The reason is very obvious. As the story of the wise men makes clear, it was foretold that the Christ would be born in Bethlehem. If someone claiming to be Christ was not born in Bethlehem, then he was not the Christ at all.

The reason that Matthew emphasises the fact that Jesus was born in Bethlehem is because most people who knew Christ during His life would have been very surprised to hear that He came from Bethlehem. He was Jesus of Nazareth – and that barred Him from being the Messiah. So Matthew in this first section of his Gospel shows us firstly that Jesus the Messiah was born in Bethlehem and also shows how He came to be known as Jesus of Nazareth. Matthew traces the moves of Christ from Bethlehem to Egypt to Nazareth to Capernaum.

Matthew reminds his readers of one of the typically callous atrocities of Herod's reign – the killing of all the male children under two years old around the town of Bethlehem. This, says Matthew, was the result of the totally unexpected and very disturbing visit of some foreigners to the court of Herod. They told Herod that the Messiah had been born. They had seen His star in the East. In fact, they were quite puzzled to find out that His own people, the Jews, knew nothing about such a birth. Surely the Jews would know if strangers and foreigners from afar had found out?

Matthew therefore shows that the Messiah's birth had really happened by recording the amazing attendant effects of His birth: the visit of the wise men, the star and, above all, Herod's paranoid order for the massacre of all the young boys around Bethlehem. Only the birth of the Messiah was sufficient to explain these events. Matthew's point is that all of these events can only be explained when traced back to the birth of Jesus, because He was the true Messiah, born in Bethlehem just as the prophet had foretold. Notice, too, that the wise men, undaunted by the troubled reaction they had received from the Jews and perhaps doubting whether the Messiah had in fact been born, were guided by the star to where they found the now nearly two-year old child Jesus. Jesus was indeed the Messiah. Mind you, we are not told where the star led them to. If Christ was still in Bethlehem we would wonder why they needed a star to guide them there. Bethlehem was only five miles away from Jerusalem – and was exactly where they had been told to go. Christ was now in a house – not in some stable. It therefore seems doubtful that Jesus and His parents were still in Bethlehem. Maybe, as Luke says, they had returned to Nazareth.

The Moral Problem

Matthew passed no comment upon the Kings from David to Jeconiah in the Genealogy. All he did was give their names. But their names were enough to provoke memories of them. We usually classify the kings of Judah as either good kings, like Hezekiah or Josiah, or bad kings, like Manasseh. The fortunes of Judah rose and fell with the lead given by their kings. It is a history that ended sadly in the Babylonian captivity because, despite the odd revivals of the fortunes of the kingdom under good men, even the good kings were not able to reverse the ongoing decline caused by the bad kings. The good kings were not good enough. They were not perfect. All of these men had their faults. What good would a Messiah be if he was only as good as men like these? If he were no better than a David or a Hezekiah or a Josiah he really would not be good enough. His Kingdom would fail too.

What about Jesus, then? If He was no better than the other kings, with the odd small faults like we all have, He could not be the Messiah. Messiah had to be above fault. He was to be the great King, ruling the wide earth for God forever. He could hardly avoid bringing God's name into contempt if His regime became corrupt. He had to be sinlessly perfect. Matthew here shows us that Christ was. God said so from Heaven at His Baptism and the Devil's fruitless temptation proved so upon earth. Who does this make Him, then? Just an angel? Surely an angel pushed to the extremes that Christ was pushed to would have buckled. It might be easy to avoid sin in Heaven but in a desert in a body without food for nearly six weeks is another matter. If Satan and his angels fell from heaven, how much more likely would it have been for an angel to fall on earth. Christ was not an angel. Christ was not capable of sinning. Christ was God with us.

This matter of Christ's moral fitness to be Messiah is what Matthew brings us to in the seventh, eighth and ninth parts of this section, Matthew introduces John's ministry, Jesus' baptism and Jesus' temptation. Jesus comes upon the scene set against the background of the preaching of repentance by John. In contrast to the confession of the peoples' sins and the protests of the proud self-righteous Pharisees, Christ's quiet baptism, without any hint of a need to confess any sin, proves His humble sinlessness. So do John's initial protests against His baptism. Finally, the opening of the heavens, the descent of the Spirit of God upon Him like a dove and the voice from out of heaven saying, 'This is my beloved Son, in whom I am well pleased' show that Christ's non-confession was not the brazen brow of impenitence. Christ's sinlessness was advertised and applauded from Heaven. Matthew is calling upon heaven's witness that the life of Christ was without sin. Finally Matthew shows that even the Devil's temptations prove that Christ was sinless.

In the last three parts of this section, we follow with interest the beginnings of Christ's ministry. He moves to Capernaum and commences preaching the message of repentance Himself. Then He starts calling disciples to leave all and follow Him, like the four fishermen. Finally, His great work of teaching and healing begins. His fame spreads far and wide and great crowds start following Him. We will leave the significance of this to the chapter dealing with Christ's teachings.

The Main Message

Let us now draw together the different strands of what Matthew's first section is teaching. The one big point Matthew is making here in this first section is that Jesus is indeed the Messiah. He is the Son of God. He is Immanuel, God with us. Matthew proves it from His genealogy, His birth, His birthplace and His sinless life. Matthew proves it from Scripture. He gives us seven prophecies that were fulfilled in Jesus in this first section – His virgin birth, His birthplace, His stay in Egypt, the slaughter of the infants, the move to Nazareth, John the Baptist's coming and His Galilean upbringing, background and ministry. This truly is the most important lesson that Matthew's Gospel teaches. There is much more that Matthew has to teach us in his Gospel but if we miss who Christ is we have really missed the main message.

But we should not miss something else about Christ here. Christ was not the sort of Messiah that we, or the Jews who heard the report of His birth, would have expected. The wise men went to Jerusalem expecting Him to have been welcomed and honoured by His own nation. Instead, they found another King occupying His throne and the Jews nonplussed about news of His birth.

He had come in secret. Why not with splendour? Furthermore, why, instead of reigning, did the Messiah have to run for it as the usurper hunted for His life? Strange Messiah, this. He had been born in Bethlehem but He later presents Himself as a looked-down-upon Galilean, a Nazarene – a Messiah who would immediately arouse disdain and doubt in the minds of His fellow-Jews. Why was it that He was exactly the opposite of what He was supposed to be? The answer, amazing as it sounds, is that His purpose in coming was to be despised and to suffer – from the start right up until the very end when He would be hanged in Jerusalem. Why?

There is one other recurring theme we have noticed in this section that explains why. It is the theme of morality. The Genealogy emphasises some people for their lack of it. The point of Christ's birth is that there was no immorality in it – although to Joseph for a moment there appeared to be. In Herod's actions in Chapter 2 we see sins of a different sort – polished deceit and demonic cruelty. In Chapter 3 we hear John's preaching of repentance and his denunciation of the phoney self-righteousness of the religious Jews. Then we hear Heaven's pleasure in a man who was without sin and we watch with admiration as He is utterly unmoved by temptation of the most extreme sort. Then finally we find Jesus Himself coming preaching the same message that John preached: Repent!

Morality pervades this whole first section. This is because Matthew wants to make it quite plain that the reason for Christ's coming was to deal with our moral problem – our sin. The angel announced, 'You shall call His name Jesus, for He will save His people from their sins.' The one who was without sin was coming to suffer and die for sinful human beings.

Matthew's message therefore is plain. Christ, God with us, has come to suffer for us to save us. We must believe in Him and we must repent. In so doing we are saved.

Chapter 3 - Excursus: The Kingdom of Heaven

N ow, before we proceed to the next section of Matthew's Gospel, we must take a slight detour and look at a subject that occurs very frequently in the Gospel and is so crucial in determining how we interpret the Gospel that we must devote a special chapter to it. The subject is the Kingdom of Heaven. In Matthew 4:17 Christ announces that the Kingdom of Heaven has drawn near. So, what is this Kingdom of Heaven?

The Kingdom of Heaven and The Kingdom of God

Firstly, we must observe that the Kingdom of Heaven is *the same* as the Kingdom of God that the other Gospel writers talk about. For example, compare Mark 1:14-15 with Matthew 4:17. Mark 1:14-15 tells us that after John was put in prison Jesus came preaching that '*the Kingdom of God is at hand. Repent and believe the Gospel*'. In Matthew 4:17 we read that after John had been put in prison Jesus came preaching '*Repent, for the Kingdom of Heaven is at hand*'. Obviously Mark is writing about exactly the same thing as Matthew, however, he uses a different term. For some other examples, compare:

• Matthew 13:31-33, Mark 4:30-32 and Luke 13:18-21: Here we have the parables about the Kingdom of God/Heaven being likened to the mustard seed and the leaven. Whereas Matthew says 'The Kingdom of Heaven is like a mustard seed, which a man took and sowed in his field', in Mark and Luke we have instead 'the Kingdom of God'.

• Matthew 19:13-15, Mark 10:13-16 and Luke 18:15-17: Whilst Matthew tells us Christ said 'Let the little children come to Me, and do not forbid them, for of such is the Kingdom of Heaven', both Mark and Luke here substitute 'the Kingdom of God'. Obviously these passages are recounting the selfsame one incident.

• Matthew 19:23-24, Mark 10:23-25 and Luke 18:24-25: Here we have the famous lines about the difficulty of a rich man entering the Kingdom of God/Heaven and the fact that it is easier for a camel to go through the eye of a needle than for a rich man to enter into the

Kingdom of God. Notice how even Matthew uses the terms Kingdom of Heaven and Kingdom of God interchangeably in verses 23 and 24.

The fact that time and time again Matthew reads 'Kingdom of Heaven' where Mark and Luke read 'Kingdom of God' shows that they are simply two different descriptions of the same Kingdom. In fact, there are many other descriptions of this same Kingdom elsewhere in the New Testament – the Kingdom of Christ and God (Ephesians 5:5), the Kingdom of His dear Son (Col 1:13), the everlasting Kingdom of our Lord and Saviour Jesus Christ (2 Peter 1), My Father's Kingdom (Matthew 26:29) plus more. Trying to define the difference between all these titles becomes absurd. They are all the one same Kingdom.

So why does Matthew use a different term to Mark and Luke? Why does he use the term the Kingdom of Heaven? It has been suggested by some that Christ originally used the term 'the Kingdom of God' but that Matthew has substituted 'Heaven' for 'God' to avoid offending Jews by referring directly to God, as the Jews feared to use the name of God. However, this is wrong for two reasons. Firstly, Matthew's Gospel refers to God directly some 55 times anyway and secondly, Matthew too uses the term 'the Kingdom of God' five times in his Gospel. I suggest the exact opposite is the case.

I suggest that Matthew's term 'the Kingdom of Heaven' did not simply come from Matthew's mind or pen. The reason I suggest this is that 'the Kingdom of *Heaven*' (literally, 'the Kingdom of *the Heavens*') sounds like a Hebraism – a Jewish way of speaking. The Old Testament's use of the word 'Heaven' gives us the clue to the meaning behind the term 'the Kingdom of Heaven'. As we near the end of the Old Testament period, God is frequently referred to as 'the God of Heaven'. Out of the 21 times God is called 'the God of Heaven' in the OT, 16 occurrences of this title are found in the books of Daniel, Ezra and Nehemiah. Daniel also writes of God as 'the King of Heaven' and 'the Lord of Heaven'. Daniel, Ezra and Nehemiah lived in the shadow of seemingly all-powerful Gentile emperors, but they feared a Higher Power and referred to God as 'the God of Heaven' to express their belief in His Heavenly Power being greater than any earthly power. In one of the most explicit of OT prophecies about the coming Kingdom, Daniel wrote 'and in the days of these Kings *the God of Heaven* will set up a Kingdom which shall never be destroyed' (Daniel 2:44). Daniel also uses the word Heaven as a synonym for God when he writes of Nebuchadnezzar learning 'that the *Heavens* rule' (4:26). The word 'Heaven/s' was sometimes used as a synonym for God, not out of some superstitious fear of saying 'God', but to emphasise God's supremacy over earthly powers and Kingdoms. John the Baptist or Christ Himself must have coined the term 'the Kingdom of Heaven', emphasising that God's Kingdom would be far more powerful than the Roman Empire or any other earthly government, for it is hard to imagine Matthew taking the liberty of inventing such a unique term. Here we have another proof of Matthew's Gospel predating Mark's. Mark and Luke, writing for Gentiles, simplified the term throughout their Gospels to 'the Kingdom of God', lest the use of 'Heavens' here might puzzle or mystify Gentile readers who were not familiar with the Jewish thinking and background behind what Christ was announcing.

What is this Kingdom?

Matthew's Gospel has announced that the Messiah – the King – had come. So, logically enough, His Kingdom was near, too. What is this Kingdom?

Before we look at what it is, let us notice two things that it is *not*. The Kingdom of Heaven is not simply another way of talking about Heaven. Christ made it quite clear in the Sermon on the Mount that those who inherit the Kingdom are going to inherit the *Earth* (Matthew 5:5) as well as Heaven (Matthew 5:12). Nor is the term 'the Kingdom of Heaven' another way of speaking about the Church. Nowhere in the New Testament do we find any statement which says The Kingdom = The Church, nor do we even read of Christ being the *King* of the Church. God's Kingdom involves far more than God simply reigning over those who love Him. God plans to reign over everything, everywhere.

> *'He shall reign from pole to pole, with illimitable sway.*
> *He shall reign, when, like a scroll, yonder heavens have passed away'.*

So then, what is this Kingdom?

There are two standard ways of viewing this Kingdom and those who hold to these two views sometimes argue against each other quite heatedly. However, like many things in the Bible, the Kingdom has two sides to it and to understand the Kingdom properly we must hold both truths.

A Present Spiritual Kingdom

Firstly, the Kingdom is clearly seen to be a present spiritual Kingdom which those of us who are believers are already in. For example, consider the verses below:

Colossians 1:13: 'He has delivered us from the power of darkness and translated us into the Kingdom of the Son of His love'.

Matthew 12:28: 'But if I cast out demons by the Spirit of God, surely the Kingdom of God has come upon you'.

Matthew 21:31: 'Assuredly, I say to you that the tax collectors and harlots enter the Kingdom of God before you'.

Luke 17:21: 'The Kingdom of God is within (or among) you'.

Romans 14:17: 'For the Kingdom of God is not eating and drinking, but righteousness, joy and peace in the Holy Spirit'. The context of the chapter shows that this refers to the way believers in this present day behave toward each other. We are not to become embroiled in arguments over trivial things like food and drink, but make it our business to pursue righteousness, joy and peace.

1 Corinthians 4:20: 'For the Kingdom of God is not in word but in power'. Again the context here shows that Paul was writing about present conditions among believers. He was going to come to Corinth and sort matters out. He warned that when he came all the idle bragging of the Corinthians about their spiritual accomplishments would not save them from the rod of Paul's chastening.

Matthew 13: The final proof of the fact that the Kingdom of Heaven has a present spiritual aspect is the fact that all the parables of Matthew 13 about the Kingdom all relate to activities that are being fulfilled in this day and age. For example, the parables about the sowing of the seed, the growth of the wheat and the tares and the fishing net being cast all refer to *present* activities.

A Future Earthly Kingdom

However, the Kingdom is also described as a future earthly realm which our Lord Jesus Christ will reign over in a future day. In fact, this aspect of the Kingdom is so important that we can say that the Kingdom is *firstly and primarily* a future earthly Kingdom.

Let us notice some verses showing that it is a *future* Kingdom:

• Christ said towards the end of the Sermon on the Mount 'Not everyone who says to me, "Lord, Lord" shall enter the Kingdom of Heaven, but he who does the will of My Father in Heaven. Many will say to me *in that day*, "Lord, have we not prophesied in Your name"'. The Kingdom is plainly here described as something in *a future day.*

• Matthew 8:11: 'Many will come from east and west and sit down with Abraham, Isaac and Jacob in the Kingdom of Heaven.' This verse again speaks of the Kingdom of Heaven in the future tense.

• The Beatitudes (i.e. blessings) with which the Sermon on the Mount commences (5:3-12) are all about the blessings of the future Kingdom which true disciples will enjoy. This is clearly seen by the fact that the first and the last of the beatitudes concern the Kingdom. The first is 'Blessed are the poor in spirit, for theirs is the Kingdom of Heaven' and the last is 'Blessed are those who are persecuted for righteousness' sake for theirs is the Kingdom of Heaven'. Notice, though, that all the blessings in between these first and last concern the future. For example, 'Blessed are those who mourn for they shall be comforted' (5:4) or 'Blessed are the pure in heart for they shall see God' (5:8). All the blessings are in the future tense. If we were to just take the first and last blessings in isolation we could perhaps argue that there is no future tense implied in the words. However, the context closes this loophole. Christ is saying that the blessing or reward of those who are poor in spirit or those who are persecuted for righteousness' sake is that they are the sorts of people who will inherit in the future the Kingdom.

• Christ tells His disciples to pray in His model prayer 'Thy Kingdom come' (6:10). The word 'come' here forces the Kingdom into the future. Thus, in one sense, the Kingdom had not yet come in Christ's day. Furthermore, this prayer is the model for a Christian in this day and age. Therefore the Kingdom has not come *yet* – for we are supposed to be still praying for its coming. The Lord's words which follow, 'Thy will be done on earth, as in heaven' are taken by some to define what 'Thy Kingdom come' means. However, 'Thy Kingdom come' involves more than sporadic or isolated outbursts of obedience to God's will. Whilst it is true that there is a present sense in the prayer for God's will to be done on earth, the words 'as in Heaven' show that this prayer will never be really answered until the Kingdom comes in the future. Only then will earth truly be like Heaven. In its world-wide scope this prayer remains unanswered in this present age of evil and injustice. A candid view of history and, better still, the later New Testament epistles tells us that our world will only become more lawless and rebellious as time runs its course. 'But know this, that in the last days perilous times will come...' (2 Tim 3:1).

There are a good few mentions of the Kingdom in the future tense in the rest of the New Testament. Notice the future tense and the words *enter* and *inherit* in the following verses:

Acts 14:22: 'We must through many tribulations *enter* the Kingdom of God.' Paul taught his new converts that persecution in this life was to be expected by a disciple *before* entrance into the Kingdom. The Kingdom is not God 'reigning in me.' It is not 'being a Christian.'

1 Corinthians 6:9: 'Do you not know that the unrighteous will not *inherit* the Kingdom of God? Do not be deceived. Neither fornicators, nor idolaters, nor adulterers, nor homosexuals, nor sodomites, not thieves, nor covetous, nor drunkards, nor revilers, nor extortioners will *inherit* the Kingdom of God.' Continuance in unrighteous living is evidence that a man is not saved and so shall never enter into the Kingdom in the future.

Galatians 5:21: '... of which I tell you beforehand, just as I also told you in time past, that those who practice such things will not *inherit* the Kingdom of God.'

Ephesians 5:5: 'For this you know, that no fornicator, unclean person, nor covetous man, who is an idolater, has any *inheritance* in the Kingdom of Christ and God.'

2 Peter 1:11: 'for so an *entrance* will be supplied to you abundantly into the everlasting Kingdom of our Lord and Saviour Jesus Christ.'

Notice also that the Kingdom is an *earthly* visible Kingdom in the future:

• In the beatitudes again we read 'Blessed are the meek, for they shall inherit *the earth.*' This gives the lie to the idea that the Kingdom of heaven simply refers to Heaven itself or to a present spiritual Kingdom in which Christ reigns from Heaven over His Church. There will be a future earthly Kingdom.

• Again, in the Sermon on the Mount we read Christ saying that His disciples should not need to make oaths. He says we are not to swear 'by Heaven for it is God's throne, nor by the earth for it is His footstool; nor by Jerusalem, for it is the city of the Great King' (5:34-35). Now the Great King is the long-promised Messiah and we are specifically told here that Jerusalem is His city. That is where His capital will be. If, on the other hand, we take the Great King to be a reference to God Himself, it amounts to the same thing anyway. If there is no earthly Kingdom and therefore no future for Israel nationally then why should God count Jerusalem any more important than Cairo? Nostalgia? No, either way, Christ is saying that there is a future for Jerusalem. It will be the seat of the Great King.

Consider some more New Testament verses that prove that the future Kingdom will be earthly:

Revelation 5:9-10: 'And they sang a new song, saying: You are worthy to take the scroll and to open its seals; for You were slain, and have redeemed us to God by Your blood out of every tribe and tongue and people and nation, and have made us kings and priests to our God; and we shall reign *on the earth.*'

Ephesians 1:9-10: 'Having made known to us the mystery of His will, according to His good pleasure which He purposed in Himself; that in the dispensation of the fullness of the times He might gather together in one all things in Christ, both which are in Heaven and which are on earth – in Him.' These verses need clarification. A literal translation of the verses reads (cutting into verse 9): '… His good pleasure which He purposed in Himself for the administration of the fullness of the times – to head up all things in the Christ – both the things in the heavens and the things upon *the earth.*' This is speaking about God's Grand Plan for all time – that at the end, called the fullness of times, the Christ – the Messiah – might head up all things both in the heavens and upon the earth. Christ is not only going to be the Head in Heaven but also *upon the Earth*.

2 Peter 3:13: 'Nevertheless we, according to His promise look for new heavens and a new earth in which righteousness dwells.' This verse is looking off to the eternal state but notice even in the eternal state there will be an earth. God has plans for planet earth!

1 Corinthians 6:2: 'Do you not know that the saints will judge the world?' This refers to the saints being given administrative responsibility during Christ's Kingdom reign. It certainly does not mean that the saints will send people to Hell at some future judgement day. Only God has the right to that sort of judgement.

Romans 4:13: 'For the promise to Abraham or to his seed that he would be the *heir of the world* was not through the law but through the righteousness of faith.' Abraham is going to inherit the *world*.

God promised many times in the Old Testament that one day He would send the Messiah, His King, who would establish a Kingdom for God on earth in the place of the kingdoms of men that have misruled Earth from its earliest days (Daniel 2:44). It would restore Earth to the Paradise it was created to be. It would be a Kingdom after God's original intentions for our world. Matthew 25:34 expresses this most beautifully: 'Then the King will say to those on His right hand, Come, you blessed of My Father, inherit the Kingdom prepared for you from the foundation of the *world*.'

How can there be Two Sides to the Kingdom?

So, we have seen on the one hand that there is a sense in which those who are the Lord's are already in the Kingdom whilst, on the other, there is a sense in which we are still going to enter the Kingdom in a future day. How can both of these two aspects of the Kingdom be possible, someone will ask? I suggest that the present spiritual aspect of the Kingdom is really *a preparatory stage* for the future Kingdom. If, as we have already suggested, the future Kingdom is likened in the Bible to a great feast, then we only have to ask any cook or farmer to learn that a feast takes a good deal of preparation before all the guests can enjoy it. There must be cooking done. Before that, there must be a crop harvested by the farmer so that there will be food to cook. In Matthew's Gospel, these preparations are pictured in Christ's parables in Ch13 where we read of the sowing of seed, the harvesting of the crop, the baking of bread and other activities. These are the present preparations for the Kingdom. The preaching of the Gospel and the salvation of men and women are the activities we are engaged in now in view of the future Kingdom.

Thus, whilst these activities are part of the preparations God is making for the coming Kingdom and are thus part of the Kingdom itself, it is not true to say that Christ's Kingdom is *simply* this Church era. It is not true to say that the Old Testament prophecies of the Kingdom are all fulfilled in the Church.

We in the Church are called to **share** ('partake' is the word used in Romans 11:17) in the blessings that God promised in the Old Testament to Israel. Remember, Old Testament Israel occupies seven ninths of the Bible. We do not replace Israel or cancel God's promises to them. They belong to Israel *and* the Church – and in that order, too. It is not a case of 'we Christians in the Church *are* the Kingdom'.

No Earthly Kingdom?

Some contend, on the basis of a few texts, that the New Testament expressly denies that the Kingdom of Christ is an earthly future Kingdom. However, in attempting to highlight these verses, some other monumental features of the New Testament which clearly teach that there will be a future earthly Kingdom are often rushed past. Let us observe four of these most obvious features that every reader of the New Testament should have noticed. After this we shall look at a few of the particular verses.

Feature 1: The Title Christ

Firstly, we must notice that Jesus is continually titled 'the Christ' – which means, the Messiah (John 1:41, 4:25). Jesus is called Christ (or Messiah) so often that it is almost used now erroneously as a surname. Jesus is given the title 'Saviour' by my count something like 15 times in the New Testament. But He is given the title 'Christ' over 500 times. Now the title Christ or Messiah means 'anointed one'. In the Old Testament Israel's kings were anointed to show that God had chosen them to be king. You will remember that David refused to kill Saul when the opportunity presented itself because Saul was 'the LORD'S anointed' (1 Samuel 24:10). The term Messiah is equivalent to 'King of Israel'. Nathanael described Jesus as the King of Israel in John 1:49. Jesus was described as 'the King of the Jews' at His birth (Matthew 2:2). He was descended from the line of the kings and was commonly referred to as 'the Son of David' during His ministry (e.g. Matthew 20:30). The term Messiah refers to a divinely appointed kingship. Why is this His most prominent and oft-used title?

For Jesus to be persistently called the Christ cannot simply mean that He reigns now from Heaven over all things – for two reasons. Firstly, this is self-evident – it would suffice to point out that Jesus is God and leave it at that. Why make so much of Jesus' Kingship, which is only a secondary implication, instead of the amazing fact of His Deity? If 'Christ' simply means He is God, 'Lord' would suffice for that purpose and 'Lord Jesus Christ' would then be tautologous – saying the same thing twice.

Secondly, the term Messiah does not refer to God's Kingship at all. The Messiah in the Old Testament was God's Vice-regent on earth. Originally God was Israel's King (1 Samuel 12:12). However, this theocratic arrangement – God ruling Israel from Heaven – did not work. Israel's sinfulness required strong spiritual leadership on earth to keep them in the right ways. During the period of the Judges Israel slipped further and further away from God. Finally, in Samuel's declining years, as Samuel tried to invest his corrupt sons in his place to continue some form of leadership, Israel's leaders presumptuously asked for a King. They wanted strong leadership on earth to save them from their enemies. They acted in unbelief without waiting for God's time. However, Israel's history teaches the lesson that there had to be a Mediator between them and God. God eventually allowed David, the man after God's own heart, to take the place of king as God's representative. Thus the title Messiah – or Anointed One – did not refer to God's Kingship. It referred to the human kingship God vested David's house with. They were to be His human Governors – ruling in His name, under His authority[5].

Some say that Jesus being Messiah only means that He was God's 'Special One' or that He was 'chosen' to be our Saviour. However, the term Messiah has little to do with salvation. It is a political office – King. Others say that His Kingship just means that He is the Head of the Church. But this is to say that He is the Messiah/King in no more than a metaphorical sense. Why then should He be called Saviour only 15 times in the New Testament whilst the metaphorical term King is used over 500 times? Why should God use as the primary title of our Lord Jesus the word Christ – meaning the King in David's Line – if it is nothing more than an honourary title with some lingering medieval pageantry? If our Lord Jesus is not King in a real sense then the name 'Christ' is superfluous.

---

[5] This explains why 1Corinthians 11:3 says that the head of the Christ is God. The Messiah is a position of authority under God's supreme authority. Christ in His *Person* is God – equal with the Father and not subordinate. But Christ, in taking upon Him the *Position* of Messiah, was taking a subordinate role – the role of an earthly human King – ruling as God's representative.

Why we Need a Messiah

Why is it that our Lord Jesus is called Christ, the Messiah, the King of Israel, then? It is a plainly admitted fact that God presently allows a serious mutiny against His rule to continue on planet Earth. God is blasphemed and wickedness flourishes. God's King was hung on a cross by His own citizenry outside His capital city. If, as some teach, Jesus being the Christ or Messiah simply involves His present reign, then it must be admitted by all that in a sense He still does not really reign here on Earth. God's will is not being done. There are many millions who are under the authority of the Devil (Ephesians 2:2). And this is the whole point of Jesus being the Messiah, the Christ. Here is the One through whom God *will* one day reign as King here on Earth. He will reign with an iron rod – the rebellion will be over. His reign will bring Heaven to Earth – Paradise will be restored as it was in the beginning instead of the sorrow, pain, tears and death of the present reign of unrighteousness.

Feature 2: The Kingdom

The second striking observation that a first-time reader of the Gospels will encounter is the enormous emphasis placed upon the Kingdom. In Matthew alone the Kingdom is mentioned approximately 50 times. Luke's Gospel has nearly as many references (about 45) and Mark's Gospel does not dodge the issue either – it has about 15. Only John's Gospel is quieter on the issue, referring to the Kingdom only about 5 times. (There are 8 references to the Kingdom in Acts and 20 in the Epistles and Revelation).

Again, the question must be asked, Why is there so much fanfare about the Kingdom if it is only a metaphor – 'God ruling in the hearts of those who love Him', etc. Is the Bible nothing more than metaphors, figures of speech and other sorts of religious poetry? Don't get me wrong: poetry, symbolism and allegory – it's all good stuff and very powerful sometimes. It has its place in the Bible. But the Bible is not *all* imagery and symbolism. Too much of the Bible becomes poetry if not only the Old Testament prophecies about the restoration of the throne of David are seen as dreamy descriptions of the Church, but also the New Testament is allegorised to mean that God's Kingdom only exists invisibly in the human heart.

It is true, of course, that God reigns over Christians who have personally submitted to His reign. But the Kingdom of God involves more than this.

God, as this world's Creator, promises that one day the Earth is going to be His again. He is going to *unite* Heaven and Earth again in one realm. He is going to undo all the damage done by sin and restore creation to the Paradise that it originally was (Romans 8:21). God is not in the business of writing off bad debts. He is not going to dump Planet Earth. He will reclaim what is His and rule universally.

Feature 3: The Resurrection

There is a third fact that I do not feel is given enough thought in discussions about the future Kingdom. There are some who admit the Kingdom is in the future, but deny that it is earthly. They hold that it is Heavenly. There are some, too, who believe that there will be a future earthly Kingdom but it will only be for Israel – the Church is destined for Heaven. However, another significant feature of the Bible has been missed.

The great emphasis in the Old and New Testaments regarding the future for believers rests upon the fact that there will be a resurrection. Now, if, when a believer dies, he is 'absent from the body, present with the Lord' – i.e. he goes to heaven, and it is 'far better', why do we need resurrected bodies at all in some future judgement day?

Of course, *theologically*, the reason for our resurrection is to demonstrate the triumph of Christ and His work over sin. Our resurrection will testify to the complete victory of Christ over sin and death. 'The last enemy that will be destroyed is death' (1 Corinthians 15:26). Yet the *practical* purpose for a body is for interaction on *Earth* and it will be on *Earth* that Christ's triumph over death will be displayed in our bodies – not just in Heaven. We do not need bodies in Heaven. Bodies are physical, even the post-resurrection spiritual body of the Lord and of the believer (1Corinthians 15:44). If we as believers were not going to inhabit a future earthly Kingdom, we could just as well be 'far better' off as spirits in Heaven.

Feature 4: Christ's Coming

All Christians accept that the Bible teaches that Christ is coming. However, where is He coming to? The answer is, obviously, that He is coming to Planet Earth. Some Christians seem to almost teach that when He comes to Earth, the Earth will instantly vaporise and dissolve and that thereafter there will only be Heaven and Hell. However, not only is this idea a bit puzzling but it is also to misunderstand the force of the Greek word 'coming' used in our NT of 'Christ's Coming'. Firstly, if it is admitted that Christ is physically returning to Earth, why should Christ return to Earth for only the briefest of stops and only to observe Earth's passing away? Why could Christ not just stay in Heaven and 'press the button' that ends Planet Earth's history. It all seems a bit needless and wasteful, if this is what is going to happen. But secondly, the word 'coming' ('parousia' in the Greek) is a very interesting word. It does not mean 'coming *again*'. Literally it means 'presence', often it means simply 'coming', but it was commonly used in NT times as a technical expression for the arrival or visit of a *King*. Special 'parousia taxes' were levied to pay for the visit's expenses, special 'parousia coins' were minted and monuments erected to commemorate the visit of an Emperor and new eras were dated from the parousia of certain kings to certain places. The modern equivalent would be a Royal Visit or Tour. The word 'parousia' in relation to Christ therefore has to do with the coming of Christ as *King* to reign rather than simply as Judge to destroy. If He only comes to end Earth's affairs, why was 'parousia' used in the New Testament to describe His coming?

A Close-up Look at Some Contentious Verses

Having thus discussed some of the big objections to a simply spiritual Heavenly Kingdom, we will look at some individual verses that are used to suggest that the Kingdom is only and solely a spiritual Kingdom. We shall look at two verses: (1) John 18:36, a verse that seems to deny a future earthly Kingdom, and (2) Galatians 6:16, a verse that seems to suggest that the Church has now taken Israel's place and therefore all the promises God made to Israel are fulfilled in the Church. These two verses are representative of two arguments used to deny a future earthly Kingdom.

Firstly, Christ's reply to Pilate in John 18:36 is sometimes half-quoted to convey the one-sided impression that the Kingdom of God is the present Christian age. Christ is normally misquoted as saying 'My Kingdom is *not* of this world. If my Kingdom were of this world, My servants would fight, so that I should not be delivered to the Jews'. However, the verse does not finish here. Notice that Christ went on to say 'but *now* My Kingdom is not *from here* (i.e. centred at Jerusalem)'. In other words, Christ was implying that although *now* His Kingdom was not based at Jerusalem, one day it will be. And so, Christ's Kingdom at the present is a spiritual Kingdom, but there is a day coming when it will be a physical, literal Kingdom on Earth. Thus this verse teaches both sides of the Kingdom. We must not become one-eyed when looking at this subject. A properly balanced binocular view of the Kingdom shows there are two sides to it.

Secondly, in Galatians 6:16 we read: 'and as many as walk according to this rule, peace and mercy be upon them, and upon the Israel of God'. Now what is this verse referring to when it mentions 'the Israel of God'? At first sighting we could take 'the Israel of God' to refer to the Church. In other words, The Church is the true Israel now that Israel has rejected God's Son. Therefore, it has been argued, the Church is really in view when we read prophecies in the Old Testament about Israel's future blessing when her Messiah reigns. However, there is another way of looking at this verse. I suggest that this verse refers to two distinct groups here – 'those who walk according to this rule (of being new creatures) *and* ... the Israel of God'. The word 'and' could possibly be used here in the sense of 'even' but it is more naturally used to distinguish a second distinct group of people. Thus, Paul is possibly blessing two distinct groups here as he closes his letter – firstly, those who walk according to the rule of being a new creation in verse 15 and 'the Israel of God'. Which way of looking at this verse is correct? We have to look elsewhere to see what the term 'the Israel of God' refers to. If we turn back to Romans 9:6-8 we are told quite clearly.

We read, 'But it is not that the word of God has taken no effect. For they are not all Israel who are of Israel, nor are they all children because they are the seed of Abraham'. This verse is often taken by some to mean that 'they are not Israel who are of Israel'. In other words, the nation of Israel, in rejecting Christ, is no longer considered by God as the true Israel, the people of God. Instead, *we* in the Church are now the true Israel, the people of God. However, this is a case of misreading the exact words. Notice that this re-reading of the verse omits the word 'all', which occurs twice in the verse. What Paul is really saying here is that not *all* Jews or *all* descendants of Abraham belong to Israel. God only considers those Israelites who believe in Christ, among whom the word of God has taken effect, to be true Israelites and true children of Abraham. The Israel of God thus refers to Jews, Israelites who believe and are truly God's children – in contrast to Israelites who are only so nationally and are not spiritually God's children. This verse thus says nothing about Gentiles at all. Nor does it really say anything about the Church being the Israel of God. The Israel of God are Jews who are true to God and believe in Christ.

Galatians 6:16 is an example of a verse that is used to try and prove that the Church is spiritually Israel and that there is no future for earthly Israel. All the Old Testament promises about Israel's glorious future are thus applied to the Church. As a result, however, Romans Chapters 9-11, which clearly teach that God's promises to ancient Israel are going to be fulfilled, end up being stretched and tangled beyond the limits of meaningful interpretation. Again, this is a one-eyed view of Scripture. Paul strictly warns us in Romans 11:11-32 against having a conceited view of the Church's importance (11:25) by assuming that God has finished with Israel. No, says Paul, 'concerning the gospel they are enemies for your sake, but concerning the election they are beloved for the sake of the fathers. For the gifts and the calling of God are irrevocable' (Romans 11:28-29). God is not finished with Israel.

The Postponed Kingdom

There is unfortunately another wrong idea about the Kingdom of Heaven that we are going to have to look at. The verse in Matthew 4:17 ('the Kingdom of Heaven is at hand') is interpreted by some to mean that Christ came announcing the imminent arrival of the Kingdom but when Israel rejected Him (by Chapter 12 of Matthew), the Kingdom had to be put off to the future. Christ changed His mind and instead of setting up the Kingdom, opted for Plan B and decided to set up His Church. One day, when the Church is complete, Christ will return to establish His Kingdom.

Now of course, again, there is some truth in this view. Nevertheless, I have caricatured it to present its obvious absurdities. In fact, I suspect that even those who sometimes advocate this view of the Kingdom will agree that when it is pushed to its logical conclusion it has certain ridiculous features.

All would agree that there was never going to be a Kingdom without the Cross. The Cross and the Church were never Plan B. Christ was never offering Himself to be King without the Cross first. In fact, it was Israel – not Christ – which wanted an immediate Kingdom. Israel wanted to make Christ their King in John 6:15 after the feeding of the five thousand. When Christ rejected their plans to make Him their King, they rejected Christ. They were quite ready to accept a miracle-working Messiah who would overthrow their enemies the Romans and usher in the golden era of Israel's glory. Their stumbling block was precisely that Christ was NOT offering an immediate Kingdom.

We shall see quite plainly when we look at the next section of Matthew's Gospel, the Sermon on the Mount, that Christ *always* envisaged a future Kingdom coming after a time of rejection and His absence. Christ was rejected long before Matthew Chapter 12 and spoke plainly of His rejection long before it too. Here are some examples:
• In the Beatitudes, Christ insisted that those who would be persecuted and reviled *for His name's sake* would be possessors of the Kingdom of Heaven (5:10-12). This implies both His absence during this period which we now live in as well as the rejection of Him and His message as delivered by His disciples.
• Christ refers to His disciples as the light of the world in the Sermon on the Mount (5:14). Later on in John's Gospel He says that as long as He is in the world *He* is the Light of the World. He is therefore implying here in Matthew that His disciples are to represent Him in His absence as light in a world that is dark – dark because it has rejected Him and He is absent.

Thus, even before Israel rejected Him, Christ spoke of the period of His absence and rejection which we now live in.

One other simple proof of the fact that Christ did not change plans midway through Matthew's Gospel and start thinking about the Church instead of the Kingdom is that 20 of the 50 references to the Kingdom of Heaven/ God in Matthew occur after Chapter 13. In other words, Christ kept on talking about the Kingdom of Heaven after He was rejected by the nation of Israel.

Restricted Area: No Christians Allowed!

This leads on to another closely related misunderstanding of Matthew's Gospel. Some teach that the Sermon on the Mount does not apply to Christians today. In fact, they teach that whole chunks of Matthew's Gospel – notably chapters 5-7, 10 and 24-25 – have nothing to do with the present Church age. Rather, they say, in the Sermon on the Mount Christ was advertising to the nation of Israel the principles upon which

His future Kingdom would be based, or that He was outlining the lifestyle required for 'Tribulation Saints' to be saved – by works. The Schofield Bible largely is responsible for spreading this idea that we must not look at the Sermon on the Mount if we are in the Church. It teaches that the Sermon on the Mount is the Constitution for the Government of the Kingdom in a future day. It says that 'the Sermon on the Mount in its primary application gives neither the privilege nor the duties of the Church'. In other words, our Lord's words here were not spoken for those of us in the Church to live by – we have to go to the Epistles. The Sermon on the Mount, rather, was spoken for Israel's sake, however, they unfortunately did not really want the Kingdom and so Christ opted instead for Plan B - the Cross and the Church.

Now this idea that the Sermon on the Mount is for Israel in the future and not for Christians today is quite easily proved wrong. I will give four reasons:

1.   We have already seen from the Beatitudes that Matthew Chapters 5-7 apply to a period when Christ is *absent* from this world – not during the future Kingdom when Christ reigns.

2.   Notice that the difficult conditions that a disciple is expected to cope with in the Sermon on the Mount apply to the days we live in – not the perfect, peaceful days of the Kingdom to come. This is plainly seen in that we, His disciples, are mourning (5:4). We will not be mourning when Christ reigns. We are to be peacemakers (5:9) and that implies conflict and war, which there will be none of when Christ reigns. We are persecuted (5:10), smote on the cheek (5:39), giving to charity (6:1-4), praying (6:5-14), fasting (6:16-18) and needy (6:25-34).

3.   It almost seems unbelievable that some teach that we as Christians are to go to the Epistles rather than the teachings of our Master. The fact that the teachings of our Lord here form the basis of all the teachings in the Epistles sinks it quickly. For example, we are taught here in the Sermon on the Mount to be like our Father in Heaven (Matthew 5:48; cf. Ephesians 5:1, 1 Peter 1:14-17), we are to return blessing for cursing (5:44; cf. Romans 12:14), we are to forgive others even as we have been forgiven (6:14-15; cf. Ephesians 4:32), we are to trust God for our needs rather than be full of care and anxiety (6:25-

34; cf. Philippians 4:6, 1 Peter 5:7) and we are not to judge our brethren (7:1-5; cf. James 4:11-12).

4.   Finally, one of the most beautiful proofs that the Sermon on the Mount is for disciples today is that it teaches us to enjoy a relationship with God as our Heavenly Father (mentioned 17 times). At the very centre and heart of the Sermon is the 'Lord's Prayer', which teaches us to address God as 'Our Father in Heaven'.

What is the Gospel of the Kingdom?

Finally, there is one further little associated misconception that needs clearing up. Some teach that Christ's message to Israel about the offer of an immediate kingdom (which we have mischievously called Plan A) is called 'the gospel of the Kingdom' and is a different gospel to the present gospel Christ has sent us into all the world to preach – 'the gospel of the grace of God'.

However, no less an authority than the Apostle Paul plainly disagrees with this notion. The 'gospel of the Kingdom' is exactly the same gospel as the 'gospel of the grace of God'. This is quickly seen in Acts 20:24-25, the only place the expression 'the gospel of the grace of God' is mentioned. There we read about Paul 'preaching the Kingdom of God' in the very same breath as speaking about the 'gospel of the grace of God'. Let me quote what the Apostle Paul said: 'But none of these things move me; nor do I count my life dear to myself, so that I may finish my race with joy, and the ministry which I received from the Lord Jesus, to testify to *the gospel of the grace of God*. And indeed, now I know that you all, among whom *I have gone preaching the Kingdom of God*, will see my face no more.'

Furthermore, Paul described his message as 'repentance toward God and faith toward our Lord Jesus Christ' just three verses before in 20:21. Thus, Paul described the preaching of the Kingdom of God, the gospel of the grace of God and the message of repentance and faith as the one and the same message. These terms are synonymous descriptions of the one gospel.

In fact, we find the apostles preaching many times about the Kingdom of God in the book of Acts. See Acts 1:3, 8:12, 14:22, 19:8, 20:25, 28:23. Notice two examples:

- In Acts 8:12 we read, 'But when they believed Philip as he preached *the things concerning the Kingdom of God* and the name of Jesus Christ, both men and women were baptized'.

- The very last verse of the book of Acts reads: 'Paul dwelt two whole years in his own rented house and received all who came to him, *preaching the Kingdom of God* and teaching the things which concern the Lord Jesus Christ with all confidence, no one forbidding him'.

The idea that there are a number of different gospels such as the gospel of the Kingdom, the gospel of the grace of God, the gospel of God, the gospel of Christ, etc, is erroneous. The Bible teaches that there is one 'everlasting gospel' (Revelation 14:6). Please observe that in Revelation 14:6 this 'everlasting gospel' is being preached by an angel *during the very period of time*, the 'great tribulation', when – according to some – the 'gospel of the Kingdom' is to be preached. This further proves that *all* men are saved by grace through faith in Christ in response to the one and only everlasting gospel. There is no other way to be saved, nor are there any other gospels – except false-gospels.

For one further disproof of the idea that the gospel of the Kingdom was only to be preached by Christ before Matthew 13 and then again in the 'tribulation' period, observe that in Luke 9:2 Christ sent the twelve disciples out to preach the gospel of the Kingdom. Here the disciples were preaching the gospel of the Kingdom *after* Christ had given His parables of the Kingdom in Luke Chapter 8. The Kingdom parables is the point (according to some) where Christ withdrew the offer of the Kingdom to Israel, stopped the preaching of the gospel of the Kingdom and instead opted for Plan B. Luke's Gospel proves that Christ still authorised His disciples to preach the gospel of the Kingdom after Matthew 13's parables.

Admittedly, these different descriptions of the one true gospel advertise different aspects of that message, but it is still the same gospel. Christ preached the Kingdom of God, His apostles preached it, and we should likewise preach that one day the King will return and reign. The message of a bright future on Planet Earth for those who repent and believe is indeed 'good news' and is *still* an important part of the message that God commissions us to preach to the world today. His Kingdom will soon be upon us. The final events that will climax in the establishment of that

Kingdom could happen at any moment! Men must therefore repent and believe in Christ. Let us not be worried, either, that Christ's announcement that the Kingdom was at hand has remained unfulfilled for 2000 years. God counts a thousand years as a watch in the night.

Chapter 4 - Christ's Teachings: 5:1 - 7:29

*M*atthew Chapters 5, 6 and 7 contain the next section of Matthew's Gospel. In these chapters we have what is popularly called the Sermon on the Mount. It consists of some of the best-known teachings of Christ. It again consists of twelve parts. They are:

1. The Beatitudes (5:3 - 5:16)
2. The Fulfilment of the Law (5:17 - 5:48)
3. Righteousness before God (6:1 - 6:18)
4. Riches (6:19 - 6:24)
5. Cares (6:25 - 6:34)
6. Judging others (7:1 - 7:5)
7. The Dogs and the Swine (7:6)
8. Asking, Seeking and Knocking (7:7 - 7:11)
9. The Golden Rule (7:12)
10. The Two Gates and Paths (7:13 - 7:14)
11. The Two Trees and Fruit (7:15 - 7:23)
12. The Two Men and their Houses (7:24 - 7:27)

True and False Disciples

The effect of the announcement of the imminent arrival of the Kingdom of God attended by the supernatural miracles of Christ had their quite foreseeable result. Great multitudes followed Him, says Matthew 4:25. And it was in response to the great numbers of followers that Christ in 5:1 climbed a mountain and gave us this sermon which comprises the second section of Matthew's Gospel.

It is very important that we notice that this sermon was directed primarily towards His *disciples*. Matthew 5:1 tells us this: 'And seeing the multitudes, He went up on a mountain, and when He was seated His *disciples* came to Him'. But it is also true that there were many of the great crowd who also heard this message. We see this from the end of the sermon in 7:28-29: 'And so it was, when Jesus had ended these sayings, that *the people* were astonished at His teaching, for He taught them as one having authority, and not as the scribes'. The Sermon on the Mount is really about what a real disciple of Christ is like. It was given for the benefit of Christ's disciples but also as a challenge to those great numbers of hangers-on who did not want to commit themselves completely to Christ.

You see, Christ had serious reservations about the great multitudes that followed Him. The crowds loved the idea of God's Kingdom coming soon. They yearned for political freedom from Rome. They had no objections to the idea of a perfect world. They needed Christ's miracles of healing. Christ, however, was not really interested in people following Him for these reasons. He had come preaching repentance as a pre-requisite for entrance into the Kingdom. The crowds did not like that so much. Neither did they like the idea of leaving all to follow Christ, like the four fishermen.

Christ did not want the sorts of 'followers' the crowds would have called themselves. And so to sort out the true followers from the false he climbed a mountain (5:1). In a way he was using the climb to illustrate what it was really going to be like to be His follower. Would they still follow if the path became narrow, steep and difficult?

Christ wanted disciples – which simply means 'learners' or 'trainees' – those who would learn to be like Him. These are true followers. They must be prepared to tread the difficult path of suffering that their Teacher was embarking upon that would lead to the glorious Kingdom. They, following after Him, would enter in. And so the Sermon on the Mount is a description of what it is to be a true follower of Christ – a disciple.

Ten Characteristics of a True Disciple

The Sermon on the Mount commences with the Beatitudes – or 'blessings'. They are a description of the character of a true follower of Christ. Christ lists ten characteristics of a disciple: They are

1. Poor in spirit - i.e. humble, not having high thoughts about themselves
2. Mourners - i.e. over their sins
3. Meek - i.e. those who do not push for their rights

4. Hungry and thirsty for righteousness – having desires to live right
5. Merciful - i.e. compassionate
6. Pure in heart - i.e. having clean thoughts
7. Peacemakers - i.e. those who are prepared to take steps to be reconciled with their enemies
8. Persecuted - for righteousness' sake and for Christ's sake[6]
9. The Salt of the earth - having a preserving moral effect by their behaviour
10. The Light of the World - pointing men to their Father in Heaven by their good works

The first seven characteristics of a disciple are *descriptions* of the righteous life that a disciple is to display, whilst the last three characteristics are the *result* of a righteous life – persecution, a preservative moral effect in the world and a light to draw others to the Father.

This second section of Matthew thus continues on from one of the major themes of the first section – morality. This section is defining more precisely what it means to repent. The first seven characteristics are the very opposites of the way men ordinarily behave. Men tend to try to promote themselves instead of being poor in spirit. They want to enjoy life rather than be mourners. They stand up for themselves rather than meekly submitting (for they say that if they don't stand up for their own interests no one else will). They hunger and thirst after all sorts of things in life except righteousness. They are too busy with their own lives to show compassion on others. They prefer uncleanness to purity of heart. They do not like to back down for the sake of peace. The disciple is to be the very opposite of the man of the world.

Christ adds to the end of each of the first seven characteristics of a disciple a blessing. In other words, he gives the reason why they are blessed. He says,

---

[6] Notice too that verse 11 ('Blessed are you when they shall revile and persecute you and say all kinds of evil against you falsely for My sake...') is simply just an expansion of the 8th blessing concerning persecution and forms part of the 8th blessing. Christ expands certain points in the Sermon on the Mount a number of times. For example, in the next part of it, he expands upon the commandment against adultery by speaking about divorce. Then in the section after that he expands upon the prohibition against ostentatious prayer by giving lengthy teaching on prayer in general, included in which is the Lord's Prayer.

Blessed are the poor in spirit,
for theirs is the Kingdom of Heaven.

Blessed are those who mourn,
for they shall be comforted.

Blessed are the meek,
for they shall inherit the earth.

Blessed are those who hunger and thirst for righteousness,
for they shall be filled.

Blessed are the merciful,
for they shall obtain mercy.

Blessed are the pure in heart,
for they shall see God.

Blessed are the peacemakers,
for they shall be called sons of God.

In short, Christ is saying that people like those He has described here in the beatitudes are going to enter into the future Kingdom and enjoy the blessings of eternal life. And that raises a problem.

The Problem with the Beatitudes

The problem with all this talk of the poor in spirit and the meek, the merciful and the mournful inheriting eternal life is that it seems to say that someone is saved by works and by living a good life. This seems to fly in the face of the message of the entire Bible that we are saved by faith.

However, this apparent contradiction is easily resolved once we remember that the Sermon on the Mount was delivered to those who already claimed to be followers and believers in Christ. The crowds would no doubt have unhesitatingly affirmed that they believed Jesus was the Messiah. Was that not why they were following Him? They had witnessed the greatest prophetic activity in over five hundred years in Israel – John the Baptist's ministry followed by Christ's miracles and message. They had little need of extraordinary intelligence to suspect that Jesus, with His message of the imminent Kingdom, was Himself the King. However, whilst the crowds would have *said* they believed, their *actions* showed that they were not true believers. They had little interest in repentance. They were not true disciples.

Christ came back to this at the very end of the Sermon on the Mount in 7:21-27 where he said 'Not everyone who says to me, Lord, Lord, shall enter the Kingdom of Heaven, but he who does the will of My Father in Heaven.' Then he proceeded to tell the parable of the wise man and the foolish man. The wise man symbolised those who heard His sayings and did them, the foolish man those who heard His sayings and did not do them. One was safe and the other came to ruin.

Christ wants real followers. If the first section of the Gospel pointed out quite clearly who Christ was and invited our belief in Him, the second section goes further. The Sermon on the Mount shows that a real believer shows by his actions that he believes. He becomes a disciple – one who hears and obeys his Teacher, thereby truly following Him.

Matthew lays enormous emphasis upon this point in his Gospel. It concludes, remember, in 28:19-20, with Christ commanding His disciples to 'Go therefore and *make disciples* of all the nations … teaching them to observe all things that I have commanded you'. Even in 7:13-14, Christ says, 'Enter by the narrow gate; for wide is the gate and broad is the way that leads to destruction and there are many who go in by it. Because narrow is the gate and difficult is the way which leads to life and there are few who find it.' Being a follower of Christ involves *two* things: firstly we enter through the gate, and then we have to walk the difficult road that leads to life. There must be faith and works, as James in his letter would put it.

Matthew also emphasises in his Gospel the fact that some people are false-disciples, particularly in his parables. For example, we have the parable of the Sower, with its fake disciples seen in the seed that fell on the stony ground (Ch13). There is the parable of the Wheat (the true disciples) and the Tares (the false) in Ch13. We have the good fish and the bad in the parable of the Net (Ch13). We have the man without the wedding garment in the parable of the Wedding (clothing speaking of lifestyle, Ch22). We have the wise and foolish Virgins (Ch25). We have the unprofitable servant cast into outer darkness in the parable of the Talents (Ch25).

Christ says in the Sermon on the Mount (7:20) 'therefore by their fruits you will know them'. Those who *say* they believe in Christ but do not do His Father's will are fakes – they are deceiving themselves and others. We have to enter through the narrow gate *and* walk the narrow, difficult path if we are going to enter into life. Mind you, we cannot get onto the narrow road except by the narrow gate. Furthermore, the only reason someone would choose to live the life of a disciple – so contrary to the normal way people live – is because of their faith. Notice that the disciple is not promised immediate blessings, but rather blessings in the future. The true disciple is someone who is not living for this life but rather for the life to come. The true disciple is someone living by faith – suffering loss now for future glory. Works follow faith. It is true faith that shows itself in works. You cannot have works without faith. And so, ultimately yet paradoxically, we are saved through faith.

What Christ was saying in the Sermon on the Mount is that a mere profession of faith is not enough. Our faith must demonstrate itself in the way we live our life. Real faith must result in works. Christ wants disciples. In fact, true disciples are the only people who are truly believers. True disciples are the only people who will enter the future Kingdom to enjoy its blessings and rewards. I know that some will baulk at this high standard for salvation – but it is Christ's standard, not mine – and we do well to take Christ's words seriously.

We must now look briefly at the body of the sermon and see how Christ describes the lifestyle of a true follower. The body of the sermon consists of another eight parts.

Five Ways a Follower of Christ Fulfils the Law

In 5:17, Christ says that He has come to fulfil the Law and the Prophets, not to destroy them. Therefore, in 5:17-48 Christ firstly teaches His disciples about the Law. He deals with five laws spanning the whole spectrum from murder to love, teaching what it really involves to keep them. They are, You shall not murder (v21), You shall not commit adultery (v27), You shall not swear falsely (v33), An eye for an eye and a tooth for a tooth (v38), and You shall love your neighbour (v43). Christ compares what Moses wrote with the higher standard that is required of His disciples. Six times Christ says '*You have heard that it was said to those of old*, 'You shall not murder' etc … *But I say to you*' (5:21-22, 27-28, 31-32, 33-34, 38-39, 43-44). Christ takes it upon Himself to add to the Law, re-interpreting, enlarging upon and explaining what the Law really involved. In so doing, Christ on His mountaintop proclaims Himself a greater Law-giver than Moses on Sinai. He in fact asserts Himself to be the very One who gave the Law to Moses!

Our Lord teaches that a disciple is to go a lot further than the commonly accepted interpretation of these laws. Just keeping the letter of the Law is not enough. It is not enough to simply avoid murder. Christ says we must not even be angry with our brother without a cause. We must not insult him (Raca - v22 - is simply an ordinary insult: 'block-head'). More seriously still, we must not level at a brother the most serious insult of all, 'You fool' – implying that he is a fool in the Old Testament sense of the word, i.e. one of the ungodly (see Psalm 14). We are thereby saying to our brother that he is not one of Christ's at all. Christ is teaching that murder involves words and thoughts of hatred as much as actions. The true follower will endeavour to fulfil this law by avoiding all of these. If he should in some way in these matters hurt his brother he will be very quick to put things right again (vs23-26).

It is the same with adultery. We must go further than the letter of the law. We must keep the spirit of the law. Christ teaches that a man who looks at a woman to lust for her has already committed adultery with her in his heart. Likewise, oaths are unnecessary for someone whose word is his bond, who is known for being as good as his word and strictly honest all the time. There is nothing wrong with oaths at all. God uses them. However, men whose honesty is in doubt use oaths to bolster their poor reputation for sincerity. We should have a reputation for honesty. By the way, Christians who refuse to take oaths in court on the basis of this teaching have missed the point of what Christ is saying here altogether. It is simply that we must have a reputation for being so completely honest that people will accept our word without an oath.

We must be those who turn the other cheek (5:38-42). That is, we must be those who demonstrate the genuine love that we have for others by even being prepared to be used and sometimes abused by others, rather than stand by our rights and insist on our pound of flesh in revenge. We must be prepared to accede to others' selfish and unreasonable requests at our expense. We are to overcome others' evil by retaliating with good. We are to return love for others' hatred. It is dead easy to return love for others love. It is the mark of a follower of Christ to show kindness to those who show us enmity. In so doing, too, we will surprise, shame, soften and finally win over our enemies.

Some consider Christ's teaching that we must turn the other cheek to be a policy bordering on madness. However, strangely enough, modern business has realised that this is the best policy to pursue when they get into a dispute. For example, some retailers, faced with an irate customer returning to the store with a defective product, have adopted the policy of not only replacing the article, but also giving the customer a voucher allowing them to spend a certain amount of money in their store. That is the quickest way to make a loyal customer for life! They go the extra mile. The benefits are lasting. Instead of telling 10-20 people what poor service they received, the customer will instead tell 10-20 other people about how well they were treated.

Christ concludes His teaching on how we are to fulfil the Law with the command to love our enemies as well as our neighbours (5:43-48). Some of us, mind you, have enough difficulty loving our fellow-Christians.

A Five-fold Description of Christian Ambition

Having thus dealt with the Law, Christ shows Himself to be greater than all the prophets. He proceeds in the next five parts of the Sermon on the Mount to give us five prohibitions:

1. Do not your righteous acts before men to be seen of them (6:1-18)
2. Do not lay up for yourselves treasures on earth (6:19-24)
3. Do not worry about your life (6:25-34)
4. Do not judge (7:1-5), and
5. Do not give what is holy to the dogs, nor cast your pearls before swine (7:6).

The Lord in these sections goes beyond the level of our actions. He probes, with the very eye of God, the motives and ambitions behind our lives. Christ does not want religious hypocrites for followers, outwardly keeping the rules but with hearts far from God.

Prohibition 1. Firstly, He warns us of doing things that are good to gain men's approval instead of doing them to please God. Christ here speaks of the particularly public aspects of religion – giving alms, praying and fasting. He reminds His disciples that their lives are based upon a belief in present resignation for future reward. Do they believe in a coming Kingdom in which God will reward them? Then let them not fall into the trap of seeking rewards or glory from men now. Let them in true faith remember that their Father sees them when they give alms, pray and fast *in secret* – even if no one else does. He will reward them richly for doing these things for Him alone.

Prohibition 2. Then Christ warns against laying up treasures on earth. Again, it is a question of whether they are living for this life or the coming Kingdom. Christ first points out the investment advantages of transferring our treasures to heaven where no thieves, rust or moths will disturb their accumulation. Then he hits at the heart of the issue. He asks where their heart really is. He says, Where your treasure is, there your heart will be also (6:21). Christ wants our hearts. He does not want us to have double-vision, having our eyes on both heavenly and earthly treasure (6:22-23). That will result in us seeing nothing clearly. He does not want us to work for two masters. That will result in us doing a bad job for both. We cannot live for earth and heaven. We cannot serve God and mammon.

Notice the theme of sight running through the first two prohibitions. We can do our righteous acts to be *seen* by men to earn their glory, or we can do them secretly, trusting in our Father who *sees* in secret to reward us openly later. Then, we have to ask ourselves what our eyes are upon – earthly treasure or heavenly. Or have we tried to focus upon both at the same time and got double vision? Our eyes symbolise our ambitions and motives – what we set our sights upon. The true follower, says Christ, has His eyes focused upon heavenly reward. The man with double vision has total darkness (6:23). He is a fake disciple.

This leaves the disciple with a question, though. If he does not live for this world's treasures, how will he survive in it? What will he eat and what will he wear? If he is so heavenly minded he will be of no earthly use. Christ anticipates this question with the warning against worry.

Prohibition 3. Christ assures the disciples that their heavenly Father who feeds the birds and clothes the fields with flowers considers them of more worth than these humbler creatures. He will feed and clothe them, as well as the birds and fields. Notice that Christ in reminding them that God feeds the birds who do not sow, reap or store and clothes the grass which does not toil or spin is not saying there is something 'unspiritual' about work. His prohibition is against *worry*, not work. There are many people in our world, who after having worked hard and honestly all day, go home and worry through the night about how their families will eat, drink and clothe themselves. It is hard to survive in our world. Christ forbids us to worry about that sort of thing. He assures us of a Heavenly Father who will attend to all of our needs if we seek first the Kingdom of God and His righteousness. Again, this warning about worry has used the imagery of the eye in the words 'seek' in vs32&33. Here our eyes are in danger of being taken off our Father and focused upon our needs.

Prohibition 4. In the next prohibition, that of judging, we are warned against turning our eyes somewhere else – on our brother. We notice all sorts of faults in our brethren betimes. Christ sternly warns us against judging them for their shortcomings. The reason he gives is that if we are in the habit of judging others, it is because we ourselves have a big problem – much bigger than those we judge. Our brother has a speck but we have a beam. The ridiculously funny thing about the story of the man with the beam in his eye is that he somehow does not realise it is there! He is a colossal hypocrite! Am I in the habit of continually judging other Christians who do not attain to the high standards I set them? Then, says Christ, I must be careful that I do not have a big beam protruding from my face that everyone sees but myself. Christ advises such a man to attend to the removal of the beam from his own eye so that he might then be of service to his brother with the speck, no doubt now in a much more humble and helpful fashion, rather than in his previous censorious style.

Prohibition 5. The last prohibition is not so easy to understand. Here is a suggestion. The warning against casting pearls before swine is usually interpreted to mean that we should not preach the gospel to rude, ugly or unfriendly people because they will not receive it. However, firstly, this is what we all were before we were saved (see Titus 3:3 and 1 Peter 4:3). It is highly suspicious theology to say that we should not preach the gospel to certain unsaved people. But secondly, the Sermon on the Mount has nothing to do with preaching to the unconverted. Matthew deals with that in depth in the fourth section of his gospel. Here Christ is teaching His disciples about how they ought to behave as His followers.

The reference to giving what is holy to the dogs refers back to the Old Testament. The priests were the only ones who were allowed to eat the holy meat from the sacrifices. If faced by a hungry snarling dog, should they pacify it by giving it some? God forbid. Let the dogs be thrown any old meat. Let not the priests surrender holy meat to the dogs. Neither should a disciple, if faced by hostile unbelievers at work or elsewhere in the world, surrender holy standards of behaviour to 'get on' or to 'fit in'. Neither should a disciple cast pearls before swine. That is, neither should he surrender those characteristics that in God's sight are beautiful and costly to an unclean world about him. The whole of the Sermon on the Mount concerns Christian character. Here we are warned against compromising Christian standards of holiness and beauty of character to get on with a world that is sinful, unholy and unclean. We are not to take our eyes off our heavenly Father and start fearing the fashions and opinions of the world.

Christ assures us that those who make compromises with the world to fit in better will earn no real respect from the world. The pearls we throw in the mud do not impress the pigs. To take a modern illustration of this, those churches which have denied the distinctive doctrines of Christianity such as Creation, the Inspiration of the Scriptures, Christ's Deity, Saving Work and Real Resurrection, or Christian moral standards are still treated by the world with contempt. These churches do not have great crowds coming to them. The world rightly considers that, having denied God, these churches should close up shop and cease to exist altogether. Or, to use another example, if we think that the world will respect us if we use the sort of filthy and unholy language they do, we are wrong. They will rightly see our lives as complete contradictions and steer clear.

Christ, in describing a disciple's righteousness in Chapter 5, has given us the most majestic of all expositions of the Law of God. Here in these five warnings in chapters 6 and 7 he has gone further and, taking the role of the Prophet, he has searched, with the very eye of God, our motives and ambitions – where we are looking.

Two Summaries of Christian Vision and Purpose

Having thus told us what to keep our eyes off, Christ next reminds us of where our eyes should be in 7:7-11. He reminds us to be asking, seeking and knocking. He is telling us to put our faith in our heavenly Father. He is telling us to persevere in prayer to God in the midst of difficult circumstances, confident that God, being good, will answer our requests. Here Christ boils down the life of faith to its essence. Let our eyes look to our Father in Heaven.

Matthew 7:12, often referred to as the Golden Rule, on the other hand, summarises our attitude, not to God, but to our fellow men. Christ says, 'Therefore, whatever you want men to do to you, do also to them, for this is the Law and the Prophets.'

Thus Christ, in teaching us to look in faith to our Father in Heaven and in teaching us to treat others the way we would hope they would treat us, is basically restating the two great commandments: Love the Lord your God and love your neighbour as yourself.

The Three Choices

Christ the master preacher concludes His sermon as all sermons should be concluded – with a call to action. A Sermon should not simply be an academic address that we can enjoy listening to. If a sermon does not spur us to action it was wasted time listening to it. God's word must not only be heard, but also obeyed. Christ brings His hearers to a crossroads at the conclusion of His sermon. He leaves them with a choice to make – between eternal life and eternal punishment. He describes this choice in three ways.

Firstly, he tells the parable of the Two Ways. We can choose to follow the world's crowds down Broadway, where there is plenty of room for whatever lifestyle we want, says Christ, but we will follow them to Hell. Alternately, we can take the narrow and difficult path, the path of true faith and true discipleship that leads to Life.

Secondly, he tells the parable of the Two Trees, the one bearing good fruit and the other bearing bad. By their fruits you will know them. The proof of a good tree is seen in its fruit. Christ says, 'Do men gather grapes from thornbushes or figs from thistles?' Good trees bear good fruit like grapes or figs. Their fruit is sweet and cheering. Bad trees bear thorns and thistles that prick and sting. What sort of fruit do I produce? Is my life full of good works which cheer the hearts of men and God? Or do I hurt and sting others? Those bearing bad fruit – although perhaps claiming to be Christ's – will be cast into the fire.

Then thirdly, Christ tells the parable of the Two Men who built their houses, the one upon the rock and the other upon the sand. Building our house upon the rock does not mean putting our faith in Christ, either, as the usual Gospel explanation of this parable would have us to believe. No, Christ says that those who *hear these sayings of Mine and do them* are those who are building their house beyond the reach of danger. Those who make the outward profession of loyalty to Christ with 'Lord, Lord' but ignore what He says and do not obey Him will perish.

Christ thus teaches here at the end of the Sermon on the Mount how serious the matter of how we live our lives really is. We can either live as disciples of His, enduring hardship and even persecution in this life, but inheriting eternal life and the blessings of His Kingdom, or we can live like the world and perish with it. Christ taught that for people to simply call Him 'Lord, Lord', would not be enough for them to enter into the Kingdom of Heaven. Mere outward profession of being a follower of Christ provides no salvation. The crowds of Christ's followers fell into this category. Christ teaches that only 'he who does the will of my Father in Heaven' will enter into the Kingdom of Heaven.

Chapter 5 - Christ's Miracles: 8:1 - 9:34

1. The Leper (8:1 - 8:4)

2. The Centurion's Servant (8:5 - 8:13)

3. Healing of Peter's Mother in Law and others (8:14 - 8:17)

4. Two Followers (8:18 - 8:22)

5. The Storm on the Lake (8:23 - 8:27)

6. The Gadarene Demoniac (8:28 - 8:34)

7. The Paralytic (9:1 - 9:8)

8. Matthew's Call (9:9)

9. Two Questions (9:10 - 9:17)

10. Jairus' Daughter and the Woman with the issue (9:18 - 9:26)

11. Two Blind Men (9:27 - 9:31)

12. The Dumb Demoniac (9:32 - 9:34)

*I*f there is one section of Matthew's Gospel that has Matthew's stamp imprinted upon it more than any other it is this section. Of course, this is where we meet Matthew himself as he meets Christ. But it is in his presentation of Christ's miracles that we see Matthew's personality and his writing style coming through more clearly than anywhere else. Here we see his characteristic brevity. Here we see his careful arrangement of material. And here we see his thematic approach to the life of Christ at its best.

Matthew's Missing Bits

Matthew's third section seems to be mostly concerned with Christ's miracles. Nine of its twelve parts describe miracles of Christ. Let us therefore briefly look at them first. There is one feature of Matthew's miracles that stands out. It is the brevity of detail that Matthew gives. The most outstanding example of this is found in the very famous story of the Paralytic at the beginning of Chapter 9. Matthew does not even mention the most interesting thing in the whole story – the fact that the paralysed man was lowered down through the roof after his four friends had found the crowd too thick to get through. All Matthew says is 'Then, behold, they brought to him a paralytic lying on a bed'. We have to go to Mark and Luke to find out that he was lowered through the roof. Why does Matthew leave this out?

Matthew's brevity of detail is seen in some of the other miracles, too. In the story of the Centurion whose servant was lying at home sick (8:5-13) Matthew tells us that the Centurion came to Jesus to request His aid. However, if we go to Luke's account we see that in fact the Centurion sent the elders of the Jews to Jesus with his request and then later as Jesus approached the house the Centurion sent other friends to Jesus. Luke tells us that the Centurion did not think himself worthy to come to Jesus or for Jesus to come under his roof. Matthew ignores all this detail and simply summarises the whole affair by saying the Centurion came to Jesus and had the conversation directly with Christ. Now some folks with only critical intentions might accuse Matthew of contradicting Luke here. What is he doing telling us half-truths like this?

In the story of the raising of Jairus' daughter he does it again. He tells us that Jairus came saying, 'My daughter has just died' (9:18). Luke, however, tells us that the little girl did not die till later on. As Jesus was travelling to the house, messengers came telling Him the girl had now died and help was useless. In the incident of Jesus healing the woman with the issue of blood, Matthew does not even tell us how Christ questioned the thronging crowd about who had touched Him. Matthew simply tells us that after the woman had touched Jesus' hem 'Jesus turned around and when he saw her He said, Be of good cheer, daughter; your faith has saved you'. Again he has ignored what seems in Luke's account to be one of the most important and most interesting parts of the story.

Even a simple comparison of the number of verses the different Gospels take to tell us the story of the Gadarene demoniacs shows Matthew's brevity. Matthew takes 7 verses, Mark takes 20 verses and Luke takes 14 verses. Mark's account is three times as long as Matthew's and Luke's is twice as long.

Matthew's abbreviation of these accounts is systematic and we can conclude from this fact that it is deliberate. If it were the case that some of Matthew's stories were shorter, but on the other hand some others were longer, we might conclude that Matthew simply was better acquainted with some stories than others. But this is not the case. Matthew deliberately prunes his accounts down to the bare minimum, leaving out facts that we can hardly believe he was unaware of, like the lowering through the roof. What is his purpose then?

Christ's Power

We see Matthew's purpose in the very first story – the cleansing of the leper. However, the point does not come out very clearly in our English translations. The point is made in the very first words of the leper to Jesus. He says, 'Lord if you are willing, you can make me clean.' Really, in the Greek, he is saying, Lord, if you are willing, you *have power* to make me clean. Matthew ignores Mark's comment on Christ's compassion and Luke's on the extent of the man's need and just simply stresses Christ's power in cleansing the leper on the spot.

This is the main point Matthew makes in this section. Time and time again Matthew ignores the interesting details that abound in these incidents to impress upon us the sheer power of Christ. By the way, if you have to do Bible studies of Christ's miracles with children who cannot read well or have poor concentration spans, use Matthew. His deliberate policy of filtering out of the picture everything else but the power of Christ hits home with enormous effect.

Christ's Authority

The most important word that Matthew emphasises is not the word power, however. It is the related word *authority*. This is the key word in the second incident in this section – that of the Centurion's servant (see 8:9). The Centurion compared his authority over his soldiers and servants to Christ's authority over the disease that was threatening the servant. This is the key to understanding this section of Matthew's Gospel. Christ has unlimited authority: over disease, the physical elements (in the storm on the sea), demons (even a whole army of them together in the Gadarene demoniacs), sins (in the story of the Paralytic) and death (in the case of Jairus' daughter). He even has the right to exercise authority over us.

Thus, in this section, Matthew strings together a catalogue of miracles, placing them side by side to show us how prolific and varied Christ's power was. Jesus is thus again shown to be Israel's Messiah. His power and authority demonstrates who he is – God with us.

Christ's Compassion

I suggest that this section of Matthew's Gospel is divided into four groups, each composed of three parts. The first group comprises the cleansing of the leper, the healing of the Centurion's servant and the further healings in 8:14-17. These three paragraphs look at Christ's healing miracles and draw from them the most obvious lessons that Christ's healing miracles teach. We have already seen the most obvious lesson already – that of Christ's power and authority. In the healings that follow however, we learn another important lesson.

I want to suggest that there is a connection between the healing of Peter's mother-in-law in verses 14 and 15 and the healing session that evening (verse 16) that tie these two incidents together. Some might accuse me of just trying to squeeze this section into twelve parts by forcing these two incidents together. However, before thus passing judgement, we must take notice of the fact that in these two chapters of Matthew's Gospel we have three other cases of two mini-incidents that are obviously tied together as one 'paragraph': the two would-be followers in 8:18-22, the two criticisms of Christ in the house in 9:10-17 and the miracle-within-a-miracle story of Jairus' daughter and the woman with the issue in 9:18-26. Notice that two people are involved in some other incidents in this section also: two Gadarene demoniacs in 8:28-34 and two blind men in 9:27-31. Maybe some bright thinker may see a reason for the repetitive references to the number two in this section.

Let us firstly notice some similarities between these two incidents of the healing of Peter's mother-in-law and the evening healings. Obviously, they are both about Christ healing sick people. Notice, too, how ordinary and unspectacular these miracles were. There seems at first little to learn from them. There seems to be little in verses 14-16 that gives away what Matthew's point was in relating these incidents. However, in verse 17 Matthew explains the point.

Matthew says that Christ's healing miracles were fulfilling the prophecy from Isaiah 53:4: 'He himself took our infirmities and bore our sicknesses'. What does this mean? For a start, is there not a mistake here? The familiar words of Isaiah in the Old Testament we read and sing are 'surely he has borne our *griefs* and carried our *sorrows*'. Why has Matthew changed it from griefs and sorrows to infirmities and sicknesses? Well, actually the reason is because that is what the words in Isaiah literally mean. Christ Himself took our infirmities and bore our sicknesses. And what does that mean? Does that mean that Christ became sick for us? Matthew does not seem to give any evidence of Christ getting sick here, nor do we even find any evidence of Christ being sick upon the Cross (seeing some say that Christ bore our sicknesses there). Even more strangely, Isaiah's prophecy, 'He Himself took our infirmities and bore our sicknesses' does not seem to have anything to do with Christ's *miraculous powers*. Isaiah does not seem to be foretelling Christ's miracles. What is the point of this puzzling quotation from Isaiah 53:4?

I suggest we see what Isaiah and Matthew meant if we look at the context of Isaiah 53 and particularly the verse before the one Matthew quotes – Isaiah 53:3. In it Isaiah prophesies of Christ's *rejection*. We read 'He is *despised* and *rejected by men*, a Man of Sorrows (lit. sicknesses, same word as in 53:4) and acquainted with grief (lit. infirmities, same word as in 53:4). And *we hid as it were our faces from Him*; He was *despised* and *we did not esteem Him*.' Now whilst Isaiah Chapter 53 is one of the great prophetic chapters on Christ's death, Isaiah is not writing so much about Christ's death in verses 3 and 4 as about Christ's life. He is writing about the sufferings of Christ in His life, particularly in His rejection. Isaiah is writing about Christ's troubles – using the words sicknesses (or infirmities) and pains in a figurative sense. He was the Man of Pains and acquainted with infirmity, as Isaiah 53:3 literally reads. His were not physical pains and weaknesses caused by disease, however, but the pains of heart, the griefs and sorrows caused by rejection.

Actually, the Greek word for 'infirmities' here also means 'weaknesses' – the exact opposite of Matthew's theme in this section – Christ's *power*. Matthew here quotes from Isaiah to emphasise that Christ understood other peoples' sufferings – particularly the sick. He sympathised with those who had pains and hurts. He had taken upon Himself frail flesh and he knew not only physical weakness (he later falls asleep in a boat) but also pains. His pains were of a different sort to the sick people He healed in this section, but

He could sympathise with others because He too suffered. He suffered for righteousness' sake. He suffered for the sake of the truth. He suffered the criticism of the religious authorities – the ones who should have realised that He was the very Messiah. He knew what it was to be without a place to lay His head. He knew, all right, what it was to suffer. The quote from Isaiah shows what motivated His healing miracles: compassion. He was prepared to take pity on a mother-in-law. He was prepared to heal all who came to Him.

So, I suggest that these two mini-stories have been linked together by Matthew's quotation from Isaiah to show this important third feature of Christ's healing miracles – His compassion. Christ had compassion on Peter's mother-in-law – the sort of person that others might not count very important. No one was unimportant to Christ. Christ's compassion extended to all the sick folk in the town that evening. No problem was too small or too great for Christ's care.

Following Christ

However, immediately after these first three parts of this section, there is an obvious and abrupt change of subject. In Part Four of this section we do not have a miracle at all – we have two conversations of Christ with would-be followers. The prophecy (8:17) has thus rounded off the first group of three incidents in this section and now we move on to the second group of incidents. In verses 18-22 we have two would-be disciples who come to Christ. The first is Mr. Too-Quick. He thinks following Christ is an easy matter. Christ warns him of the difficulties of the journey. 'Foxes have holes and birds of the air have nests but the Son of Man has nowhere to lay His head.' Then we meet Mr. Too-Slow. Ties to family members who were uninterested in Christ were holding him back. They urged upon him his family responsibilities – the burial of his father, either literally or possibly the care of an aged father – to stop him following the Lord. Christ warned this man that following Him must come before family. In fact, why was this man so tied to those who were so obviously spiritually dead? The spiritually dead were better suited to burying their dead. Christ's disciple was better leaving them if they were as spiritually dead as this.

But why does Matthew abruptly change subject from Christ's miracles to the matter of discipleship and following Christ? Where is the connection? The answer is that Christ's power, authority and care have been emphasised in the opening group of miracles in this section because they provide the reason why we should follow Christ. Christ's call to discipleship in the Sermon on the Mount is followed by Christ's miracles, power and authority to assure us that we can trust Christ when we give up our own ambitions for this little life and follow His call. He gives us two very good reasons for following in His pathway of suffering: He has authority over every difficulty that we might meet along the way and He cares about us.

Thus, in the Fifth Part of this section (verse 23) we read that Christ got into a boat and His disciples *followed* Him. Where did they follow Him? Into a storm in which they thought they were going to perish. Following Christ will sometimes land us in situations like this in life. And where was Christ during the storm? He was asleep! Did Christ not care? Does Christ not sometimes seem to us to be remote and uncaring during the storms of life? Did Christ not realise that He was leading His disciples into a storm when He commanded them to go to the other side? Of course He knew what He was doing – and still today He knows the way we take. Christ showed His disciples that He was in control and upbraided the disciples for their lack of faith: 'Why are you fearful, O you of little faith? Then He arose and rebuked the winds and the sea and there was a great calm.' Christ calls us to follow Him, trusting Him to bring us through safely to the 'other side'. We will have difficulties in our life of discipleship, but the one thing that should embolden us to follow Christ's call is the fact that, as Master of All, he can look after the problems.

The next incident again continues this theme. Matthew tells us something about the Gadarene demoniacs that neither Mark nor Luke do. In Matthew 8:28, we read that the demoniacs were so wild that 'no one could pass that way'. We, as disciples are called to follow Christ where He leads. We will come up against seemingly impassable mountains of opposition – perhaps even spiritual and Satanic opposition of the stiffest sort. However Christ, in all His Divine power and authority over all things, is in control. We must simply follow.

Christ and Sin

In the next three parts of this section (9:1-17), the emphasis changes slightly yet again. The three parts to this next group of incidents are:

• The raising of the Paralytic

- The call of Matthew

- The two questions that Christ's critics threw at Him

Firstly, Christ, in healing the paralytic, raises the issue of the forgiveness of sins. He claims to forgive the man's sins and proves that He has the authority to forgive sins by physically healing the man as well. Only God can do these sorts of things.

The point of this here in this section of Matthew's Gospel is obvious. Christ has been healing people of their sicknesses in the first three parts of this section. Here, he turns to healing our spiritual sickness. Christ shows that as God he has authority to forgive sins and thus to heal us of what is far more serious than any physical sickness.

Then secondly there is the call of Matthew. Again, we have Christ's compassion for sinners seen in His call of the tax-collector. But here the call to follow Christ involves something more than just faith. Matthew, being a taxman, was being called not just to leave his job, but the sinful life that went along with it. Following Christ involves us leaving our sins behind. We must repent.

After this, in the two questions Christ's critics asked while he was in Matthew's house in 9:9-17, Christ again teaches us about His attitude toward sins and sinners.

Christ was firstly questioned by the Pharisees on why he companied with disreputable people. Christ gave the well-known reply that those who are sick have need of the physician – not those who are strong. He had come to call sinners to repentance. Again we have the issue of sin brought up. Christ came in great love, not to condemn and ostracise sinners, but to bring them back to God in repentance. He came to heal us of our sin problem, not to congratulate those who deluded themselves they were free from sin.

The second question addressed to Christ was about why He didn't fast like other religious people did – for their sins. Christ's reply to this second question about fasting teaches that the Christian, forgiven of his sins through the love of the Heavenly Bridegroom, has reason to rejoice – not mourn.

But Christ not only teaches us about sin here. He also teaches about His attitude to society. Christ did not come to 'fit in'. He very publicly and provocatively forgave the paralytic's sins. He publicly called Matthew the sinful tax-collector to follow Him, and then publicly associated with the whole town's tax-collecting community. This was scandalous behaviour in the eyes of the religious Jews.

Christ teaches that following Him means leaving even the established traditions and attitudes of the people around us in society – even the religious and moral people around about us. Christ had come to bring a revolutionary and very radical way of life. Some Christians today think that the essence of being a Christian is being as crusty a conservative as possible. Christ instead shows us that following Him means being as radically different as He was.

The Pharisees were of the sort of religion which really consisted in earning the praise of others. Christ, in refusing to compliment them with His company, earned their hatred. Christ was not afraid of stepping out of the very comfortable little circle of mutual admiration and self-congratulation that made being a Pharisee bearable. In companying with sinners, however, Christ was getting Himself into serious trouble. He was breaking the taboos and traditions of Jewish religious society.

Becoming Christ's follower means leaving behind the ruts of human religious tradition. It means leaving fasting for feasting (9:15). It involves tossing out the patched up, starchy, old robes of respectable tradition and trying on Christ's rather more comfortable, new, clean festal attire (9:16). It involves replacing the dried up, tight, old inflexible wineskins for new ones capable of containing the new wine He gives us (9:17). But, with all that, it means enduring the criticism of those whose love for their 'old ways' outweighs the little love they have for the ways of God. Christ had not come to reform human religion. He came with no attempt to resurface the 'old-paths'. He came to bring in something radically new.

Christ was no conservative. He did not bend down to kiss the bootstraps of the religious establishment. The Scribes and Pharisees were outraged with virtually everything He ever said or did. He stood for the truth and eventually died for the truth. To the Scribes and the Pharisees he said in this section, 'Go and learn what this means: *I desire mercy and not sacrifice*' (9:13). He was quoting Hosea's simple message. The people of Hosea's day performed their outward religious sacrifices and rituals most punctually. However, their religion was no inward reality. There was no truth or mercy or knowledge of God (Hosea 4:1). The streets ran red with blood. There was no mercy (i.e. compassion) for their fellow men. Their behaviour towards their fellow men showed up the hypocrisy of the religious pretence they played at. Christ was not going to have His followers become the slaves of hypocritical religious dictators and kill-joys.

Notice, however, that Christ was a radical for the cause of Truth – Truth based on Scripture. He said in 9:13 '*Go and learn what this means*: I desire mercy and not sacrifice'. He was telling them to go and look up their Bibles. Christ was not licensing us to be radicals in whatever way we want just for the sake of thumbing our noses at religious authority. He based everything He did upon Scripture. However, notice further that He implied here that the Pharisees, although they *said* they had a high view of Scripture, were rather ignorant of it. They thought they knew it better than any others. In fact they thought they knew it so well that they had stopped reading it altogether. All they did nowadays was debate with each other interpretations of instructions in their little religious rulebook – 'Principles of Sabbath-keeping and Sundry other Strictures'.

Notice how difficult is the pathway that Christ calls us to follow Him on. He was accused of blasphemy when he forgave sins in the incident of the paralytic. Then He was criticised for eating with tax collectors and sinners. Then He was questioned on why he did not conform to the religious traditions of the Pharisees and the disciples of John. It would have been very easy for Christ to simply conform to the religious system of the Pharisees for the sake of peace. Christ instead chose to stand for the truth and eventually to die for it. This is the sort of pathway we are called to follow Christ along. Why would anyone want to be a disciple and follow along this difficult road? Only because we believe, on the basis of Christ's authority, that the blessings He promised in the Sermon on the Mount will certainly follow the suffering we experience for His name's sake now.

Faith

The final three parts of this section concentrate on what we need if we are going to firstly experience the salvation and spiritual healing we need because of our sins and if we are secondly going to follow Christ in the pathway of discipleship. We need faith. The first incident here is the raising of Jairus' dead daughter with the embedded incident about the healing of the woman with the flow of blood. Here we have two of the supreme examples of faith in the Bible. Firstly, Jairus asked Christ to lay His hand on his dead daughter so that she might live. What great faith! Then we have the woman who counted Christ's power so great that she reckoned all that would be needed would be for her touch the edge of His coat. Christ turned to her and said, 'Be of good cheer, daughter, your faith has saved you.' This is what we need. We need to be saved or we will perish in our sins – forever. We therefore need faith because it is the only way we can come into the blessing of salvation.

Then we have two blind men who came to Christ crying out for healing. Christ turned to them and asked, 'Do you believe that I am able to do this?' They replied 'Yes, Lord.' Christ touched their eyes and said, 'According to your faith, let it be to you.'

Then finally, we have a case of **_unbelief_** in the healing of the dumb demoniac, who once healed, spoke. The crowds were amazed and said that there had never been anything like this in Israel. However, in spite of the evidence right in front of their noses and indeed throughout this whole section, the Pharisees refused to believe. They said, 'He casts out demons by the ruler of demons.'

Here in Chapters 8 and 9 we therefore see Matthew's Gospel at its thematic best. Matthew shows us who Christ is in His miraculous power, authority and compassion. Then Matthew shows that Christ's authority provides the firm footing for following Christ in a life of discipleship. Then Matthew looks at a spiritual dimension of Christ's miracles, showing that we need spiritual healing from sin. Matthew shows us that Christ alone can deal with our problem and bring us salvation from our sins. Finally he shows what our salvation hinges upon – our faith. He does all this without any editorial commentary. It is accomplished simply by the arrangement of the incidents.

Chapter 6 - Christ's Preaching: 9:35 - 12:50

1.   Christ's Call of the Twelve (9:35 - 10:4)

2.   Christ's Commissioning of the Twelve (10:5 - 10:42)

3.   John's Question (11:1 - 11:6)

4.   Jesus on John and His Generation (11:7 - 11:19)

5.   Jesus rebukes the cities of Galilee (11:20 - 11:24)

6.   Christ's Gospel Invitation (11:25 - 11:30)

7.   Plucking Grain on the Sabbath (12:1 - 12:8)

8.   Healing on the Sabbath (12:9 - 12:14)

9.   Jesus' Withdrawal (12:15 - 12:21)

10.   The Unforgivable Sin (12:22 - 12:37)

11.   A Sign Requested (12:38 - 12:45)

12.   Jesus' Family (12:46 - 12:50)

*I*n Chapters 10-12 Matthew's Gospel reaches a mini-climax. In these chapters the Religious Establishment rejects Christ. Christ, for His part, also rejects not only the religious leaders but the crowds who follow Him but refuse to repent.

This fourth section of Matthew's Gospel also examines the next great area of Christ's teachings – His instructions regarding the preaching of the gospel. Matthew's Gospel thus presents the preaching of the gospel as the second great responsibility of a disciple – after that of living a life of discipleship as described in the Sermon on the Mount. Notice that our gospel witness comes after our personal righteousness. This teaches us the lesson that our preaching will have little effect unless we are first living the life of a disciple. Someone who truly imitates Christ should also respond to the tremendous spiritual need of men and women around him or her in the same way that Christ did: 'When (Christ) saw the multitudes He was moved with compassion for them' (Matthew 9:36).

But is this really what this whole section is all about, asks the sceptic. What has the incident about Christ's disciples plucking grain on the Sabbath, for example, got to do with evangelism? Let us briefly examine the contents of this section.

Connections

The central part of this section is the long talk Christ gave to the twelve disciples before He sent them out on their evangelistic journey (Chapter 10). The rest of Chapters 11 and 12, however, are very neatly summarised for us by Matthew in the words of 11:1 'Now it came to pass, when Jesus finished commanding His twelve disciples, that *He departed from there to teach and to preach in their cities'*.

In other words, whereas in Chapter 10 we have Christ commanding His disciples to preach, in Chapters 11 and 12 we have the record of Christ Himself going and doing the business. The connections between Christ's teaching in Ch10 and Christ's actions in the following two chapters become very clear once we start comparing these chapters. Let us briefly observe seven similarities between Christ's teaching in Chapter 10 and Christ's demonstration of the principles He taught in Chapters 11 and 12.

1.   In the first verse of Chapter 10, Christ gives His disciples *power over demons and disease*. Then He tells them in 10:7-8, 'as you go, preach, saying, The Kingdom of Heaven is at hand. *Heal the sick, cleanse the lepers, raise the dead, cast out demons.'*

Now, come over to the beginning of Chapter 11, to the very first incident recording Christ's own evangelism. John's question about whether Jesus was the Coming One is answered by Christ in verses 4 and 5 with the words 'Go and tell John the things which you hear and see: *the blind see and the lame walk; the lepers are cleansed and the deaf hear; the dead are raised up and the poor have the gospel preached to them'*. Both the Evangelistic instructions and the demonstration start with miracles. They are signs that authenticate the message of the gospel and demonstrate concern for the practical and physical needs of those hearing the message.

2.   Christ in His teaching in 10:9-10 describes the evangelist's *clothing* and equipment. Christ stresses the fact that the evangelist is *not* to take any

money or spare clothing or equipment for emergencies. The evangelist is to be a man who lives by faith. He is working for God and God will see to it that His worker gets his food (10:10).

We find the parallel to Christ's directions for the clothing and the supply of a preacher's physical needs in the next incident in Chapter 11. Christ starts to talk to the crowds about John the Baptist (11:7-19). In particular, he reminds them of the lack of 'mod-cons' that John had. Christ particularly describes the ***clothing*** that John wore and the harshness of the environment he lived in. Christ's main point was to show that John was indeed a prophet. Indeed, Christ says that he was more than a prophet – he was Elijah who was to come – that is, the messenger who would come before the Messiah. However, Matthew, in addition to making this point, seems to be also using John as a role model for an evangelist. John was no reed shaken by the wind. He was no wishy-washy crowd-pleaser, swaying this way and that. Self-denial and fearlessness marked the man, the very qualities that Christ was calling for in those he sent out.

3.   Christ talks about the reaction His evangelists will receive in ***the cities and towns*** in 10:11-15. If they were received in a city or house they were to bless it with their peace (v13) but if they were not received they were to shake the very dust from their feet (v14). Notice particularly that Christ said in verse 15 that it would be more tolerable for ***Sodom and Gomorrah*** in the day of judgement than for the city that did not receive His messengers.

Back over in Chapter 11 now, the next thing we have recorded is ***Christ's rebuke of the cities*** in which His mighty works had been done but which did not repent (11:20-24). Notice that He uses the very words in 10:15 again of Capernaum: 'it shall be more tolerable for the land of ***Sodom*** in the day of judgement than for you'.

4.   The rest of Christ's discourse in Chapter 10 takes on a more foreboding aspect. He speaks of the evangelists being delivered up to councils and scourged in their synagogues (v17). They would be also brought before governors and kings for a testimony to the Gentiles (v18). Notice particularly that their ***opposition*** would come ***from religious quarters*** – in verse 17, the synagogues.

The parallels continue in Christ's own evangelistic ministry. The next two incidents Matthew relates (12:1-14) deal with the **opposition** that Christ received *from the Pharisees*. They accused Christ of breaking the Sabbath by allowing His disciples to pluck grain on it and in healing the man in the synagogue. Their strict and inflexible religious ideas would deny Christ's poor and hungry disciples the grain they had to pluck as they walked by the side of the field on the Sabbath. Even when Christ did a *good deed* in healing a man they managed to find fault rather than rejoice. When Christ did not meekly and quietly fall into line they plotted against Him, how they might destroy Him[7].

5.   Notice that when Christ was warning His disciples of this sort of opposition in Matthew 10:19-20 He assured them that the '*Spirit of your Father*' would give them what to speak when they were put on trial. In the aftermath of Christ's clash with the Pharisees in 12:15-21 Matthew quotes the prophet's words of Him too, 'I will put my Spirit upon Him'.

6.   As Christ's warnings of the rejection His disciples will have to face as they preach the Gospel comes to its culmination, Christ says in 10:25 'It is enough for a disciple that he be like his teacher, and a servant like his master. If they have called the master of the house **Beelzebub**, how much more will they call those of his house.' Looking again over in Ch12, the next story (12:22-37) shows Christ's rejection coming to a head with the incident in which Christ's casting out of a demon drew the response from the Pharisees, 'This fellow does not cast out demons except by **Beelzebub**, the ruler of the demons.' Christ then responds at length to the accusation that He has Beelzebub, patiently showing how illogical it is – and how blasphemous it is.

7.   For a final comparison between Christ's teaching in Chapter 10 and ministry in Chapters 11 and 12, we find Christ speaking towards the end of Chapter 10 about the rejection that a disciple would have to face from his

---

[7] The puzzling words in 10:23, 'When they persecute you in this city, flee to another, for assuredly, I say to you, you will not have gone through the cities of Israel before the Son of Man comes' make sense once we realise the connection between Matthew Chapters 10, 11 and 12. These words do not refer to Christ's Second Coming, but to the Lord's approaching death. Whilst the disciples would face persecution on their evangelistic journey, their persecution would be small compared to the sufferings Christ Himself would face within a very short period of time. The disciples would not have managed to cover all the cities of Israel before the Messiah Himself would be finally rejected and crucified. Thus the disciples are again being pointed to Christ Himself as their example in evangelism.

own family. He said, 'I have come to set a man against his father, a daughter against her mother and a daughter-in-law against her mother-in-law' (10:35).

Then the final incident in this section (12:46-50) is the story of how the members of Christ's own family were not among His followers. They stood without, seeking to speak with Him. They obviously were not with Him, and were thus against Him, to use His words in 12:30. Christ accordingly publicly disowned them. He stretched out His hand toward His disciples and said, 'Here are my mother and my brothers!'

Chapters 9:35 to 12:50 thus stand together to form a complete unit, with a striking correspondence between Christ's instructions concerning evangelism and the incidents that Matthew retells about Christ's example of evangelism.

Twelve Parts

Furthermore, this section is clearly split up into twelve parts. Even in Chapter 11, which consists mostly of words of Christ and appears at the first difficult to split up, Matthew has interposed little editorial remarks in verses 7, 20 and 25 to guide us into a correct division of the parts. The twelve incidents are not split up into four sets of three here, you will notice. Rather, the section is split up into six pairs of two, just as the twelve disciples were split up and sent out as six groups of two in 10:2-5 (notice the use of 'and' in those verses). Let us notice the six sets of pairs:

1.   In the first two parts, Christ presents the need of the lost and then sends out His disciples to meet the need.

2.   In the third and fourth parts of this section John the Baptist is the common factor. These two parts present the evidence for Jesus' Messiahship, firstly in Christ's miracles and secondly in John himself and his ministry. If John was 'the messenger' who would 'prepare the way', then who could Jesus be other than the Messiah?

3.   In the fifth and sixth parts of this section we have the two reactions to the gospel message: the rejection of Christ's message by the cities on the Lake of Galilee and Jesus' thanksgiving for the reception of it by His disciples.

4.   The seventh and eighth parts are both about Christ falling foul of the Pharisees over the Sabbath Day. This is the spark that ignites their desire to destroy Him.

5.   In the ninth and tenth parts of the section we have the brewing confrontation between Christ and the Pharisees. Firstly, Christ quietly withdraws from confrontation with the Pharisees and secondly, the Pharisees blaspheme by saying that Christ casts out demons by Beelzebub. Both these parts are about the Holy Spirit. In the first, Matthew quotes Isaiah's prophecy about Christ having the Holy Spirit upon Him. In the second, after the Pharisees attribute Christ's power to Satan, Christ says they have committed the unforgivable sin of blasphemy against the Spirit.

6.   Finally, in the last two parts of this section, we have the request for a sign from the Pharisees and Scribes and secondly the visit of Jesus' family. These incidents show the culmination of the nation's rejection of Christ. In reply to the unbelieving request for a sign, Christ offers them only the sign of Jonah's three days and nights and promises that the Gentile Ninevites and the Queen of Sheba will stand up in the judgement to condemn the unbelief of their generation. Finally, even His own family are not with Him or on His side. They are 'standing outside' the circle of His followers. Christ henceforth refers to His disciples as 'My mother and My brothers'.

Preaching the Gospel

Let us now turn to learn some of the lessons Christ teaches us about preaching the Gospel.

1.   Preaching Christ Firstly, we learn here the lesson that we must preach Christ. 'We preach not ourselves but Christ Jesus the Lord' (2 Corinthians 4:5), 'whom we preach' (Colossians 1:28). Here is the attractive power of the gospel message. Notice that Christ is the central figure in this section of the Gospel. Here we have some of the greatest titles of Christ in the Scriptures:

*   the Coming One (11:3)
        – the One fulfilling all the prophecies;

*   the One greater than the Temple (12:6)
        – surpassing and superseding the Old Testament religion;

*   the Lord of the Sabbath (12:8)
        – the God of Creation;

*   'My Servant whom I have chosen, My Beloved, in whom My soul is well pleased' (12:18-21)
        – the Perfect Man;

- the One stronger than the Strong Man (12:29)
  - the Victor over the Devil;

- the One greater than Jonah (12:41)
  - the greatest preacher and evangelist of all time;

- the One greater than Solomon (12:42)
  - the wisest teacher of all time.

Yet, it is at this high point of Matthew's revelation of Christ's person that we reach the crucial point in Christ's life of His rejection. He is rejected for showing mercy to His hungry disciples, allowing them to pluck the grain on the Sabbath day and even for doing good on the Sabbath day, healing the man with the withered hand. They say He has Beelzebub. They call Him 'a glutton and a winebibber, a friend of tax collectors and sinners'. Even His own brothers do not believe in Him. How incredible!

2.   Defending the Gospel Notice that the first thing that Christ did for His apostles was to give them evidence that would convince men of their message. In 10:1 we read, 'and when He had called His twelve disciples to Him, He gave them power over unclean spirits, to cast them out, and to heal all kinds of sickness and all kinds of disease'. Notice again that this was precisely the sort of evidence Christ reassured John the Baptist with in Chapter 11. Notice thirdly that this section on Evangelism follows directly on from the section on Christ's Miracles. When we preach the Gospel Christ intends that we too offer credible evidence to the world. Here at the end of this section we have the ultimate (and God's final) sign that we are to preach – the sign of the resurrection. This was the sign Christ Himself offered when asked for a sign from heaven in Matthew 12. The book of Acts shows the Apostles preaching the resurrection of Christ even more than His Death. For example, in Acts 2, Peter devotes 1 verse to Christ's death but 12 to His resurrection. We in our preaching must likewise present the evidence and the reasons for our belief in Jesus being the Son of God. Not only so, but our day and age requires that we strenuously defend belief in God, Creation, God's Laws and the Bible itself.

Some suggest that 'apologetics', which means defending Christ and the Bible by showing evidence and using reasoning, is not a spiritual activity. We should just say 'thus saith the Lord' with a take-it-or-leave it attitude.

However, we live in a world where there are many people who have sincere doubts about the Bible, even about God. They may not admit to these doubts straight away, but usually reserve them for when they are being pressed with the gospel. Then they start firing questions back about whether God is really there. Sincere questions deserve respectful, and therefore solid, answers. It will not always do to just say 'Because the Bible says so'. Sometimes we must be prepared to give reasons why the Bible can be trusted. Of course, there is a point at which faith must reach out and feel for God as Acts 17:27 tells us. But there are good reasons for a person to believe in God, Christ, the Bible and the gospel. Peter wrote 'But sanctify the Lord God in your hearts and always be ready to give a defence (or answer, Greek 'apologia') to everyone who asks you a reason for the hope that is in you, with meekness and fear' (1 Peter 3:15). Paul wrote about the necessity not only of 'the furtherance of the gospel' (Philippians 1:12) but also of 'the defence (Gk. 'apologia') of the gospel' (Philippians 1:17).

3.   **Persecution** Christ devotes the most of His teaching on evangelism to the subject of dealing with rejection and persecution. The twenty-four verses from 10:16-39 deal with this subject. This teaches us a number of lessons. It teaches us that we must not be surprised, disappointed or put off our mission by opposition to the Gospel. The early apostles were ready for opposition (Acts 4:24-30) and we shall have to overcome this hurdle like them. Opposition is inevitable. A big part of Christ's message was the preaching of repentance, a message not exactly calculated to entertain. Admittedly, we must not stumble people by being rude, culturally insensitive or out of date or touch when presenting the Gospel. However, if we water the Gospel message down or hide it behind so much entertainment that nobody gets *mad* as well as glad (John Wesley) then maybe we are not presenting the true Gospel at all.

4.   **The Means of Salvation** What means will bring people to Christ, then? How do we see fruit in the preaching of the gospel? The power of the Holy Spirit. Out of twelve references to the Holy Spirit in Matthew's Gospel, five are found in this section on Evangelism (1:18, 20, 3:11, 16, 4:1, **10:20, 12:18, 28, 31, 32**, 22:43, 28:19). It is by God the Holy Spirit's activity and power that people are born again. We need to learn dependence upon God's power in prayer if we are to see God working. In 11:25-30 we have Christ's thanksgiving to His Father for having hidden His truth from the wise and

115

prudent and revealed it instead to 'babes'. Christ in this paragraph speaks of the absolute necessity of God revealing His truth to men for them to be saved. Salvation is God's work. He is the Lord of the harvest and He is working alongside us as we preach the Gospel. We must preach the gospel in faith, trusting God to bless the message. In the very same breath Christ gives His glorious gospel invitation 'Come to me, all you who labour and are heavy-laden and I will give you rest'. Theological heavyweights can take on the job of reconciling God's election and man's responsibility at this point. The rest of us will pass on.

5.   Labourers in the Harvest Whilst we are all called to be witnesses for Christ, yet it is true that there are certain disciples whom God calls to full-time evangelism. We have a case here: the twelve were sent out by Christ as apostles (which means 'ones sent on a mission', or 'missionaries'). Being a missionary is not something a person decides they would like to do for a living, like a career choice. Nor do missionary societies or committees send out missionaries (in the Bible, that is), nor even Churches (they *release* them – *apelusan*, Acts 13:3). Christ chose, called, prepared and sent out these men. He told them in 9:38, 'Therefore pray the Lord of the harvest to send out labourers into His harvest'. If we acknowledge that God is 'the Lord of the harvest' and that it is 'His harvest' – not ours, then it follows that He alone has the authority to send out labourers into it.

Notice next that Christ, in 10:9-15, gave instructions for the support of His disciples. They were not told to go and scrape together their hoarded resources to buy provisions for their trip. Nor were they told to go round their friends and gather subscriptions or pledges of support or negotiate some salary with a sending committee. Indeed, they were told not to take any money or bag or spare clothing or spare equipment. Christ assured them that 'a worker is worthy of his food' (10:10). Christ, their Master, would see to it that their needs of food and shelter would be met as they journeyed. Christ's provision for their needs, however, was not going to drop from the sky. These needs were to be met in the various places they went, through the provision of 'those who are worthy' – 10:11, which seems to mean those who are *spiritually* worthy – i.e. devout fellow-believers. Christ concluded His teaching on evangelism in 10:40-42 with a promise of reward for those who receive Christ's evangelists, particularly those who look after their material needs. Even a cup of cold water given to one of them will not be forgotten or go unrewarded.

Some will plead that for a missionary or minister of the gospel to depend upon such means for a living is somehow inapplicable in today's situation. But Christ expects His servants to put their faith in Him for the little things, like their material support, as much as for the big things like the accomplishment of the task of evangelism. Faith delights to prove God, not to murmur and complain. The later New Testament shows this principle in action and provides the solutions to some problems in this regard (for instance, how a pioneer is to be supported). Why should principles that were practised by Christ and Paul not be good enough for us today?

Chapter 7 - Christ's Parables: 13:1 - 13:52

1. The Parable of the Sower (13:1 – 13:9)

2. The Disciples' Perplexity (13:10 – 13:17)

3. The Interpretation of the Parable (13:18 – 13:23)

4. The Parable of the Wheat and the Tares (13:24 – 13:30)

5. The Parable of the Mustard Seed (13:31 – 13:32)

6. The Parable of the Leaven (13:33)

7. The Fulfilment of the Prophecy (13:34 – 13:35)

8. The Interpretation of the Second Parable (13:36 – 13:43)

9. The Parable of the Treasure in the Field (13:44)

10. The Parable of the Pearl of Great Price (13:45 – 13:46)

11. The Parable of the Net (13:47 – 13:50)

12. The Parable of the Householder (13:51 – 13:52)

*T*he next section of Matthew's Gospel is again a very clearly defined and distinct unit. In it Matthew records some of Christ's parables. And once again, without any forcing or squeezing, we are able to split the section up into twelve parts.

This is a crucial section in Matthew's Gospel. It marks a major turning-point in the life of Christ. As we saw in the last section, the religious leaders have rejected Christ's person and the crowds themselves have paid little attention to His message. There has been neither faith nor repentance. However the crowds still follow Christ. Matthew 13:2 tells us that when Christ went out of the house and sat by the sea, great multitudes were gathered together to Him. They saw in Jesus the material for a potential Messiah. They liked the idea of the Jewish nation regaining its freedom from Rome and ruling the world. They had no particular objections to paradise on earth. They wanted the coming Kingdom. They thought that any day now Christ would call them to follow Him up to Jerusalem where, with their popular support, He would somehow seize power.

Something queer is going on here

Christ here starts to speak to them about His Kingdom. However, he starts to speak to them in a rather strange and confusing way. He speaks to them in parables. Now we tend to have a slightly wrong idea of parables. We like to think of parables being like a preacher's illustrations – the interesting stories preachers tell to keep us from going to sleep. They use the illustration of something we are very familiar with from everyday life to help us to understand rather more complicated spiritual ideas. And in a sense Christ's parables are illustrations. But they are very strange ones.

Notice two things about Christ's parables here. Firstly, notice that Matthew is not giving us here a sample selection of Christ's parables so we will see how wonderful were His powers of storytelling. Matthew does not tell us some of Christ's parables which are rightly considered the most famous – like the Good Samaritan or the Prodigal Son. Matthew's parables are not a representative spread of Christ's parables at all. Most of them are not great story-parables at all. Three of the seven parables here are only two verses long and two are only one verse long. They are not the sort of illustrations that grip you with a good story-line and then deliver a dramatic punch-line at the end. They are about the most down-to-earth affairs of life – farmers sowing their seed, a woman baking bread, merchants trading in pearls and fishermen casting nets – and nothing particularly startling happens in them. Mind you, there are one or two exceptions. But by and large, there is not a great deal a novelist would consider worthy of a plot for a best-selling book. They are not very interesting or exciting. They don't even go on long enough to be boring. They must have been a great anti-climax for these listeners used to the majestic and gracious words of Christ. What had happened? Christ must have appeared to the multitudes to have lost His gift. After having listened not long ago to the lucid, logical and powerful words of Christ's Sermon on the Mount, His parables here seem to be a pale imitation of His prior oratory. That is the first thing that is strange about these parables.

The second and really peculiar thing about these parables is that Christ did not tell His audience what His parables meant. A preacher normally relates his illustrations to the truths he is trying to explain. Imagine a preacher who spun off a long string of illustrations one after another, illustrations that did not seem to have any lessons we could learn from them and did not seem to have anything to do with each other. We would politely enquire after the health of the man. He certainly would not be invited back to preach. To be true, Christ did tell the people what the parables were about. They were about the Kingdom. But the crowds must have wondered what Christ's Kingdom had to do with a woman baking bread or fishermen going to their daily work.

The crowds were left puzzled. If Christ was speaking in riddles, why was He not telling the crowds what the riddles meant? Worse still, if He was not speaking in riddles, it was about time they stopped regarding Him as a teacher worth listening to. And this is precisely what started to happen. The crowds of followers who had up till this point flocked to hear Christ preach, began to drift away. John relates this very thing happening at the same point in Christ's life in John Chapter 6.

The Riddle Explained

However, Christ's parables here were not the poor quality illustrations that they at first appeared to be. They were in fact full of meaning and significance. The brilliance of these parables lies in the fact that Christ was able to do two things at once. He was giving the impression of having lost His talent for teaching. Yet at the same time he was speaking, not silly nonsense, but sober truth. His parables, as some preachers have said, both conceal and reveal. They illustrate as well as causing those there solely for the sermon-tasting to lose interest.

Even the disciples were puzzled. They asked in v10, 'Why do you speak to them in parables'? Christ's reply was that these people had stopped listening to Him long before He started speaking in parables. He said in v13 'therefore I speak to them in parables, because seeing they do not see, and hearing they do not hear, nor do they understand'. They saw His miracles but did not see the significance of them. They did not see that here was the Son of God. They heard His words but did not really listen to Him. They did not obey Him. Christ had become to the crowds a bit like Ezekiel in Ezekiel 33:32. God said to Ezekiel, 'Indeed you are to them as a very lovely song of one who has a pleasant voice and can play well on an instrument; for they hear your words but they do not do them.' Christ was not interested in popularity or in crowds. He wanted real followers. He wanted disciples who heard His words and obeyed them. And so, by speaking in riddles, He started turning away the crowds who were not really interested in what He was teaching.

Furthermore, the crowds were quite seriously mistaken about Christ's Kingdom. There could be no Kingdom on earth until sin, which had spoilt God's creation, was dealt with. Christ could not be King unless He was first crucified. There could be no glory without the suffering. And for these crowds, there would be no Kingdom at all because they did not take responsibility for their own personal sins – and repent. Christ's Kingdom was not going to come the way the crowds thought it should.

Christ's movements in the chapter are a parable in themselves. I suggest that Christ symbolises His response to Israel's rejection of Himself by His actions in this chapter. We read in 13:1 that 'Jesus went out of the *house* and sat by the sea'. This (for reasons we will see later) symbolises His rejection in His own 'house' – Israel, His departure from it, and the good news of salvation going out to the Gentile nations, symbolised by the sea.

Then, after having told the first four parables to the crowds outside by the sea, in v36 'Jesus sent the multitude away and went into the house'. There He told the last three parables to the disciples inside the house. This return to the house, where only His disciples were with Him, symbolises Christ's rejection of the multitudes of false-disciples. Instead He turns to the few He can truly call His own, making a new home for Himself in the Church, where those who are prepared to hear Him are told the secrets of God.

The Point of the Parables
Now let us have a look at the seven parables themselves briefly. They are

1.   the Parable of the Sower
2.   the Parable of the Wheat and the Tares
3.   the Parable of the Mustard Seed
4.   the Parable of the Woman putting the Leaven in the Flour
5.   the Parable of the Treasure hid in the field
6.   the Parable of the Pearl of Great Price
7.   the Parable of the Net.

Now the parables run in pairs up until they reach the seventh parable. The first two parables have to do with a man who sows seed in his field. The first parable concentrates on the sowing of the seed, whilst the second parable's focus shifts to the harvesting of the crop.

In the first parable the seed falls on four sorts of surface – the pathway, the shallow and rocky soil, the weed-choked soil and the good soil, producing a crop of different quality in each case. In the second parable the man sows good seed in his field but an enemy sows fake wheat – called tares. The interest here centres on the fact that the farmer chooses to only separate the wheat from the tares at harvest.

The third and fourth parables are both about growth. The third parable is about the mustard seed which, although it is so small a seed, yet grows to produce, not a vegetable, but a small tree sizeable enough for the birds to perch in. The fourth parable concerns the woman baking bread who takes the leaven, the yeast, and hides it in three measures of flour. The leaven itself spreads throughout the whole and causes its growth.

The fifth and sixth parables are commercial. They both concern loss for ultimate gain. The fifth parable concerns a man who sells all that he has to buy a field which he knows has treasure hidden in it. The sixth parable concerns a pearl merchant searching for beautiful pearls who found one pearl of great value and likewise sold all that he had to buy it.

The seventh parable is about a fishing net which was cast into the sea and indiscriminately caught good fish which were kept and bad fish which were thrown away.

Christ Himself only explained three of the seven parables in this section to His disciples – the first, the second and the last. These three parables really teach the same general truths. They are about how in this present age the message of the gospel is being spread. Sowing and fishing are both used as pictures in the New Testament of preaching the gospel. Also, in all three parables, there are true disciples and false disciples produced. These are pictured in the seed fallen on stony and thorny ground, the tares, and the bad fish. Christ says that they shall stay mingled and not be told apart until the end of the age when the 'righteous will shine forth as the sun in the Kingdom of their Father' (v43).

Therefore, I suggest these parables teach two truths. The most important thing we must notice from these parables is that Christ is teaching that His Kingdom will be preceded by a period in which the gospel will be preached. This is the period which we live in. Our job now is to spread the gospel.

Those who truly believe and are real disciples will eventually – at the end of the age – enjoy the blessings of Christ's Kingdom. The Kingdom was not to immediately appear. There would be a delay as the necessary preparations for its eventual coming took place. Secondly, these parables remind us again of the possibility of false discipleship.

The Keys that unlock Christ's Treasure-Chamber

What, however, about the other four parables that Christ did not explain? We have to be careful about being too dogmatic in expressing what we think some of these parables teach. However, I want to suggest that Matthew himself gives us the answers to what the unexplained parables mean. Throughout the next two sections of his Gospel (chapters 14-18) there are numerous parallels with Christ's parables. For example, notice the general parallel between Christ's first four 'agricultural' parables about 'growth' and the outstanding feature of the next section of Matthew's Gospel: how Christ twice miraculously **multiplied** the loaves and fish.

Then, notice in Chapter 15 we have an explanation of the second parable. The second parable is about the farmer who sowed wheat only to find his enemy had come and sown tares. His servants came and asked if they should root up the tares. The farmer replied that this might cause some of the wheat to be accidentally pulled up as well. Instead, all was to be left till harvest when the wheat would be gathered into the barn but the tares would be burned. Now the key to what this parable teaches is found in Chapter 15. There we have the incident where Christ was criticised for paying no attention to the Pharisees' tradition of hand-washing. When Christ talked about the true nature of defilement saying 'Not what goes into the mouth defiles a man; but what comes out of the mouth, this defiles a man' the Pharisees, misunderstanding Him, were offended. The disciples came and told Christ but Christ replied, 'Every **plant** which my heavenly Father has not planted will be rooted up.' Christ is quite pointedly referring back to the second parable when He talks about unwanted plants being rooted up. The tares represent religious counterfeits. And Christ in Chapter 15 points out the Pharisees as a case in point.

So too, Christ explains the fourth parable about the woman hiding leaven in three measures of flour in Matthew's next section. Several quite different interpretations have been placed upon this parable, but when we come to

Chapter 16, Christ again comes back to the subject of leaven and we see in what way He was referring to it in the parable. He says in Ch.16:6, quite out of the blue, 'Take heed and beware of the **leaven** of the Pharisees and the Sadducees'. Here Christ tells us what He meant by leaven in the parable in Chapter 13: the infiltrating work of evil doctrines (16:12).

Then, in the section after that, Matthew is still illuminating and explaining Christ's parables when, following the incident involving the demon-possessed son, he relates Christ's words concerning the mustard seed (17:20), which Christ talked about in the third parable in Chapter 13. He says, 'If you have faith as a **mustard seed**, you will say to this mountain, Move from here to there and it will move; and nothing will be impossible for you.' He is speaking about the power of faith to do things thought impossible, like feeding the multitudes or Peter walking on water (Ch14).

So I suggest that the third and fourth parables deal with the astonishing spread of the true gospel in the present age by the power of God through our faith on the one hand, and, more sadly, on the other, the significant infiltration of evil within it, which itself has a great capacity to cause growth and to spread rapidly (remember Galatians 5:9). Just on that note, it's very possible that we might use the parable of the leaven as a rod to beat others with. This, however, is not quite the purpose for which Christ told the parable. Many Christians avow (1) that their particular brand of Christianity is the correct, uncorrupted version, and (2) that all other versions of Christianity are seriously contaminated with error. The truth is that **every** version of Christianity, says Christ's parable, is more or less corrupted with the leaven – wrong doctrine – of either the Sadducee sort (denying truths of Scripture) or, perhaps more commonly, the Pharisee sort (adding all sorts of human traditions to Scripture). There are other sorts of leaven, too (see 1 Corinthians 5:7). It does not take much searching to find faults with any Christian communion – none are perfect. Christ carefully points out the infiltration of evil, not to give us ammunition with which to criticise other Christians, or so that we complacently treat corruption as an inevitability, but that we might more humbly appreciate our own failings. A little more humility, self-scrutiny, self-correction and tolerance (not of evil doctrines, but of other similarly failing Christians) is our responsibility.

In the fifth and sixth parables we have stories about businessmen who sell all they have to gain something. In chapter 16, Christ talks again about the commercial subjects of loss, exchange and profit when He says, 'If anyone desires to come after Me, let him deny himself, and take up his cross and follow Me. For whoever desires to save his life will *lose* it, but whoever loses his life for My sake will *find* it. For what *profit* is it to a man if he *gains* the whole world and *loses* his own soul? Or what will a man give in *exchange* for his soul?' (verses 24-26).

Christ had just announced (16:21-23) that He Himself must die. He is the great example of sacrifice for greater gain that He calls His disciple to follow. So I suggest that the fifth and sixth parables refer to:

(1) Christ having to sacrifice Himself before He could reign,

(2) Christ giving Himself so that the Church could be His (for in the Chapters 16 to 18 Christ introduces His disciples to the Church), and

(3) the disciple's similar resignation of his life for Christ's sake if he is to follow Christ into that Kingdom, as required by Christ in Chapter 16.

Matthew goes on in the next section of the Gospel to explain more fully what the Kingdom is all about.

Chapter 8 - Christ's Kingdom and Israel: 13:53 - 16:12

1. Rejection in Nazareth (13:54 – 13:58)

2. Herod's Opinion (14:1 – 14:2)

3. John's Beheading (14:3 – 14:12)

4. Feeding the Five Thousand (14:13 – 14:21)

5. Walking on the Water (14:22 – 14:33)

6. Healing in Gennesaret (14:34 – 14:36)

7. Eating with Unwashed Hands (15:1 – 15:9)

8. True Defilement (15:10 – 15:20)

9. The Canaanite Woman's Daughter (15:21 – 15:28)

10. Feeding the Four Thousand (15:29 – 15:39)

11. Pharisees and Sadducees desire a Sign (16:1 – 16:4)

12. Disciples forget to take Bread (16:5 – 16:12)

*R*eaders of Matthew's Gospel sometimes complain that when they get to certain spots in the Gospel they 'lose the plot'. That is, they do not understand what the main thrust of a series of chapters is. After Christ's parables we come to a series of narratives that leave us wondering what connection they have with each other, what connection they have with what has already happened in the first thirteen chapters and what part they play in the overall storyline of the Gospel. This section is split up into two halves of six parts each. We shall see that this section presents us with two principal messages about the relationship of Christ's Kingdom with the nation of Israel. Let us notice, first of all though, some connecting features of the entire section.

Feasting

The first feature that we must notice is that this section is full of stories about **bread**.

• There are the two occasions where Christ fed the five thousand and the four thousand.

• Then we have the Pharisees' question to Christ stated in 15:2, 'Why do your disciples transgress the tradition of the elders? For they do not wash their hands when they eat bread.'

• Then we have the story about the Canaanite woman's request for Christ to cast out the demon from her daughter. The climax of the conversation is reached when Christ says in 15:26, 'It is not good to take the children's bread and throw it to the little dogs,' to which the woman replies, 'Yes, Lord, yet even the little dogs eat the crumbs which fall from their masters' table.'

• Then, following the visit of the Pharisees and Sadducees, Christ warned His disciples, 'Take heed and beware of the leaven of the Pharisees and the Sadducees' (16:6). The disciples had no idea what Christ was talking about, but suspected it was a sniping criticism of them for having forgotten to bring bread with them. They said 'It is because we have taken no bread' (16:7).

Thus we have five stories in which bread is directly involved. Furthermore, we could add to this list the story of John the Baptist's execution. It was all about a birthday feast – at which the last dish brought out had John's head on it. Finally, we must add the two other stories directly linked with two of the five stories already listed which direct mention bread: Christ's assessment of true defilement (part 8 of this section) and the Pharisees and Sadducees seeking a sign (part 11). That makes eight out of the twelve parts that directly or indirectly involve bread and feasting.

A Parable in Actions

This seems to be a rather high proportion of stories that have bread or eating as a prominent part of them. It seems too high to be simply coincidental. What is this all about? Well, we see the answer if we look carefully at the last story in this section. Christ, speaking to the disciples following the disciples' misunderstanding of His warning about the leaven of the Pharisees and the Sadducees, asks in 16:11, 'How is it that you do not understand that I did not speak to you concerning **bread**? – but to beware of the leaven of the Pharisees and Sadducees'. Christ was not speaking about literal bread, He tells them. He was using bread as a parable. I suggest, on the basis of Christ's own words here, that bread is used throughout this section as a parable.

Christ's Kingdom is often spoken of in the Gospels as a great feast. For example, in Matthew 8:11, following the Centurion's statement of faith in the authority of Christ to heal his sick servant, Christ said, 'And I say to you that many will come from east and west and sit down with Abraham, Isaac and Jacob in the Kingdom of heaven.' The words 'sit down' in the original Greek here literally refer to reclining at a meal. The Kingdom of Heaven is pictured as a grand feast. Christ Himself told the parable of the great supper in response to the comment in Luke's Gospel from one of His fellow diners 'Blessed is he who shall eat bread in the Kingdom of God' (Luke 14:15). Isaiah spoke of the day when 'in this mountain the LORD of hosts will make for all people a feast of choice pieces, a feast of wines on the lees...'(Isaiah 26:6). I suggest that this whole section is an enacted parable. It is all about feasts. Underneath it all we have important teaching about the Kingdom of heaven – God's great future feast when God's King, the Messiah, the Christ, comes again to reign over the earth.

This section thus follows logically on from the last section in which we had Christ's **spoken parables** about His Kingdom. Here we have a series of incidents which are really **parables in action**. The parables in the last section described the Kingdom of heaven using activities that are involved in the **preparations** for putting on a feast. There was the sowing and harvesting, there was the baking of the bread and the mustard seed used for seasoning, there was the cost of the feast described in the two parables about the men who sold everything to buy something else more precious and there was the fishing. Christ's parables were teaching that this present age we are in is but God's preparation time for God's great eternal feast.

Thus, this next section continues to teach us about Christ's Kingdom. In particular, this section teaches us about Christ's Kingdom's relationship to the nation of Israel. Israel had by this stage in the Gospel, by and large, rejected both Christ's claims for Himself and His message of repentance. What is Christ's reaction to such a perverse nation? And what does the future hold for the nation of Israel?

Leaving Home

To answer these last two questions, let us notice that in this section Christ repeatedly *departs*. After the news of John's execution came in 14:13, 'Jesus departed from there by boat to a deserted place by Himself'. After the Pharisees' criticism of Him for not keeping their tradition of washing their hands before eating we read again in 15:21 that 'Jesus went out from there and departed to the region of Tyre and Sidon'. Then, after the Pharisees and Sadducees had come testing Him in Chapter 16 we read in v4 'he left them and departed', going to the other side of the lake (v5). This is reminiscent of Christ, at the beginning of the parables in Chapter 13, leaving the house and going down to the seashore.

The reason I suggest the repetition of the symbolism of 'leaving the house' in Chapter 13 is because we run up against it again in the first story in this section. Christ goes to Nazareth, where His old townsfolk despise their onetime carpenter's son in unbelief and ask 'Where did this man get all these things (i.e. His wisdom and miraculous powers)?' Christ's answer is, 'A prophet is not without honour except in His own country and in His own *house*' (13:57). Luke puts the story of Christ's visit to Nazareth right at the beginning of Christ's public ministry (Luke 4). It was a fact that Christ had gone back to Nazareth and then left His hometown right at the beginning of His public ministry, as Luke and even Matthew tell us (Matthew 4:13). Matthew, however, has deliberately left the story of Christ's rejection in Nazareth until here immediately after the parables, to focus attention upon Christ's rejection in His own house – Israel. Christ had been rejected in His own house – not just in Nazareth but in the nation of Israel as a whole. As a result, Christ leaves home (the Jewish nation) in this section.

Politics and Religion

This section looks at Christ's reaction to the nation of Israel from two perspectives. In the first six parts of this section we look at the nation of Israel politically and nationally. In the second six parts of this section we look at the nation of Israel religiously.

This section firstly aims to deliver us from the standard Jewish misconceptions of Christ's Kingdom that were held by the crowds who followed Jesus. They hoped that Jesus would lead a political insurrection and thus secure His Kingdom. They were justifiably unimpressed with the political arrangements under which they had to live and hoped that Christ would rescue them from the Romans. In this they were to be so disappointed that they would soon desert Him in droves.

For Christ was not going to rescue Israel nationally. In fact, He was going to abandon it! At least, He was going to leave it stuck with its own rejection of Him until, in a day yet future, He will come again and Israel (nationally) will be saved.

The second half of this section deals with Christ's Kingdom's relationship with Israel's religion. Was the state religion of Christ's Kingdom going to be the Jewish religion? You would have thought so – God Himself had established the Jewish religion. Surely Christ would confirm it to be the One True Religion. No, it was not to be. The Jewish religion had failed God and now turned their back on His Son. Christ was going to leave Jewish religion behind.

This section therefore deals with the two hottest topics in any society – politics and religion. It shows how Christ rejected the current popular views on these important topics.

The Kingdom of Heaven and the Politics of Planet Earth

In the second and third parts of this section we meet Herod, the ruler of Galilee. In the second story, Herod hears of the fame of Christ and says to his servants that it is John the Baptist risen from the dead. I suggest Herod is trying to laugh off the reports of Christ here. He is mocking – he has not turned religious. He is trying (as usual) to play the big man in front of his servants. See Luke's parallel account (Luke 9:7-9) for a more private and sincere expression of Herod's puzzled and perhaps fearful reaction to the reports of Jesus. Then in the third story we have the account of John's beheading. Now it is very strange that we are told the details of John's death. God rarely ever relates stories for their human-interest value like newspapers hoping to increase their circulation. We are not told of the death of Mary, Jesus' mother or Joseph, her husband. Neither are we told of the end of the lives of most of the prominent figures in the apostolic period. The reason is simple. These people are not the central figures in the Bible story in God's eyes, however much religious people will make heroes of them. There is only One important figure – Christ. So why are we told about John's death in all its gruesome detail? And why are we told right here? It would perhaps have been more in keeping with chronology to tell us about it a bit earlier.

I suggest these two stories teach us important truths about the relationship of the Kingdom of the Heavens to this world's politics. They firstly teach us of the attitude of this world's political systems to Christ: Herod derisively dismissed reports of Christ. And secondly, these stories teach us of Christ's attitude to this world's political scene: He walked away from it. Christ was not interested in using this world's political systems for the purposes of His Kingdom. We should not be either. Christian double-standards on this issue are worrying. We protest about religious persecution of Christians overseas, but then try to legislate our beliefs – on homosexuality, for example – on others. Do we only want tolerance for Christian viewpoints and values? We ought to know that those who take the sword of political activism die by it. If we use it, it will be used on us.

Notice Herod's response to the fame of Jesus. He mocked at news of miracles from God. Hoping the political process will remedy the corruption of our society is unrealistic. The Herods of this world are only interested in holding onto power. This world is just as corrupt at the top as it is at the bottom. We are not here to reform it. We pray 'Thy Kingdom come' and wait for the time when God's Kingdom sweeps away all human misgovernment. This does not mean that we should not speak out against this world's sins. John bravely did. But we should not expect to be hailed as the world's political saviours. We will never 'build the New Jerusalem in England's green and pleasant land' until Christ returns. We were not left here to try to, either. We have a different mission.

Notice Christ's reaction to the news of John's death. Did he arrange a popular protest march and call for the abdication of Herod? He could have. There would probably have been quite a successful turn-out. He could have taken on Herod as the first stage of a run for power. Instead, He departed (14:13). He left Herod to continue his little life. Christ departed for the other side of the lake. He had a different mission. There He healed the great multitude's sick, and then through His disciples, miraculously fed them. This is a picture parable of what our present job is in this world.

Our job is to meet the needs of the multitudes with the gospel. Christ invited the participation of the disciples in the feeding of the crowds. He gave the disciples an opportunity to put their faith into action. He said, 'They do not need to go away. *You* give them something to eat.' Christ in His power worked through the disciples' faith to meet the needs of the multitude. It was the disciples' five loaves and two fish that were given to Christ in faith to feed the five thousand. It was their hands that passed the food out. So Christ similarly calls us today to put our faith in Him into action as through us Christ in His power meets the needs of the many in our world who are perishing.

In the next story, the parable is taken a stage further. It is now evening and Christ urges His disciples to cross over to the other side before Him. No doubt they wondered to themselves how Christ was going to get over to the other side of the lake. But they had enough problems of their own to think about, crossing a lake in the middle of the night with the wind against them. Meanwhile, Christ was on the mountain top praying.

How like the present position in which we are found. Our present position in this world is compared to night a number of times in the New Testament epistles (Romans 13:11-14, 1 Thessalonians 5:1-11, 2 Peter 1:19). The glorious Day of God's Kingdom is not yet come. Christ's disciples are found on the sea – picturing the fact that the small band of Christ's loyal disciples are now no longer confined to Israel but are tossed amidst the sea of sinful Gentile nations (see Isaiah 57:20). Israel has been left behind and we are on our own in the struggle against the wind and the tossing waves – except for the fact that Christ has left us for the mountaintop of intercession. He cares about our struggles and difficulties down below. He is coming back just before the break of day (the fourth watch – v25) to relieve us of the struggle against the elements. When He gets into the boat the wind ceases and the scene on the shore of Gennesaret (part 6 of the section) is perhaps a picture of the wonderful blessings Christ's Kingdom will bring. Night has given place to day and we read that 'when the men of that place recognised Him, they sent out into all that surrounding region, brought to Him all who were sick, and begged Him that they might only touch the hem of His garment. And as many as touched it were made perfectly well' (Matthew 14:34-35). It seems to me to be a beautiful picture of future Jewish faith in Christ and the resultant Millenial blessing of Christ's reign.

Of course, I will not mind if you see this as being a little too allegorical. The primary interest in the story of the Lord walking on the water is that it reveals Christ in all His power and authority. The disciples recapture their sense of wonder as they exclaim, 'Truly You are the Son of God.' It was not a case of them not knowing who He was before this. It was rather a case of them needing a fresh vision of Christ's power to remind them of who He was. The doubts and troubles of their voyage and Christ's absence had taken their minds off Christ in all His glory.

The story of Christ walking on the water teaches us a lesson too. It is again the lesson of the need for our faith. Christ invited Peter to walk to Him upon the water. But Peter's faith faltered as he took his eyes off Christ and felt the strength of the wind, strangely forgetting that he had already overcome the biggest part of the problem – walking on water. He began to sink and Christ reproached his lack of faith. 'Why did you doubt?' Christ calls upon us to overcome the problems that face us in this struggle we are called to navigate through. We are not to let our eyes look upon the magnitude of the problems so much as the power of Christ to overcome them. Christ challenges us still to attempt great things for God and to expect great things from God.

The Kingdom of Heaven and the Jewish Religion

The second half of this section commences with the visit of the scribes and Pharisees from Jerusalem. No doubt they were treated as VIPs in provincial Galilee and knew how to throw their weight around. They confronted Jesus over His neglect of the worthy principle of hand-washing before eating. Jesus replied by pointing out that here was the whole problem with Pharisees: their own time-honoured traditions had not only been placed *alongside* God's commandments, but had progressively *replaced* God's commandments. Christ gave the example of the way they allowed gifts to the Temple (a worthy cause) to let someone off from having to keep God's commandment to honour and financially support elderly parents (15:4-6).

It is always the case: if we add anything to God's Word – even something that seems good, like washing one's hands, we end up substituting our rule for God's. Christ proceeded to point out that God was not as silent on the subject of cleanliness and defilement as they ignorantly thought. It was true that God had not said in the Scriptures anything about whether we should wash our hands before a meal. However, that was because God required cleanliness of a completely different and far more important sort. God required internal rather than external purity (15:11, 16-20).

Human Traditions, Sea-Shells and Sunday Schools

Human traditions and man-made rules seem to be an unavoidable trap - so unavoidable that some people even try to defend 'good' traditions. They come in two varieties, either prohibiting things that God's Word does not or adding additional commands to those God has given.

A preacher who was dying of cancer was giving a series of nightly studies in the Book of Revelation. Someone asked if it would be all right to tape the messages, seeing the preacher would probably never again deliver the series. The Convenors' reply was: 'Anything in a black box is of the Devil,' meaning that no tape recording was going to be allowed. That little rule, of course, was neither from the Bible nor is it true: some Bibles even come in black boxes. It falls into the category of a tradition of man. Perhaps a rule that more accurately represents what Christ was teaching here is: Beware of any *Rule* not found in your Bible. Now there are some human rules that it is advisable to keep, like your mother's table manner rules. There are even some rules from men that the Bible commands you to keep, like the laws of the land. However, when it comes to our Christian lives, we must obey God and be very wary of the traditions of men. Human traditions are dangerous precisely because they tend to displace God's commands.

Notice that I emphasised that any *Rule* that you do not find in your Bible is something to be wary of. I did not say that you should be wary of any *Thing* that you do not find in your Bible. Let me explain because this is where it is possible to make a simple but serious mistake, even from the best of motives. Some people actually insist that rubber tyres on tractors are worldly, presumably because the Bible does not mention rubber tyres anywhere. However, to ban anything *simply* because it is not explicitly mentioned in the Bible - like collecting sea-shells or having a Sunday School or a yearly Conference - is to seriously misunderstand the nature of the New Testament. There might be dangers in these non-biblical practices. However, the New Testament is not like the Old Testament, which spelt out innumerable rules governing every little detail of life. The New Testament instead gives us more basic, overarching, fundamental principles. Under the New Testament God no longer treats us as immature, unintelligent *infants* needing a rulebook to find out what we must or must not do (see Galatians 4). Instead, the believer is treated as a mature **Son** in the family of God and is given the responsibility to think spiritually for himself under the New Testament **Law (or Rule) of Freedom** - see James 1:25 & 2:12, Galatians 5:1, 2 Corinthians 3:17. This is not to encourage the flippant abuse of that freedom like a rebellious teenager or to allow an anything-goes attitude but to develop personal spiritual maturity, intelligence and responsibility before God. God encourages us to live out the principles of His Word, not as unthinking, fearful robots but as loving Sons and Daughters, maturing in spiritual intelligence, wisdom and the knowledge of God. Rule-bound infants are no better than **Slaves** (Galatians 4). And this is why extra-Biblical **Rules** are so dangerous - they enslave us. It is a sad reality that some Christians want to rule others as their slaves but what is stranger still is that some Christians feel happier as slaves tagging along behind other men and their rules. God, however, wants us for Himself. 'You were bought with a price. Do not be the slaves of men' (1 Cor.7:23). What then should be our attitude to such human rules? The same zero-tolerance our Lord showed the Scribes.

Defilement

This incident of the Scribes and Pharisees criticising Christ for being unclean and His subsequent explanation to the crowds of what true defilement consists of has another important lesson. One of the most important aspects of any religion is what it says about dealing with defilement. Most religions prescribe various treatments for human purity. Christ teaches here that defilement is an important matter. To continue the parable, if we are going to sit down to the table of the Great Eternal Feast, we are going to need clean hands. But Christ here teaches that the defilement that really matters is the internal defilement of sin. 'Out of the heart proceed evil thoughts – murders, adulteries, fornications, thefts, false witness, blasphemies' (v19). Performing outward religious rituals will not cleanse us or fit us for God's banquet – we need internal cleansing. We need our sins forgiven – by God. And how do we get that? We read on.

Christ's reaction to the Pharisees' twisted religious ideas was again to depart. He went to the region around Tyre and Sidon where the Canaanite woman pleaded with Him to cast the demon out of her daughter. Christ had left the boundaries of Israel because He had been rejected there. But this did not mean that He was now going to commence a mission to the Gentiles. His mission was to the lost sheep of the house of Israel. And, that being the case, He ignored the woman's cry for help. However, her faith in His ability to save her daughter was not deterred. She persisted by pestering His disciples. She was not even put off by Christ's reply 'It is not good to take the children's bread and throw it to the little dogs'. She replied that the little dogs were allowed the crumbs that fell from the table. Her faith would not be denied. Christ said, 'O woman, great is your faith! Let it be to you as you desire,' and healed her daughter. Israel's lack of faith is contrasted with this Gentile woman's great faith. But here too we see someone receiving instant healing of the indwelling uncleanness of demon possession through faith in Christ's work. Here is the way to cleansing.

Faith

The next story, the tenth, is the feeding of the four thousand (15:29-39). What a contrast we have here between Christ's concern for the multitudes to be fed and the Scribes who earlier in the chapter were obsessed with their little rules about the way bread had to be eaten. Notice that again here there seems to have been a sizeable Gentile element in the crowd. When Christ had healed their sick before He fed them we read that they 'glorified the God of Israel' (15:31). Christ thus again was allowing the Gentiles to experience His blessings. And again, in feeding the multitude, Christ calls upon His disciples to exercise their faith. Christ hints at the need for the multitudes to be fed by reminding the disciples of how hungry the crowds were and how dangerous it would be to send them away without eating (v32). The disciples' response shows that they had learned little in the school of faith. They said, 'Where could we get enough bread in the wilderness to fill such a great multitude?' Christ proceeded to feed the four thousand families with just the seven loaves and a few little fish. What an encouragement for us! Even with our little resources and faith, Christ wants to meet the needs of a perishing world!

The second last story is about faith too. The Sadducees and Pharisees, Israel's two main opposing religious groups, together combine to try and test Christ, showing just how united was Israel's unbelief. They call for Christ to produce a sign from heaven – some miracle in the sky. They were sure, of course, that Jesus, being a fraud, would not be able to produce one. They were unbelievers still in spite of all His miracles. If they were genuine they would have been convinced already. But they had closed minds. So Christ gave them no miracle. Instead He issued a blunt warning of judgement in terms suited to their insincerity, mocking them with what today is a children's rhyme, 'Red sky at night is a shepherds' delight, red sky at morning's a sailor's warning'. How was it, He warned, that they could foretell the weather but could not see the storm of God's wrath coming? Then He offered them again the sign of the prophet Jonah in his watery 'resurrection' and his subsequent warning of imminent judgement. Then He left them.

The final story is about faith too. Only this time it is about the lack of faith of the disciples. They had forgotten bread and feared Christ's upbraiding for having left such a necessary item behind. Then Christ warned them about the leaven of the Pharisees and the Sadducees. They completely misunderstood what He meant. But before Christ told them that by leaven He was meaning the spreading corruption of false-religion, He stopped to enquire of their faith. How many baskets did you take up for yourselves after the feeding of the multitudes, he asked. Was I not able to provide for your needs as well as the great crowds – O you of little faith?

Christ had departed from Israel now. The reason, at its root, was that they had no faith. Were His own disciples no better? Still today Christ trains and disciplines us so that we will have a resilient personal faith in Himself, a faith prepared to step out and accomplish great things for God.

Conclusion

Christ's ministry in this section of the Gospel has now dramatically altered course. Instead of rallying great crowds with their Messianic expectations, Christ has tried to get away from Galilee altogether. He was not interested in their political goals. Instead of teaching the great crowds which followed Him earlier in the Gospel, Christ has instead devoted Himself to privately training His own disciples in the school of faith. Instead of continuing His confrontation with the corrupt religious traditions of the Pharisees and Scribes, Christ has turned His back on Judaism altogether. Along the way, Christ's actions here teach us what His Kingdom is all about. It is all about meeting the needs of the perishing multitudes through faith in Him and individual cleansing from sin through faith in Him. Christ rounds off this series of lessons by reinforcing again the importance of faith: could His disciples not even have faith in Him to meet their own physical needs?

Chapter 9 - Christ's Secrets: 16:13 - 18:35

1. The Question in Caesarea Philippi (16:13 – 16:20)

2. The Announcement of Christ's Sufferings (16:21 – 16:23)

3. The Requirements of Discipleship (16:24 – 16:28)

4. The Transfiguration (17:1 – 17:8)

5. The Disciples' Question about Elijah (17:9 – 17:13)

6. The Healing of the Demoniac Boy (17:14 – 17:21)

7. Further Announcement of Sufferings (17:22 – 17:23)

8. On Paying Tax (17:24 – 17:27)

9. Christ's Teaching on Little Children (18:1 – 18:11)

10. The Parable of the Lost Sheep (18:12 – 18:14)

11. Christ's Teaching on Brothers (18:15 – 18:20)

12. The Parable about Forgiveness (18:21 – 18:35)

*I*n Matthew 13 Christ told His parables to the crowds. Then, later, when He was alone with His disciples He privately explained the meanings of the parables to them. Chapters 13 to 16, as we have just seen, are rather like one big parable. This next section (Chapters 16-18) corresponds to an explanation. In this section, Christ starts revealing His mysteries – His hidden secrets – to His disciples. Thus, Christ's revelation in Caesarea Philippi marks the start of a significant new development in Christ's ministry.

The Big Secret

The first revelation of Christ's in this section is the most important of them all. In Caesarea Philippi Christ asks His disciples who men say He is. They reply that some say He is John the Baptist, some say He is Elijah and others say He is Jeremiah or one of the prophets. He then asks His disciples the great question, 'But who do you say that I am?' Simon Peter replies, 'You are the Christ, the Son of the Living God.' Christ replied, 'Blessed are you, Simon Bar-Jonah, for flesh and blood has not revealed this to you, but my Father who is in heaven' (16:13-17).

The crowds no doubt thought they were paying Christ the highest of compliments when they called Him a prophet. But Christ was not another prophet. There are still some today who would like to think they are complimenting Christ by calling Him the modern equivalents: a great thinker and communicator. However, this is to make the greatest mistake of all. Christ here acknowledged He was the Son of God and to call Him simply a prophet is not a compliment, it is a calculated put-down. Further, it is inconsistent. How can we even call Christ a prophet if we refuse to accept what He said about Himself? We must either admit both His prophetic and His Divine claim or we must deny both. And could there be any sin more serious than this? It is to directly insult our Creator.

It was to these men who believed in Him that Christ started to reveal His secrets. Notice where He did it. Christ chose to reveal to His disciples the most important of His secrets in Caesarea Philippi. Instead of heading for Jerusalem to take power like the crowds hoped He might, Christ went in the very opposite direction right out of the land of Israel altogether. Israel had by and large rejected Him. Israel had not wanted the truth and the light. Israel was therefore going to be left in the dark. Israel was not going to be told God's secrets. Instead, it was going to be in Gentile territory that Christ would make His most far-reaching revelations.

More Mysteries

Christ makes a whole series of revelations in this section. In Chapter 16 he proceeds to reveal the secret of *His Church* built upon the rock, not of unstable Peter, but of the truth of who He truly is, as Peter had confessed. All who believe are part of the Church and rest upon that foundation, which as Peter himself later wrote, is Christ Himself (1 Peter 2:7). Then He started to tell them about His *death and resurrection* in Jerusalem (16:11). This was almost incomprehensible to disciples jockeying for cabinet positions in Christ's soon-coming Kingdom. Then He revealed *the requirement of discipleship* – a disciple must deny himself, take up his cross and follow Christ. It would mean losing our lives, if not physically then certainly figuratively, but paradoxically finding them in the process (16:24-25). Then He further revealed His *future coming in glory* to bring reward (16:27).

In the next three parts of this section concerning the Mount of Transfiguration, Christ reinforced these lessons. Firstly He gave the three disciples a glimpse of His personal glory. They, and in particular Peter, seemed to be more impressed by the presence of Moses and Elijah, putting Christ on the same level as them just like the crowds did. Peter said, 'Let us make here three tabernacles – one for you, one for Moses and one for Elijah.' The voice from the cloud sternly interrupted, reminding Peter of who Christ was.

Then on the way down, Christ reminded the disciples that in spite of His majesty and glory which they had just been privileged to witness, He was nevertheless going to die. Christ told the disciples to 'tell the vision to no man until the Son of Man is risen from the dead' (17:9). For the disciples who were no doubt struggling to comprehend Jesus' death, the announcement of His resurrection must have been completely mind-boggling. They did not seem to be able to take it in. Besides, they were still thinking about the mountain scene. They asked about Elijah. Now the scribes obviously taught that before the Messiah would come, Elijah would come back (17:10). That obviously posed some difficulties for any hopeful Messiah. He needed an Elijah to first return. Christ proceeded to confirm the scribes teaching, quoting their own words: 'Indeed, Elijah is coming first and will restore all things' (v11). However in verses 12 and 13 He told the disciples that what the scribes were talking about had already come to pass – the Elijah they were referring to was John the Baptist. Most importantly, though, Christ assured them that just as the Jews did not know John but did what they wished with him in putting him to death, so it would happen to Himself also. Christ was again referring to His death.

Then, to complete the first half of this section, Matthew recounts the scene that confronted Christ when he reached the disciples at the bottom of the mountain. A man came to Christ explaining that he had brought his demon-possessed son to the disciples in Christ's absence but they had been unable to cast the demon out. Christ lamented the faithlessness and perversity of His generation asking, 'How long shall I be with you?' He was again making a passing reference to His death and departure. He cast out the demon but then the disciples came and privately asked Him to explain why they had been unable to cast out the demon. Christ's reply to His disciples emphasised the two things that this part of Matthew's Gospel had been calling for in a disciple – firstly, the necessity of faith 'like mustard seed', capable of moving mountains (v20), and secondly, the necessity of a life of self-denial, prayer and fasting (v21).

So the first six parts of this section teach three lessons twice over:

Matt. 16:13-28	Matt. 17:1-21	The Three Lessons
Question in C. Philippi	Transfiguration	Who Christ is
Announcement of Death	Descending Mountain	Christ's death and resurrection
Requirements of followers	Healing of Demoniac	Discipleship

The Church

The second half of this section sees Christ and His disciples back in Galilee just before the final move to Judea and eventually Jerusalem. In this second half of this section Matthew devotes special attention to one feature of Christ's revelation in the first half of the section – the Church. Matthew alone of the Gospel writers mentions the Church and he only mentions it in two places, both in this section: 16:18 ('I will build my church') and 18:17 ('tell it to the church').

In part seven of this section, which concerns Christ's further announcement of His sufferings, we read that He made it 'while they were *staying* in Galilee' (v22). Now the manuscripts are divided over this word 'staying'. The majority of the manuscripts read 'staying' but some of the older manuscripts plus virtually all of the Latin manuscripts have 'while they were *gathering* in Galilee'. Whichever of the words is right we are correct in thinking of Christ and His band of followers now as a rather smaller close-knit group than before. Christ's ministry was not as public as it had previously been in Galilee. The band resembled much more closely the modern church community 'gathering' together with each other in the midst of the general unbelieving population.

Christ's further announcement of His sufferings is notable for one thing. Christ now tells the disciples something about His sufferings that He has not mentioned yet – He is going to be *betrayed*. We read that the disciples were exceedingly sorrowful (17:23). This is something that can only really affect those who are on the 'inside'. It is only an insider that can betray. And so, it is in the seclusion of the little group in quiet, rural Galilee that Christ particularly announces to His disciples that inside the group there is a traitor, a false-disciple.

Furthermore, in the next incident about the taxmen and their question to Peter, we read in v25 that Christ asked Peter about his conversation with the taxmen when Peter 'had come into the *house*'. Forgive me if you think I am reading too much into one word here, but this is again reminiscent of the symbolism we noticed involving the house in the parables in Chapter 13 and at the end of Chapter 13 where Christ went to Nazareth. Christ has now left the house of Israel and He has taken up His abode in a new house – the church. And, as we shall see, Chapter 18 deals in some depth with a Christian's relations with his fellow-Christians – the other 'little children', the 'brothers' – in the family of God or the household of God, if you like. Let us briefly notice some of the lessons that this incident over tax teaches.

The incident concerning the paying of the temple tax deals with the relationship of the Christian community with the outside world. Every Jewish man had to pay the temple tax. And so the taxmen politely enquired of Peter whether Jesus was going to pay or not. Peter had not thought about this much before and with a hint of embarrassment he replied 'Of course!' Once he was in the house, Christ asked him, in a sort of parable, whether He – being God's Son – should have to pay tax to God. Of course *not*! But, said Christ, we do not want to stumble them. We do not want them to think, with all their fanciful and misinformed suspicions about our little band, that we Christians are a lawless bunch of breakaways or opt-outs from normal society. Therefore we shall pay the tax. And with that Christ sent him to catch a fish, wherein Christ promised him he would find a coin that would pay the tax for the two of them. There are sufficient practical implications in this little story to write a book about: A Christian's attitude to monasteries, paying tax, serving on juries, compulsory voting, etc. But I shall leave that for someone more down-to-earth.

Little Children and Brothers

Chapter 18 appears at first to be one long unbroken speech of Christ's except for Peter's question in 18:21. Where do we get four parts from? Is this another attempt to make Matthew's Gospel fit a pre-arranged pattern? I trust not. Judge for yourself. Notice first of all the two main expressions that dominate this chapter.

The first expression is 'little children'. Notice how much reference is made to it. After the disciples had asked in 18:1 who was the greatest in the Kingdom of heaven, Christ in v2 called *a little child* to Him and set him in the midst. Christ then assured them that unless they were converted, which means 'turned about' or 'changed', and became as *little children* they would never enter into the Kingdom (v3). Then he said in v4 that whoever humbled himself as the *little child* was the greatest in the Kingdom of heaven. In v5 he said that whoever received one *little child* like this 'in my name' received Christ Himself. In v6, if you will forgive my modern paraphrase, He warned it were better to be thrown off the back of a boat with a fridge tied around the neck than to cause one of these *little ones* to stumble. Then in v10 Christ talked again about the little child saying, 'Take heed that you do not despise one of these *little ones*.' In v14, after the parable about the lost sheep He finally said, 'Even so it is not the will of your Father who is in Heaven that one of these *little ones* should perish.' That makes seven references to little children up to verse 14.

But from 18:15 to the end of the chapter Christ starts to talk about something else. We have four mentions of the word 'brother'. Christ says in v15, 'Moreover if your *brother* sins against you, go and tell him his fault between you and him alone. If he hears you, you have gained your *brother*.' Then Peter asks in v21, 'Lord, how often shall my *brother* sin against me and I forgive him?' Then finally, after the parable about the unforgiving servant Christ says, 'So my heavenly Father also will do to you if each of you, from his heart, does not forgive his *brother* his trespasses.'

So the first half of Chapter 18 is all about little children and the second half is all about brothers. Now of course you have already worked out that Christ is not talking about literal 'little children' and literal 'brothers' here. He is using these terms to describe what His followers should be like. We are little children if we have been born of our *Father* in heaven (mentioned four times in this chapter).

Now to reinforce His message in each of these two sections Christ told a parable – first the parable of the lost sheep after the teaching about 'little children' and then the parable of the unforgiving servant after the teaching about 'brothers'. And so we have four parts to this chapter: the teaching regarding 'little children', followed by a parable reinforcing the message, then the teaching regarding 'brothers', followed by another parable reinforcing the lesson of Christ's teaching.

Fellowship

Why is there all this talk then about 'little children', 'brothers' and 'our Father in Heaven'? Simply because Christ's Church is supposed to be like a family – and a family where we all get along with each other. The primary characteristic of Christ's Church was that it should be a place where we would have fellowship with each other and with our Father in Heaven.

Notice that here in this chapter we have all that is recorded of what Christ said on the subject of the local Church while on earth. What He said here must have been infinitely important if it was all that God recorded of Christ on this subject. And has not this matter of Christians getting along with each other been one of greatest areas of Christian failure down the Centuries? Has it not caused untold damage to the reputation of Christ Himself? No wonder then that the matter of Christian fellowship should occupy Christ's attention here in the only chapter in the Gospels where we have His teachings on the Church. No wonder either that in the Lord's great prayer in John 17 as He left His disciples and as He looked into the future course of His Church He should pray for the unity of those who should believe on Him. The subject was dear to His heart. If it is not to ours, then maybe it is a good thing we have returned to look at this chapter of Matthew's Gospel. We are going to look at the whole subject of fellowship here *Scripturally*. We are not interested in listening to human reasoning or arguments that certain policies are 'Practical'. Since when was the Practical more important than the Scriptural?

Christ tells us we need to be like little children. That is, we need to be humble. However, just like the disciples in Matthew 18:1, we instead tend to think of ourselves as greater than others. This in turn leads on to some of the most serious of all problems between Christians. Look at v5: Christ taught that whoever *received* one little child like this 'in My name' *received* Christ Himself. We can become so proud of how great we are (!) that we refuse to receive other Christians we deem less worthy than ourselves, cutting them off from our fellowship. Usually, it is because of our pride that we cannot get along with them or we fear losing our position on the top perch. We divide up Christ's Church, ruining local witness, but even more seriously, denying the One Mystical Body of Christ comprising all believers. Is Christ divided? Christ here warns sternly against the sectarian sin of a 'union-ticket-only' clubbishness.

Reception

Christ teaches here about reception. He says that we must receive all those who are 'little children'. That is, they are in the family. We are to receive those who are truly His. Look at v6. Christ goes to some pains here to define a 'little child' here for us as 'one of these little ones who *believe* in me'. Christ did not teach that we are to receive only those who are in our select circle or club. Christ's words are intended to expressly forbid us receiving only those who are as spiritually superior as we are! Christ assures us that if we receive one little child *in His name* (i.e. if we receive one of Christ's little ones because they are *His representative* through their simple, childlike faith in Him) we are really receiving Christ Himself (v5). On the other hand, we can harm the spiritual life of a fragile 'little child' of His, particularly by the serious offence of refusing them the status of someone worthy of our fellowship. If a representative of Christ is not good enough for our company, who is? Christ says that those behaving like this would have been better being thrown into the sea tied to a millstone. Do you get the general idea? Christ uses extremely angry language to describe His reaction to those who harm His 'little children'. By refusing to have fellowship with them we can hurt their feelings so badly that they stumble in their Christian walk. We must not despise *one* of these 'little ones' (v10). This issue of fellowship/reception is a major cause of much heartache amongst Christians today. What does the New Testament say about it?

Here in Matthew 18:5 we have the *general principle* of Christian reception: 'Whoever receives one little child like this in My name receives Me'. It is a general principle that we find restated time and time again in the remainder of the New Testament. Of course, *individual cases* of reception in the real world are all different and much wisdom is needed.

Firstly, we find Christ stating this truth in every single one of the Gospels:

- In Matthew 10:40, in relation to the preaching of the gospel, Christ says, 'He who receives you receives Me and he who receives Me receives Him who sent Me.' Christ Himself knew the pain of not being received in this world and heightened the seriousness of whether someone receives Him or not in the gospel message by reminding us that we are thus signalling our response to God Himself.

• Mark and Luke both also repeat Christ's words: 'Whoever receives one of these little ones in My name receives Me; and whoever receives Me, receives not Me but Him who sent me' (Mark 9:37, Luke 9:48). Notice that reception is on an individual basis – Christ emphasises the word 'one' here and throughout Matthew Chapter 18. Who my *family* is related to or what *other people I know* are irrelevant issues when it comes to reception. Fellowship is on an *individual* basis. Nor do Denominations have any Divine or Scriptural legitimacy. There is One Church. There is to be no 'tarring everyone with the same brush'.

• On the other hand, in John 13:20, after Christ has washed the disciples' feet, we read Him saying, 'He who receives whoever I send receives Me; and he who receives Me receives Him who sent Me.' Notice the slight difference here, please. Christ has just alerted the disciples to the fact that one of them is a fraud. Judas was not a true 'little child' or 'brother'. Christ does not say that we should receive a Judas into our fellowship. He says that we should receive 'whoever He sends'. Yes, we should receive every one of God's 'little children' that God sends to us, but a Judas does not really qualify as a 'little child'. There are limits to who we should receive.

Reception involves more than throwing open our arms and doors to anybody. The very word 'reception' implies the exercise of some discernment and some evaluation of the person who wishes to have fellowship with us. It certainly means more than 'welcome' – as some Bibles translate it and as many Churches indiscriminately practise it. 'Receiving' someone involves an appraisal before acceptance of the person. The New Testament also provides a means for those who are total strangers to us to be received if they come to us – by a letter of commendation (Acts 18:27, Romans 16:2, Philippians 2:29, Philemon 1:12). Mind you, some of God's 'little children', honest and sincere believers, have not been taught about bringing this New Testament idea into this day and age. It is not their fault they have not been taught. Letters of commendation are not a ticket system meant to debar those not in our club. They are meant as an aid to help in the business of reception.

The later New Testament provides examples of those who should have been kept out as 'false-brethren and spies' (Galatians 2:4), 'wolves amongst the flock' (Acts 20:29) and 'ungodly men who crept in unnoticed' (Jude 4). There are some who must be kept out, even though they claim to be Christians. However, we must be careful that in our zeal to weed out the tares we do not 'also uproot the wheat with them' (13:29) as the Lord very carefully warned the servants in His parable. Every plant that our Father has planted is important to Him. They are His 'little children', infinitely dear to Him.

There is ample anecdotal evidence supporting the contention that mistakes can be made in swinging to either extreme in this matter. Painful stories could be told of what has happened when true 'little children' have not been received when they should have been. Equally painful stories could be told of occasions where there has been a lack of proper care in reception and much damage has resulted in the Church. It is necessary that appropriate enquiries be made 'at the door' and this is no easy task. It is an extremely difficult job that must be done with a shepherd's heart. Care must be shown for the flock that wolves are not let in, and also for the 'little child' that he is not despised and stumbled. One bad experience can wound for life.

Some will object that the principle of reception in Matthew Chapter 18 does not apply to Church reception. However, if you look at Matthew 18 you will see that Christ is speaking all the way from verse 3 down to verse 20 without a break or interruption. Christ mentions this principle of reception in the very same paragraph as He mentions the word 'Church' in verse 17 and in verse 20 where He says 'where two or three are gathered together in My name, I am there in the midst of them'. Who are we to separate the principle of reception from Christ's teaching about the Church if Christ has not? We can either refuse one of God's 'little children' and so refuse admission to Christ Himself. Or we can receive His 'little one' and so receive Christ. Shall we leave Christ outside or invite Him in?

The same principle continues to be repeated throughout the later New Testament writings:

- In Romans 14 and the first few verses of 15 we find the subject of reception dealt with in great detail by the Apostle Paul. Paul's treatment of the subject commences in Romans 14:1 with the words '***Receive*** one who is weak in the faith' and it concludes with the words in 15:7, 'Therefore ***receive*** one another, just as Christ also ***received*** us, to the glory of God'.

In between these two 'book-end' verses bounding this section, Paul outlines all sorts of differences that might exist between believers. Yes, we might have our differences of opinion and some differences of practice. But we are still to receive other believers. In 14:3 we read that we should receive the other brother, despite our differences 'because God has *received* him'. What could be plainer? This same argument is repeated in another way in 15:7. We are to receive other believers because Christ *received* us. If you think you have something against some other believer, please remember how much the Lord could have held against you in your sins. He could have refused to receive you. But in Divine grace, Christ also received us in salvation. He requests His followers to likewise receive each other. The basis of reception in the NT is Faith and Godliness of Life – not shared trivial distinctives.

Again, some would argue that Romans 14-15 does not apply to Church reception. Actually, the NT does not use the term 'Church Reception' at all. This, however, does not license us to invent our own 'Principles of Church Reception'. The fact is that the NT teaches *One General Principle of Reception* that is found throughout the NT and is applicable to all situations, including Church Reception. Here we find Romans 14-15 reiterating that principle again, just like in Matthew 18.

• The Church in Jerusalem's reluctance to receive Paul after his conversion in Acts 9:26 is sometimes spoken of approvingly as an example for how we should receive others. However, whilst their caution was understandable, maybe even commendable, Paul's case was an exceptional case that still proves the rule. If they had not received Paul they might just have made one of the biggest mistakes in history.

• Exclusion was a favourite tactic of the Judaisers. Paul warned the Galatians in Ch4:17 (lit.): 'They are zealous after you – not rightly; but they want to exclude you that you may be zealous after them'. Exclusion was used as blackmail and an attempt at reverse-psychology: 'tell the Galatians Gentiles that they are not worthy of our fellowship and they will meekly fall into line with our doctrines'. Who wants to be compared to such accursed Judaising predecessors?

•• Paul's Letter to Philemon, which is essentially an inspired Letter of

Commendation, provides a beautiful example of the principle of reception in action. Listen to Paul's reason for why Onesimus should be received: 'You therefore receive him – that is, my own heart' (Philemon 12) and 'receive him as you would me' (verse 17). Paul's argument was that in receiving Onesimus, Philemon (and his family and the Church) were in fact receiving Paul himself. The godly Paul, imitating Christ, patterns his request on Christ's principle of reception: to receive a true child of God is in fact to receive Christ Himself.

• One final example will suffice: In John's Second and Third Letters we have two warnings about the principle of reception. In 2 John we are told who *not* to receive. In 3 John God warns against being like Diotrephes who did not receive those who he *should*. He would not even receive the apostle John! Notice how the apostle John's own attitude to reception had changed with time. In Luke 9:49-56 he first showed a hard, cold attitude in rebuking a man who was casting out demons in Christ's name (which the disciples themselves could not do in verses 37-42 of the same chapter!). The Lord Jesus gently rebuked him. Then, in verses 51-56 when some Samaritan villages refused to receive Christ out of sectarian bigotry, John returned the same sectarian bigotry in suggesting that fire be called down from Heaven upon them. What was it that caused the heart of John, the Son of Thunder, to so thaw out that he became the apostle of love? I think the answer is seen in 3 John 11 just after the Diotrephes verses: John had 'seen God'. He had learned what Christ was really like. He had leant on Christ's bosom for so long that any narrow, hard-heartedness had finally gone.

The Parable of the Lost Sheep

The parable of the lost sheep gives us the reason why we should treat each of Christ's little children with special care. Notice that the parable concerns *one* sheep that went astray. Christ has already emphasised '*one* little child' in verses 5, 6 and 10 in relation to receiving, stumbling and despising them. In the parable the shepherd is prepared to leave the ninety-nine sheep and go to the mountains to find the one lost sheep. Christ is telling us that every single one of His 'little children' were so important to Him that He came from Heaven as the shepherd to save them. Therefore we must receive each *one* of His 'little ones', we must not stumble them and we must not despise even one of them. If that 'little child' who you refuse fellowship with was the only sinner that needed saving Christ would have come to save that one person. Each *one* of His little ones is infinitely dear to Him – the apple of His eye. As Paul put it in Romans 14:15 in exactly the same context, 'Do not destroy … the one for whom Christ died'.

Occasionally today we hear some say that the Gospels do not have much of God's teaching for believers in them – God has given us the Epistles to explain to us the deeper truths of the New Testament revelation. Our Lord's teaching was, as He Himself said on the eve of His death, limited by time. He was going to have to send the Spirit of Truth. However, He Himself was the Master Teacher. His teaching is more than just the seed-plot for all of the New Testament doctrines. It is the all-important, high-priority teaching of the whole Bible. Those matters Christ did expound are the most important and most serious matters of all. Dare we ignore the teachings of Christ we find in the Gospels? This matter of our Lord's teaching on fellowship is one of a number of cases where we cannot afford to ignore, misunderstand or disobey our Lord's commands.

Forgiveness

In the second half of Chapter 18 the boot is on the other foot. What happens if, instead of me hurting my brother, my brother sins against me? If, having pointed out the matter to him privately, he pays no heed, I am to take another one or two more to hear the case. If he does not heed them, it is to be told to the church. If he refuses even to hear the church he is to be to me as a heathen or a tax collector. In other words, I am to treat him as if he were not a believer. I am to discontinue fellowship. That seems to contradict what we just learned, though, does it not?

There is no contradiction between the rules of fellowship we observed in the first part of this chapter and the rules we learn here. Fellowship is based upon the fact that we share the common salvation – that we are in the family. However, whenever someone who claims to be in the family gives us grave cause to doubt that he is saved – that he is a brother at all – either by his *behaviour* or *beliefs*, we are to treat him like he is not in the family. We are to put him out of fellowship. Christ is here investing the Church with His own authority. He says, 'Where two or three are gathered together in My name there am I in the midst of them.' If therefore, in the first part of the chapter, in receiving each one of these little ones 'in My name' we are receiving Christ Himself, so too when someone is put out of fellowship, the Church is acting on Christ's own behalf, as His representative.[8]

The Parable of the Unforgiving Servant

Peter's question and the Lord's parable in reply about forgiveness complete this section. Forgiveness and reconciliation is what we should aim for. Discipline is a last resort. Peter considers himself quite generous in offering forgiveness seven times to a brother who has sinned against him. Christ stunningly replies that seventy times seven would be a little more appropriate. Some of us can hardly forgive once. How are we to manage with this?

Christ told a parable to help us see why we should forgive so generously. It concerned a King who decided to do some bookkeeping and came across a servant who owed him ten thousand talents. Now this was a rather big sum of money. It is equivalent to ten billion pounds Sterling at current rates. Yet he pleaded for his Lord's forgiveness and it was granted! On the way home, however, he met another servant who owed him one hundred denarii, about ten thousand pounds worth of debt. Now this was no small sum either and he collared the fellow and had him thrown into prison. The King, hearing of it, was incensed and sent the man off to the torturers.

Of course, this sort of situation would never happen in real life. A man who had just been forgiven for so much could not forget so quickly and treat another so harshly. This is the point of the parable. Such a situation should not ever happen in Christian life either. Either such a person was never saved at all or alternatively, if they were saved, they would never do such a thing. The moral is clear. We have been forgiven so much that we must forgive the much smaller sins of others against us. If we do not forgive, there must be a real doubt over whether we were ever forgiven.

---

[8] There is perhaps a third reason for being dis-fellowshipped, found in Titus 3:10: 'Reject a divisive man (not 'a heretic') after the first and second admonition'. Notice the similarity with Matthew 18 in the 'three chances policy'. This verse teaches that the Church is authorised to put out of fellowship someone who is a divisive troublemaker and not subject to Church government. Notice that it does not say that the Church is to refuse to *receive* people it suspects might turn out to be troublemakers. The man is not even to be dis-fellowshipped until the third offence! Being received into a Church that teaches the truth in love and that exercises strong Church government (by not being afraid to deal with divisive troublemakers) is precisely the cure that God prescribes for believers with spiritual sicknesses of any sort. In such a good, healthy, normal Church environment they will learn the truth, feel the love, fear the consequences of causing problems and finally start to make some progress in their Christian lives. Titus 3:10 therefore shows that anarchy is not the result of putting into practice NT principles of reception. Rather, strong Church government is required and thereby encouraged.

Chapter 10 - Christ and Life: 19:1 - 21:11

1. Marriage and Divorce (19:1 – 19:9)
2. Christ on Celibacy (19:10 – 19:12)
3. Christ prays for the Little Children (19:13 – 19:15)
4. The Rich Young Man (19:16 – 19:22)
5. Christ on Riches (19:23 – 19:26)
6. Peter's Question concerning Reward (19:27 – 19:30)
7. Parable of the First and Last (20:1 – 20:16
8. Announcement of Sufferings in Jerusalem (20:17 – 20:19)
9. Mother of Zebedee's Children's Request (20:20 – 20:28)
10. The Two Blind Men (20:29 – 20:34)
11. Two sent to Fetch Colt (21:1 – 21:6)
12. The Entry into Jerusalem (21:7 – 21:11)

*C*hrist has spent the best part of the past two sections of Matthew's Gospel out of the way of trouble with the religious leaders and out of the way of the popularity of the crowds. He has turned his back on the path of the ordinary political or military Messiah by getting away from the crowds rather than rallying them and leading them towards Jerusalem. Yet now Christ makes a decisive change in direction. He moves out of quiet Galilee and comes into the region of Judea beyond the Jordan (19:1). He starts moving slowly and deliberately towards Jerusalem. He moves into territory where He immediately arouses Messianic hopes among the crowds and where He cannot but come into conflict with the religious leaders. The journey to His destiny has begun. This section concludes with Christ entering Jerusalem where His final conflict begins.

But this section appears to be simply a string of incidents that bear little relation to each other. They just seem like odd incidents that happened along the way to Jerusalem. They seem too diverse to be part of a unit or section like some of the other easily identifiable sections in Matthew. Do these separate stories really make up a self-contained section? We shall find, on closer inspection, that this section yet again presents us with strong confirmation of the fact that Matthew's Gospel is divided up into definite blocks of material which are all dealing with the one big topic.

Family and Financial matters

This section has a lot to do with rather ordinary matters of life – at least in the first half of it. The first three parts of it have to do with family life. First of all, the Pharisees throw Christ the knotty problem of marriage and divorce to unravel. Then having shocked even His own disciples with His denial of the divorce option – provoking them to exclaim that it would therefore be better not to get married at all – Christ secondly talked about celibacy. He said that celibacy is only for those to whom it has been given – those who are physically unfit for marriage from birth, those rendered physically unfit by men and those who have themselves chosen to remain single for the sake of the Kingdom of heaven. Christ says it is a personal choice – 'he who is able to accept it, let him accept it' (19:12). Then thirdly Matthew relates how little children were brought to Him to be blessed and, in spite of the disciples' rebuke, Christ called for them and laid His hands upon them. Christ therefore upheld marriage, said celibacy was good (but only optional) and finally blessed children, the fruit of marriage.

The next three parts have to do with money – how we finance life. In Part Four the rich young man came to Christ sure of himself that he had perfectly kept the commandments and was good enough to gain eternal life. But when Christ said that if he wanted to be perfect he should go, sell his possessions and give to the poor he went away sad, not willing to give them up (19:22). In Christ's teachings on riches in Part Five after he had gone, Christ commented that it was harder for a camel to go through the eye of a needle than for a rich man to enter the Kingdom of heaven (v24) which again produced astonishment amongst the disciples. They themselves felt the lure of riches and worried that they might not be saved if being saved was as difficult as this. But then in Part Six the thought dawned in Peter's mind with some comfort and then growing pride that he and his fellow-disciples *had* indeed left all to follow Jesus. Precisely what were they going to receive for all their sacrifice for Christ? Christ told him that when He would return to reign, sitting upon the throne of His glory, they would sit on twelve thrones judging the tribes of Israel.

Likewise everyone who left all for Christ's sake would receive a hundredfold and inherit eternal life.

But why is Christ talking about these mundane matters of everyday life like marriage and money?

The Kingdom of Heaven and it's Social Agenda

I am not altogether satisfied with using the title 'Christ and Life' to describe this section. An alternative title would be 'Christ and Society', although that too would be insufficient to encompass what Matthew is presenting here. In this section, Christ's Kingdom is asked to issue, not its political or religious agenda but its *social policy*. In this section, Matthew addresses the reaction of Christ to our world's chief social problems.

• In the first incident we are presented, not so much with marriage but with *divorce*. Now remember that Matthew has already recorded Christ's attitude to divorce in the Sermon on the Mount. There Christ dealt with divorce morally. Here he comes back to deal with it again – this time socially.

• Next Matthew touches on the social problem of *disabilities* – genetic and man-made, 'there are eunuchs who were born thus from their mother's womb and there are eunuchs who were made eunuchs by men' (19:12).

• Then we come in the fourth story to another one of the world's big social issues – wealth and *poverty*. Christ said the rich young man had a moral obligation to sell his possessions and give to the poor if he would be counted morally perfect.

• Later, we come to the parable of the labourers in the vineyard in which we have a classic case of a *workplace dispute* over wages.

• Then we have the incident where James and John want the best places in Christ's Kingdom. The subject under discussion in the ensuing conversation is *government*, which some people consider the solution to our world's social problems. Christ had to teach His disciples that His sort of government involved humility and service – exactly the opposite of normal human government (or even most systems of Church government!).

• Lastly, Christ is brought face to face with a whole package of social problems – ***disease, disability, poverty and discrimination*** – when He passes two blind beggars on His journey.

Social issues like these dominate the editorials of newspapers and the arguments on radio talk-back shows. And these problems just will not go away, however much our politicians promise at election time. Our world is faced with enormous and seemingly insoluble social problems. If the Messiah is God's King, surely He has an answer to these problems, we enquire. What does God's King offer in the way of improving the quality of our lives?

In part six of this section Christ uses a big word to announce what he intends to do about all our problems. He says in response to Peter's question about the disciples' reward for their sacrificial following of Christ that 'in the ***regeneration***, when the Son of Man sits on the throne of His glory, you also will sit on twelve thrones...'(19:28). What does he mean by 'the regeneration'? Literally in the Greek the word means 'the start-again'. Christ's purpose is to ultimately restore Paradise. Christ has no desire to simply manage or cope with our social problems. Christ is not interested in band-aid solutions. Christ recalls to our attention that we once lived in Paradise. He has already referred to that state we enjoyed 'in the beginning' when speaking about divorce (19:4,8). He intends to bring us back to it again.

Nor is this some wistful, nostalgic daydream. Christ's social programme is made of more solid stuff than the well-meaning but unworkable solutions of politicians. There is only one person who can fix Earth's problems. God (who created it and who alone has the power and the wisdom to deal with its problems) must re-create it anew. This, Christ is happy to tell us, has always been the very plan of God Himself. Christ later on tells us that His Kingdom was 'prepared from the foundation of the world' (Matthew 25:34). Christ's coming Kingdom will give our world its start again. God foresaw the Fall and was not going to allow it to disturb or thwart His plans for this world. Long before the creation of this world he plotted the eventual triumph of good over evil, beauty over ugliness and joy over tears.

Christ offers us the most magnificent answer imaginable to the problems of life. He preaches Eternal Life. He offers Life that is perfect and Life that never ends. That is Christ's Kingdom's social policy.

In the mean time, by the way, the moral principles that underpin Paradise still apply. God still expects us to build by His original plans for marriage. Christ did not pronounce a blessing upon Divorce like the little children brought to Him soon after, did He? Nor can we ignore the world's suffering groans by pleading diplomatic immunity as ambassadors of God's Kingdom. Alleviation of the problem of poverty is a Christian responsibility. We are not here to preach a 'social gospel', but neither does Christ's own example of healing and helping others leave us any option but to help others in need. Life won't be perfect till His Kingdom comes, but Paradise is built on righteousness and that is how we must live until it comes.

The Kingdom of Heaven and Eternal Life

Christ is indeed offering Eternal Life. But why then is He devoting so much attention to wordly and mundane matters like marriage and money at this point in time? He is on the most important journey that any man ever made. Why is He stopping to pat babies' heads? Shouldn't He be a bit more concerned with eternal verities instead of the temporary problems of this life?

Let us look a little closer at these incidents. Christ is not just teaching here about Life. He is teaching us about how to get Eternal Life. The reason Christ blessed the children is given in His own words in 19:14: 'Let the little children come to me, and do not forbid them; for of such is the Kingdom of Heaven'. Christ was teaching that little children perfectly picture the sort of person we have to be to enter into Christ's Kingdom. Notice that the story of the rich young man is similarly about how to have eternal life. The word 'enter' is mentioned here three times. Christ told the young man 'If you want to *enter* into life, keep the commandments' (v17). Then in verses 23 and 24 Christ said it twice again: 'Assuredly I say to you that it is hard for a rich man to *enter* the Kingdom of heaven. Again I say to you, it is easier for a camel to go through the eye of a needle than for a rich man to *enter* the Kingdom of God'. Here Christ was teaching that if we would enter the Kingdom of heaven we would have to admit our moral poverty – our sinfulness.

Again in a way this section is a bit of a parable. Life for us is like a journey – just like Christ here was on a journey up to Jerusalem. The culmination of this section is Christ's entrance into Jerusalem – with His faithful followers.

This whole section, I suggest, is about how to *enter* into eternal life. And that is going to be determined by the way we live in this little life. If we would enter into eternal life with Christ at the end of *our* journey we must imitate those characters who, following Christ, entered into Jerusalem and, on the other hand, avoid the example of those who desired to follow but turned back when they heard what the journey involved.

This section teaches that the following characteristics -

• soul-humility like that of little children,

• poverty of spirit – unlike that of the rich young man,

• acceptance of suffering before glory (20:17-19, 22),

• servant-likeness in the image of Christ who came not to beserved but to serve (20:28) and

• abandonment of our natural self-sufficiency, which must be replaced instead by dependence of faith like the blind beggars (20:29-34) are required if we would enter into the future Kingdom.

In other words, we must humbly repent and believe. It is as simple as that. Yet, for many people, this is not simple at all. They would rather try to accumulate as much credit with Heaven in good deeds as they can like the rich young man in Jesus' day. They find it hard to stomach that they are not good enough on their own merits for eternal life. The rich young man had to have this hard lesson taught to him by having his moral failure pointed out to him – he did not love others perfectly. We have to learn that we are like the impoverished beggars beside the road – dependant upon God showing us mercy. But we must take another step and, like them, be willing to believe that God in His Love is willing to show us mercy. We have simply got to trust what God says about how to get eternal life – by believing in His Son who He sent to save us.

Christ entered into Jerusalem humbly and poorly on a borrowed donkey. He Himself is presented in this section as the chief example for all those wanting to enter into eternal life and future glory. If you want a text for this section I would suggest the disciples' question in 19:25: 'Who then can be saved?'

Thus I call this section 'Christ and life' slightly apologetically. I could have called it 'Christ and eternal life'.

Future Glory and Reward

This section also goes a step further. In it Christ pulls back the curtain and allows those of us who are saved a brief glimpse of what our future eternal reward is like. If having eternal life were not enough, we are promised rewards on top!

Peter broaches the subject in 19:27: 'We have left all and followed You. Therefore, what shall we have?' Christ replies that their reward will involve a privileged position in His Kingdom – sitting on twelve thrones judging the twelve tribes of Israel, one hundredfold on all the losses they have suffered for Christ and – strange that He should put it last – eternal life. James and John bring up the same subject again through their mother when they ask if Christ might grant them to be able to sit on His right hand and left hand in His Kingdom. They seemingly were not content with the future benefits of having eternal life and of being one of the twelve. They wanted the added prestige of being Christ's favourites.

Of course, they were thinking of the more immediate Kingdom that they still hoped Christ would establish upon His arrival at Jerusalem. It was really in the 'here and now' that James and John wanted to be seen as Christ's favourites. Christ taught here that His followers are to take the lowest place as servants and least of all if we really want the best reward in the future. Sadly, we are more like the disciples. We may talk or dream of living so as to earn the best places in Heaven, but mostly we just try to get the best places on earth.

The Parable of the First and Last

Christ told a parable in this section (20:1-16) which helps us to see what our attitude as followers of Christ should be to future reward and glory. The parable is about a landowner who went out early in the morning to the marketplace to hire labourers to work in his vineyard, agreeing to give them a denarius - the day's wage - for their day's work. He went out again at the third, sixth, ninth and even the eleventh hours and hired others also, promising to pay them what was right. When the evening had come he gave them all their wages starting with those who had only worked the one hour. To the surprise of some and to the envy of others he gave them all one denarius. Those who had worked all day complained that they were made equal with the ones who had only worked one hour. But the master reminded them that they had agreed to their wages and that he was perfectly entitled to be good and to show extra kindness to whoever he wished. Christ finished the parable by saying 'So the last will be first and the first will be last. For many are called, but few chosen'.

The primary lesson I suppose we should take from Christ's statement about the last being first and the first being last is that those who take last place in this world will be given first place in the future one. That is, those who humbly admit their moral poverty and sinfulness and accept like the two blind men that they are beggars dependant upon God's mercy and call out in faith to God for it are the ones who inherit eternal life. Then, having become a follower of Christ, those who seek to be the servant and the least of all in this life will be first in the next. Peter, James and John wanted the best places in future glory as if they had a right to them. This is the wrong attitude. We have no *right* to eternal life at all, let alone any additional benefits.

The interest in this parable focuses largely on the bad attitude of the twelve-hour labourers. They had received their wages and should have said their thank yous and whistled their way home. Likewise, Christ's disciples were getting things a little bit out of perspective in forgetting how fortunate they were to be receiving eternal life and starting to ask for extras on top. Notice again that the rewards promised to Peter were in exactly the wrong order. There were thrones, one hundredfold and eternal life. The first was last and the last was first. If we were allowed only one we would choose eternal life and quit while we were ahead. But not Peter, James, John or the other disciples. Why? Because they had forgotten how unworthy they were of the least of God's mercies. They had started thinking themselves somewhat important and were calculating their reward accordingly. They were forgetting the principle upon which they entered the Kingdom – humble, repentant, undeserving, faith. Christ is teaching from the parable that those who see that they least deserve eternal life will regard it so highly that they hardly notice any additional rewards. True humility and thankfulness will result in the greatest enjoyment of the blessings promised us in the future.

Grace

I suggest that Christ teaches another extremely important lesson from this parable. The parable is all about *grace*. The landowner, in giving the same wage to all the labourers, was accused of treating some unfairly. They said, 'These last men have worked only one hour, and you have made them equal to us who have borne the burden and the heat of the day.' However, the landowner – badly misunderstood man that he was – had shown grace and kindness, not unfairness. He replied, 'Friend, I am doing you no wrong. Did you not agree with me for a denarius? Take what is yours and go your way. I wish to give to this last man the same as to you. Is it not lawful for me to do what I wish with my own things? Or is your eye evil because I am good?' The landowner was not depriving the early workers of anything that they had agreed upon. Out of the goodness of his heart he was simply giving more to the late workers than what they really deserved.

This is grace – God giving us what we have not earned. It is one of the most important principles of God. It is one of the most important principles we have to understand if we are to be saved, for it is by grace that we are saved, say the later New Testament writings. Eternal life is not earned, merited, won or attained by our good works, charitable attitudes, performance of religious rituals or honorary (or even active) membership of religious organisations. It is not a case of us earning enough points for a place in Heaven. It is a case of God giving to beggars what they do not, nor ever will deserve. In fact, if God were to simply give us the wages we deserved, we would all be in Hell. Those who will one day find themselves in Hell will not be able to complain against God for treating them harshly – they will be getting the wages of their sins.

The lesson of this parable is very important. Some feel that God should (or even will) eventually take us *all* into His eternal rest – because Christ has died for the sins of the whole world (1 John 2:2). But this is to quite misunderstand the nature of salvation. God does not owe *any* of us anything – except the due reward of our deeds. We are all sinners and we all deserve the same wages for our sins: Hell. Therefore, for some to be saved and others to perish is a case of God on the one hand showing grace and on the other hand giving others the well-earned wages of their sin.

'Many are Called but Few are Chosen'

Now I want here to talk for a moment about Election – one of the most avoided and therefore misunderstood subjects of the Bible. The Scriptures clearly teach that God *chooses* individuals to be saved[9]. However, this idea attracts suspicions of unfairness on God's part – just as the landowner was accused of unfairness in the parable – and so some people reject the idea of Election outright.

Notice that Christ says at the end of the parable 'Many are called but few are chosen'. I suggest that this parable teaches us a valuable lesson about grace that unlocks the puzzling doctrine of election. Here it is – you might have to mull over it for a bit: *Someone who shows grace – even in a discriminatory way – is not being unfair to those who are not shown it.* This line does not go down well in the anti-discriminatory times we live in, which just shows that the grumpy labourers of the parable are still alive and well today. God is only unfair if he gives *less* than what is right or what we deserve – not if He in grace gives more than what is deserved – even to a select few. The others get their dues. God is not being unfair in choosing some to be saved whilst others perish. Those who perish are getting the wages they rightly *deserve* – the due reward of their sins. God is quite free to discriminate in dispensing undeserved kindness if He wants to. It's His Grace. Is our eye evil because God is being good? He could have sent all men to Hell. No one complains that God discriminates against the angels who fell by providing neither sacrifice nor salvation for them. God does not owe any man salvation. He is free to show grace to whom He will.

[9] See for example verses like 2 Thessalonians 2:12, 13: 'But we are bound to give thanks to God always for you, brethren beloved by the Lord, because *God from the beginning chose you for salvation* through sanctification by the Spirit and belief in the truth, to which He called you by our Gospel'. See also John 6:37,44,65, 15:16, Romans 8:29,33, 9:11,15,16,22-23, 11:5-7, 1 Cor.1:26-28, Ephesians 1:3-5, Col. 3:12, 1 Thessalonians 1:4, 2 Tim. 2:10, Titus 1:1, 1 Peter 1:2, 2:8-9, 2 Peter 1:10, Revelation 17:14. Attempts are sometimes made to say that 'God chose those who He knew would later believe'. However, this robs the word 'choose' of any force or meaning. This is to really say that God did **NO** choosing whatsoever. 'Election' means to 'choose' or 'select' certain out of a greater number. The Bible does not even simply say that God chose *certain blessings for us*. It says that God chose *us for the blessings*. Nor is the idea that God chose the Church corporately but not individual Christians either (a) Scriptural (see Acts 13:48, Romans 16:13) or (b) logical. If selectors choose a team, they choose the individuals who make it up.

But why are 'many called', then?

Why then, someone will ask, does God bother with the preaching of the gospel? Those who are chosen will obviously be saved whether we preach or not and those who are not chosen cannot respond to the message and be saved anyway. Does this doctrine not make preaching the Gospel a futile business? Does it not mock the afflicted, teasing those not chosen with the offer of salvation that they can never have?[10]

In reply to this question, let us first notice that in the Lord's words here He places Election alongside the Gospel call. 'Many are *called*, but few are *chosen*.' Obviously Christ does not find any clash between the two principles. As so they must be reconcilable. The problem really lies in the reasoning of the grumpy labourers, not in the grace of the landowner.

Two Verses that Resolve the so-called 'Contradiction'

(1) In John 5:40 Christ says, 'But *you are not willing* to come to me that you may have life.' The fact is that there is no sinner who *naturally* wants to be saved. The proof of this is seen in that the vast majority of the world's population is not saved despite God's universal provision and offer of salvation. Who of us that are saved cannot look back in life to remember how we resisted the Holy Spirit – how we were fearful of taking Christ and made many excuses why we should not? Do we forgetfully think that when we were perishing we were somehow different to – or even better than – the other ordinary unsaved people around us who did not want to repent, believe and come? No, we were exactly the same as others (see Titus 3:3). Do we think that it was because we were better sinners than others (more honest, more humble, more moral) that we believed? This is obviously false. All sinners are basically the same.

---

[10] Some who believe in Election deny that God has provided for the salvation of All, or that God commands the gospel to be preached to All or that God commands All to repent or 'whosoever will' to come. But these truths are as plainly taught as the verses about Election. See 1 John 2:2, Mark 16:15, 1 Timothy 2:4-6, 2 Peter 3:8, Acts 17:30 and Acts 10:43 for starters. God in making such a universal offer of salvation is underlining the fact that *He* is not at fault for men not coming to Christ to be saved, but *man himself in his sinfulness* for not wanting to repent, believe and come. Nor is God under any obligation to draw men into such faith. If He does so, it is of His Grace, not Duty. And because it is of Grace, God is free to dispense it to whoever *He* wills.

What then made the difference by which some are saved and others are not? We certainly cannot claim the credit ourselves. It did not come from within us. The difference came from outside us. It was God's grace in our lives. This leads us on to the second verse.

(2) Christ's words in John 6:44 tell us: '***No one can come to me unless the Father who sent me draws him***'. God has intervened in grace in our lives, drawing us to Christ. It was God's working in us that led to our salvation. It was of God's choosing grace that we believed. He made us willing. He drew us into His salvation – some of us fighting every inch of the way up until our final surrender. Who of us that are saved do not look back and thank God for the way He worked in our lives to bring us to faith? Or do we congratulate ourselves? God must have all the glory! Salvation is all of Grace! Not only did God show us grace in Christ's death, thus making a **Way of Salvation**, but God also had to show us grace in individually singling us out and drawing us – as stubborn unrepentant sinners with wills opposing Him – to Christ in faith. God had to bestow grace on us in the **Reception of Salvation**.

We must Personally Believe

You see, there are two things needed for our salvation: God's provision of it in Christ and our acceptance of it in faith. If we are going to be saved we must personally believe. We do not have it in ourselves to do our second part of the bargain entirely on our own – and we justly deserve God's holy wrath and punishment for failing to do so. It is our responsibility as moral creatures to repent and believe. Sinners will get their fair wage. Yet none of the saved would ever have repented and believed if it were not for God's Spirit having set us apart in grace, convicting of sin and striving with us till we eventually personally believed and accepted Christ.

It's There for the Asking

Notice one final feature of this section. Four times in this section someone requests a **petition** from Christ – the mothers request His blessing, the rich young man seeks eternal life, the mother of James and John seeks a place for her sons and the blind beggars request their eyesight. Some mothers' petition is granted and another mother's is denied. The rich young man went away sorrowful and two beggars followed Christ, their petition having been granted. We too must come and ask Christ, acknowledging our moral poverty as sinners, for what we do not deserve but what God, in His incredible grace, is willing to give us: eternal life. He will grant it. Christ turns no one away if they come with all their need in faith to Him. He did not turn the mothers with their little children away. He did not turn the late labourers away. He did not turn the blind men away. He will turn none away who come to Him in their need, depending not upon their own spiritual or moral wealth or standing, but begging His grace – His undeserved kindness. 'Whoever calls on the name of the Lord shall be saved' (Romans 10:13).

Chapter 11 - Christ and Religion: 21:12 - 23:39

1. Cleansing of the Temple (21:12 – 21:17)
2. Cursing of the Fig Tree (21:18 – 21:22)
3. Christ Questioned concerning Authority (21:23 – 21:27)
4. Parable of the Two Sons (21:28 – 21:32)
5. Parable of the Vineyard (21:33 – 21:46)
6. Parable of the Wedding (22:1 – 22:14)
7. The Pharisees' Question (22:15 – 22:22)
8. The Sadducees' Question (22:23 – 22:33)
9. The Lawyer's Question (22:34 – 22:40)
10. Christ's Question (22:41 – 22:46)
11. Christ's Warns the crowds of the Scribes and Pharisees (23:1 – 23:12)
12. The Woes upon the Scribes and Pharisees (23:13 – 23:39)

e now come with Matthew to view Christ's great final clash with the religious authorities in Jerusalem that precipitated His death.

Instead of coming up to Jerusalem to overthrow the Roman military machine in the accepted mould of a Jewish military Messiah, Christ instead surprisingly launched a furious attack on His own nation's religion and its leaders. Christ reacted angrily to the religious corruption and hypocrisy He found in the Temple – the very seat of the religious authorities. It was a direct challenge that they could not ignore.

The initial reaction of the religious authorities to Christ's cleansing of the Temple was to tell Him to steady on a bit. They didn't like to see someone taking religion so seriously. They didn't like religious excitement and became disturbed as the children in the Temple crying aloud, acclaimed Jesus as the Messiah. But as they called for Christ to restrain such cries He coldly replied: 'Have you never read, Out of the mouths of babes and nursing infants You have perfected praise?' Christ was not quite the broadminded, softly-spoken, peace-preaching, moderate and tolerant type the religious authorities appealed to Him as. Christ had little time for the sort of religious don't-rock-the-boat wishy-washy sentimentality that some people consider religion nowadays. For Christ, religion was a serious matter. It was not so much over His political views but over His religious views that Christ made Himself enemies. Lukewarm, half-hearted religion was play-acting hypocrisy to Christ and He came to Jerusalem to expose the Jewish religion's corruption.

How would Christ react to the religious situation today, then? We shall see in this section what Christ counts as true religion and what Christ condemns as hypocrisy. How strange it would be if we were to find that Christianity today had returned to the state that Christ criticised the Jewish religion for being in. But it was precisely because Christ did not want His disciples to become like the Chief Priests, Scribes, Pharisees and Sadducees that He criticised them in so much detail. It is high time we who claim to be Christ's stand with Him for what He said God wanted out of religion. That takes courage. But if there is any feature of Christ's that stands out here in this section it is His bravery.

In the reaction of the religious leaders to Christ in this section they completely underestimated Him. They looked down upon Him as 'Jesus of Nazareth', a radical young Galilean idealist with a big following amongst the ignorant masses but with no experience in the big, wide world of complex issues. They decided that it would be sufficient (and a relatively simple matter) to publicly humiliate him before the crowds. One after another, the different religious parties came to Christ, smugly sure of the cleverness of their insoluble problems, inviting Him to help them. One by one they fired their questions at Christ, confident He would quickly flounder in problems their best brains could not solve and entangle Himself in the most sensitive political and religious issues of the day. One by one they exited dazed and humiliated by Christ's replies, their conceited reputations deflated. What we have in this section is the war of words. Christ dealt with their challenges so comfortably and then turned around and publicly exposed their corruption so completely that they realised that words were never going to get rid of Him.

Now we must not miss the main point of this whole section. The big fault for which Christ criticised their religion was its complete pretence. This was the very word Christ used in the first of the Woes in 23:14, 'Woe to you Scribes and Pharisees, hypocrites! For you devour widow's houses and for a pretence make long prayers'. The Jewish religion was perfectly pictured by the fig tree with nice leaves but no fruit. God got no fruit from it, to quote Christ's parable of the vineyard later on in this section. Their religion was just a front for all sorts of corruption. It was like a whitewashed sepulchre (23:27). Inside it was full of rottenness, decay and corruption.

Fake Religion (Episode I) – The Almighty Dollar

In the first part of this section – Christ's cleansing of the Temple – the merchants and money-changers used religion as a front for making money. Christ reacted violently to the idea of people using religion for commercial gain. He said, 'It is written, My house shall be called a house of *prayer*, but you have made it a den of thieves.' He then healed the blind and the lame in the temple and acknowledged the praise of the little children crying 'Hosanna to the Son of David' with the words 'Have you never read, Out of the mouths of babes and nursing infants You have perfected *praise*'. Religion is to be for prayer and praise to God and for doing good to our fellow men, not for milking money. And yet today the Christian church is one of the wealthiest organisations in the world. The wealth it has laid up in architectural extravaganzas and art treasures, which exist for the glory of architects and artists and not for God's, should be used to relieve the world's problems. God would get more glory from that sort of behaviour than from tourists paying money as they walk through the turnstiles of St. Paul's or from peasants in the 1400's paying money to buy pardons from Purgatory to finance the building of St. Peter's.

The next story – the cursing of the fig tree – continues the emphasis upon the true nature of religion. Following the cursing of the tree the disciples marvelled at the suddenness of the fig tree withering away and Christ taught them further about prayer. He said, 'Assuredly, I say to you, if you have faith and do not doubt, you will not only do what was done to the fig tree, but also if you say to this mountain, "Be removed and be cast into the sea" it will be done. And whatever things you ask in prayer, believing, you will receive.' True religion consists of real faith in a real God, expressed by us as needy creatures dependent upon God in prayer. Of course, those of us who do not have a God to rely upon have to resort to the accumulation of wealth for our security. Money-making is in many ways the very opposite of true religion.

These two incidents, I suggest, are therefore linked together by three shared features. Firstly, there is the common emphasis upon pretence; that of the Temple religion and the fruitless fig tree. Secondly, both incidents show Christ's violent reaction – overturning the tables and cursing the tree. Thirdly, both incidents present us with teaching on true religion. The important feature of true religion presented here is prayer: 'My house shall be called a house of prayer' (21:13) and 'whatever you ask in prayer, believing, you will receive' (21:22). We will see that the other incidents in this section similarly follow in pairs.

Fake Religion (Episode II) – Power Politics

The third part of this section is the confrontation with the elders and chief priests. Christ was teaching in the Temple precincts. He was confronted by a delegation of the chief priests and elders, the most senior figures in the nation. They asked, 'By what authority are you doing these things? And who gave you this authority?' They were asking what right Christ – to them a Nazareth nobody with no human qualifications – had to teach in the Temple. Their very presence as the nation's leaders was intended to intimidate and humble Christ. Also, their question in itself was intended to be unanswerable. Christ had no human authority for what He was doing. He had not been to their Bible Colleges. He had sat at the feet of none of the respected Rabbis. He had no letters after His name. He had been a simple carpenter. He had no human right to be sitting in the Temple of God in Jerusalem teaching the nation.

Christ showed little sign of being intimidated by their stature or the authority they wielded. He asked them to first answer Him a question. What did they make of John's baptism? Was it from Heaven or of men? They were too popularity-conscious to say it was NOT from Heaven before the crowds and were too proud to say it was from Heaven because that would be to admit they were wrong – they had not acknowledged John or submitted to his baptism. And so, they evasively answered, 'We do not know.' In His question, though, Christ had thus given away the answer to their question by mentioning the possibility of having authority from Heaven, instead of authority from men, which was all they could conceive of. But at the same time He publicly exposed their crowd-pleasing and power-hungry hypocrisy.

This episode shows up another problem of the Jewish religion. It was out of envy that these men confronted Christ and later killed Him (Matthew 27:18). They were afraid they were going to lose their hold over the masses. They were afraid of losing power. Religion was just a front for their prestige and power. They were big bullies. They enjoyed the cushy club atmosphere where they kept power within a small group of men whose only interest was in perpetuating their position. A man had to wear the school tie to get anywhere in this institution. God's own Son could not even get into His own Temple! The real authority in their religion was no longer vested in God. It rested in the lap of a small group of powerful men who cared little for God or true religion. The Jewish religion had become a front for the lust for power and position among the religious aristocracy. That is all they were in it for.

Their religion was not of God or from Heaven. It was of men. The religious leaders held their positions because they were men-pleasers. They lusted for the praise and popularity of the crowds. They got their positions because of the approval of their peers. They boasted in the qualifications that other men had conferred upon them. They did not care much for the praise that comes from God alone.

It is very strange therefore that Christianity has now for almost as long as it has existed been exactly the same (for the problem reappeared very early on). It is, in most quarters, so structured as to inevitably breed pride in a hierarchical position and even nowadays in an academic position. Christ strictly forbad His disciples at the end of this section taking to themselves titles like Rabbi, Leader, Father and Teacher (23:8-10) but Christianity today is full of people aspiring for special positions with special titles. We have Popes and Patriarchs (i.e. Fathers), Doctors (i.e. Teachers) and umpteen titles for different sorts of leaders. We put men on pedestals. Mind you, we need Church government, but Christian leadership involves humble servanthood, not hierarchical systems which result in men basking in the glory of having climbed to the top of their tree. This is what breeds a man like Diotrephes (3 John) lording it over God's people (1 Peter 5). We have returned to the standards of the corrupt sort of religion that Christ criticised. Christ stood up to all of this and suffered for it. We paint the Sepulchre. Is 2000 years too late to call for reform? Is it not even just plain naïve of me to call upon the current crew of chief Priests to rid themselves of their grand titles? In a way it is not strange that Christianity has become so leavened with this. We are all failing and sinful. We are particularly susceptible to pride. But that is why Christ made such a point about forbidding titles – we are not to even open the door to allow pride an opportunity.

The fourth part of this section, Christ's parable of the two sons, shows just how far the Jewish religious leaders were from submitting to the only true authority there is in religion – God's authority. In the parable, the man told his two sons to work in his vineyard. The first son said no but later regretted it and went. The second son said he would go and work but he didn't. He was a pretender. Christ proceeded to draw a parallel between the second son and the hypocritical religious leaders.

Christ compared the reactions of the religious leaders and, at the other end of the religious spectrum, the worst sinners in society, to John's message of repentance. 'John came to you in the way of righteousness' said Christ 'and you did not believe him'. What could they have possibly held against a man who preached righteousness? Yet they had not acknowledged that John was from God or listened to him. John was not in their little club. Christ was not only calling them religious frauds and pretenders to their face. Christ was saying that the tax-collectors and prostitutes in their repentance were better than the Priests who ruled the people.

Fake Religion (Episode III) – God-less Religion

The fifth and sixth parts of this section are the parables of the vineyard and the wedding. Christ continued to show that the Jewish religion was a religion without God – a God-less religion.

In the first parable, God received nothing from their religion. The vinedressers did not hand on the fruits of the vineyard to the owner of the vineyard. The vinedressers were simply the workers in the fields – they did not own the crop. Yet they refused to give the fruits of the vineyard to the messengers sent from the owner and instead started killing the owner's messengers. They even killed his son. It was almost as if they denied there was someone who owned the vineyard.

It was exactly the same with the Jews. They ignored God's messengers. They even killed them. They did not want God interfering in their affairs. It was almost as if they denied that God existed or owned them or had brought them out of Egyptian slavery into all the blessings of the land of Canaan. Consequently, they acted as if they owed God nothing. The leaders were determined to get as much from their positions as they could. Forget about God! Strangely, the Jews still thought that they were the most God-pleasing people on Earth. Christ said that God was being robbed.

In the second parable, they refused to receive what God wanted to give them. The King graciously invited the guests to the marriage of his son. Yet they would not come. Upon further invitation, they made light of the matter and went instead to their businesses and their farms. Some even started killing the King's servants! People do not normally respond like this to a wedding invitation. The people preferred anything to the company and kindness of the King.

In these parables the people had a poor estimation of the landowner and the King. In the case of the landowner the vinedressers had inflated ideas of their importance. They acted as if they owned the vineyard instead of just being workers there. They acted as if there was no landowner to whom the vineyard owed its existence, to whom they owed their jobs and to whom the fruits belonged. In the case of the King, the invited guests 'made light' of the King's kind invitation and costly preparation for the feast. They again were ungrateful for the privilege they were being given. Who would turn down an invitation to the wedding feast of a King's son nowadays? The reason why they didn't come was again because they had a low appreciation of the King.

And so it was with the Jewish religion. At the root of their problem was a lack of proper reverence for God. They little esteemed the privilege God had bestowed on them in calling Himself the God of Israel. The religious leaders were so full of their own importance and interests that they pushed God out of His rightful position. They got so much from their comfy jobs that they did not feel the need of God or any responsibility to Him.

Notice too that both of these parables concerned a son. The son was sent to the vinedressers because the landowner thought 'they will respect my son'. Here was God's Son in God's Temple, not being given the respect He deserved. In turning down an invitation to the King's Son's wedding, the guests were insulting both the King and his son. It is not exactly surprising then to notice the reaction of the landowner and the King to the ill-treatment of his servants and his son. The landowner would miserably destroy the wicked vinedressers. The King ordered the armies in to destroy and burn the city of the men who had killed his servants sent with the invitation. So too God's Son was giving Israel official warning of what they should expect from God if they rejected His Son – Destruction.

Fake Religion (Episode IV) - Truth

The first half of this section has dealt with the religious establishment in its structured hypocrisy and Godlessness. The second half that we shall now look at deals more with the Pharisees, Sadducees and Scribes. These were the religious pacesetters. They dictated what was believed and practised. They were the think-tanks, the learned doctors and theologians. Religion must be concerned with matters of belief and matters of lifestyle. Of course, for some impoverished souls, religion is all about the outward decorations of architecture and music, ritual and ceremony – summed up here in the Temple. But even a Herod can build a Temple. Real religion consists in matters of real life. And this was where the Pharisees, Sadducees and Scribes came into their own. Yet Christ criticised these men for the same thing as He criticised the Priests and elders for – hypocrisy.

The seventh and eighth incidents are paired together. They are about the visits of firstly the Pharisees with the Herodians and then secondly the Sadducees to try to trip up Christ in His words. Their trick questions were clothed with the outward cloak of humble sincerity. Again, in trying to humiliate Christ they only ended up being exposed themselves as the hypocrites they really were.

The Pharisees tried to trap Christ by asking whether tax should be paid to Caesar or not. To say yes was to acquiesce with the heavy taxes which the Jews hated. It would put Him offside with the general people. It was not the sort of thing a Messiah was supposed to say. It would rob Him of the great asset of the support and protection of the great crowds. On the other hand, to say that the people should refuse to pay the taxes would be to invite charges of inciting revolt against Rome. It was an offence a man might die for. The Pharisees dressed this very sensitive political question up as a religious enquiry to draw from Christ, who heretofore had shown no evidence of an interest in political matters, a response on the question. Of course, there was not much religious sincerity in the question.

Christ in reply asked for a coin and innocently asked them who it was who was pictured on the back. When told it was Caesar, Christ suggested they should give to Caesar what belonged to him – and likewise to God what belonged to God. The Pharisees were silenced by the ingenuity of Christ's reply and had no come back.

The Sadducees then decided they would take Christ on and show that they were a superior set to their enemies the Pharisees who Christ had silenced. Being as cocksure of their intellectual superiority as only humanists can be, they proceeded to tell their drawn out story of the woman whose husband died and was then, under the terms of Moses' law, married to a succession of his brothers as they successively died too. Their question was, To whom was she to be the wife in the resurrection? Their complicated little story was supposed to show the absurdity of the resurrection. It was a strange and tortuous route they took to get there. Christ dealt with their question with an ease and simplicity that there always is about the truth. He told them that people don't get married in the resurrection. They are like the angels of God – a completely different class of being to a mortal human and therefore above earthly needs such as marriage. Then to prove the matter of the resurrection which was what they really denied, Christ reminded them that God would have been downgrading Himself to tell Moses that He was the God of Abraham, Isaac and Jacob if the Patriarchs were no more than three dead men whose bodies had decomposed. For the Eternal and Living God to name Himself after three men was proof positive that they were more than dust. God is not the God of the dead but the God of the living.

Now quite apart from the lessons about taxation and resurrection, these two stories deal with some more important issues. They teach us lessons about the matter of truth. Religion is first and foremost about truth. A religion's primary purpose is to offer an answer to the big questions of our existence. The Pharisees came and tried to flatter Christ by saying, 'Teacher, we know that you are *true* and teach the way of God in *truth*; nor do you care about anyone, for you do not regard the person of men.' Here we learn lessons about what is truth and how we work out what is the truth. Christ's constant criticism of the Jewish religion in this section is expressed time and time again in His words 'Have you not read?' (21:16, 21:42, 22:31). That is, they liked to boast that they were Bible-based and Scriptural but in reality they had long ago stopped searching the Scriptures and had instead substituted their own standards. Christ continually reminded them of Scriptures that disproved their views and showed up their true ignorance of the Bible. His standard for evaluating truth was 'It is written' (21:13) and 'in the Scriptures' (21:42). He said here to the Sadducees, 'You are mistaken, not knowing the Scriptures' (22:29). The Jewish religion had substituted its own standards of truth for God's. They had pushed God's Word to one side and substituted their own cleverness.

The Pharisees, pious sorts that they were, were very concerned with moment by moment matters of what they could and could not do. They asked here whether it was *lawful* to pay tax to Caesar or not. They had added lots of little rules to the Scriptures where they thought the Scriptures were not explicit enough. Their traditions had become so important that eventually they did not need the Scriptures anymore. They spent their days quibbling over matters that the Scriptures did not consider important enough to enlarge upon. Notice here that they made no appeal to the Scriptures as to what they might do. They relied upon their 'sanctified common sense' as some today call it. And so Christ's reply showed them how little common sense they had. The money belonged to Caesar and so it was all right to give it back to him. But, he added, do not forget to pay to God what God was due. The Pharisees were so busy with their little religious rules that they had effectively left what God was telling them to do out of their religion.

The Sadducees too, were so sure of their intelligence that they would go even further and disagree with Scripture. The little matters they found in Scripture that puzzled them, they were sure, were problems with Scripture rather than with their reasoning. They had all their little conundrums and contradictions that they could call upon to belittle the Scriptures. They only used Scripture to show how silly it was to rely upon it.

Both of these groups were basically at fault in their understanding and knowledge of God. They did not think highly enough of God. The Pharisees thought that God had overlooked certain matters that would be best left to people as pious as themselves to legislate upon. The Sadducees, in Christ's words, were mistaken 'not knowing the Scriptures nor the power of God'. Resurrection was too much for their puny brains to comprehend. And so man's limited knowledge became the test of what was true.

Our Society is not so much different to that of Christ's day. Our society's Sadducees tell us that we should not go to the Bible to find out about history or science. It is just about religion, by which they mean myths and morals – and who today wants that sort of religion? Instead, to find the truth, it is better to take the majority opinion of the academic establishment upon a question.

Christ had no time for the Pharisees or Sadducees of human religion. He came as the Word to bring us God's message of Truth. In fact, He could say, I am the Truth. We should believe Him rather than the academic establishment, whose only measure of truth is the volume of applause they receive from each other.

The really scary thing is not that our modern society has treated God's Truth like this – but that large sections of Christendom have done it. Our modern-day churches are run by the accepted opinions of the theologians in their seminaries and Universities – and many of these people leave the Sadducees miles behind in their unbelief. We now have Priests who are atheists. At the other end of the spectrum there is no shortage of Pharisees either. God's Word is not held in much regard today. Christ could say to His Father of the Scriptures 'Your word is Truth'. Trust Christ's word for it.

Real Religion (Episode V) - Priorities

The ninth and tenth parts of this section again show similarities. In Part Nine Christ was given another question to test Him. He was asked what was the great commandment, the most important commandment. Christ's reply was 'You shall love the LORD your God with all your heart, with all your soul and with all your mind'. He was not expected to say this. He had the reputation for being a bit loose with the Law. He did things on the Sabbath Day that they forbad. Again therefore Christ's answer surprised them. Christ went further, though, and added the second commandment 'You shall love your neighbour as yourself'. Then in Part Ten Christ turned round and asked a question of the Pharisees. 'What do you think about the Christ? Whose Son is he?' They returned the standard answer 'the Son of David'. Christ then proceeded to question why in the Scriptures David referred to the Messiah as 'my Lord' if the Messiah was simply his descendant. 'No one was able to answer Him a word' is the Divine commentary upon their reply.

These two parts again deal with Scripture. Here the Scribes and Pharisees, seeing Christ had placed so much emphasis upon the Scriptures in dealing with the Sadducees, tried to show how superior their Bible knowledge was to Christ's. Their question about the great commandment was a bit like a Bible Trivia game question. The Bible was just a way to show off their knowledge. They did not worry about doing what it said. Nor did they even love it enough to really seek to understand it. Part Ten shows this. When Christ turned round and asked them a hard question they did not even put up a showing. Their knowledge of the Scriptures consisted of nothing more than quoting from commentaries. There was never any serious searching of the Scriptures to find the truth. Christ time and again sarcastically asked them 'Have you never read…?' They thought they knew so much that they never bothered to read the Book. They made such a fuss of their famous Rabbis that they never learned anything more than what the Great Teachers said. Once they ventured off the narrow by-paths that their Rabbis had cut through the untouched forest of Scripture they were hopelessly lost.

But these two parts also have something else in common. They both deal with priorities. The Pharisees in particular, as we shall see in Christ's criticism of them in Chapter 23, were obsessed with the most trivial matters and managed to completely overlook and ignore the weightiest responsibilities. It can sadly be true of us today as well that we can become obsessed with fine points of Prophecy or Church Government and treat them as the most all-important matters of religion. Some Christians today even go so far as to refuse to have fellowship with other children of God who do not share their eccentricities. If that is our case, we have become Pharisees. The cure for such a spiritual illness is to rebalance our spiritual diet by letting 'all the counsel of God' (Acts 20:27) shape our thinking so that we see the different features of Scriptural landscape in their proper place and in perspective.

Part Nine deals with the foremost place that God must have in our lives. Nothing must be allowed to take a higher place in our lives than a cultivation of a real and demonstrated love for God and our fellow man. The great problem with the Jewish religion was, as we have seen, that God was not in it. It was a case of making money rather than praying to God, the approval of men rather than the authority of God and the ideas of men rather than the truth of God. God got nothing from their religion and they had so many spin-offs and perks from their religion that they felt no need for God. They did not love God.

Part Ten shows us the other great problem with their religion. It was their attitude to God's Son. This was the final proof of the utter emptiness of their religion. They were on the very tip-toe of expectancy for God's Messiah but for all their talk about their Messiah they were actually going to unknowingly put Him to death within a week or so. They were ready to crucify God's own Son – in the name of religion. This is how corrupt religion can become – even a religion originally from God.

Christ's Warning

The last two parts of this section, in Chapter 23, contain Christ's criticism of the Scribes and Pharisees. Firstly, in verses 1 to 12, Christ addressed the crowds, warning them against the hypocritical behaviour of their teachers, the Scribes and Pharisees. Christ made sure His disciples heard His criticism too. He did not want them becoming teachers like the Pharisees amongst His own people after His departure. Then in the last part of this section (verses 13 to 39), Christ turned and directly addressed the Scribes and Pharisees, exposing their hypocrisy and calling down eight woes upon them.

Christ in verses 1-12 warned the crowds and His disciples of the Scribes' and Pharisees' hypocrisy in teaching the law but not practising it (verses 3&4). He warned of doing works to show off so men might think well of them (verses 5-7). Lastly, He warned of desiring to be addressed with special titles like Rabbi, Father and Leader, and in so doing taking the place of God and Christ over God's people (verses 8-12).

Christ's Curse

This last section consists of the eight Woes Christ called down upon the Scribes and Pharisees. What a serious and sobering thought that Christ, who did not come to condemn the world but to save the world, could curse any man, let alone religious men. Yet religious sins are maybe the most serious of all human sins. Let us not think that we as Christians are somehow spiritually protected against ever becoming like the Pharisees of Christ's day. Matthew records Christ's condemnation of the Pharisees and Scribes precisely so that we may avoid any resemblance to them in our religious observances.

These curses are the exact opposite of Christ's eight blessings upon the true disciple in the Sermon on the Mount. And, just as in the Sermon on the Mount, where the eight Beatitudes were followed by the two illustrations (the salt of the earth – to preserve – and the city set upon a hill – to enlighten) so too here Christ concludes the curses with two little illustrations. The first is about the hen gathering the chicks under her wing to save them. Christ said he wanted to likewise preserve the Jewish nation from coming disaster, but they were not willing. The second illustration is about an empty and derelict house. Just as Christ called upon us to be like a city set on a hill to guide men to God, so the city of Jerusalem with its Temple was supposed to point the nations around to the true and living God. But it did not. It was going to be left empty. God's Son had been rejected in God's own house and so not only was He leaving it, but God was too. The Jewish religion was finished.

The woes in verses 13-39 run in pairs – albeit not in quite the way we might at first think. The second woe in verse 14 should actually be the first of the woes. Virtually all the Greek manuscripts place this verse before v13. The first woe in v14 teaches the same lesson as the last woe in verses 29-36, and the remaining woes in between run in pairs in perfect symmetry.

Woes on Scribes and Pharisees (verses in brackets)		Cursing their:
1. Devour widow's houses (14)	8. Build prophets' tombs (29-36)	Pretence
2. Shut up the Kingdom (13)	3. Travel overseas, little fruit (15)	Proselytism
4. Gold or Temple? (16-22)	5. Gnats and camels (23-24)	Priorities
6. Clean: Inside or Out? (25-26)	7. Whitened tombs (27-28)	Outward Appearances

The first and eighth woes were about the Pharisees' double-standards and hypocrisy. They devoured widows' houses and in pretence made long prayers (Woe 1). They built the tombs of prophets (Woe 8), honouring those their fathers killed. Yet they were on the very verge of outdoing anything their fathers had done in the way of persecution. They were blind hypocrites and fools. The initial and concluding woes on their hypocrisy really summarise all the woes. Christ called them hypocrites seven times in the Woes.

The second and third woes were about their proselytism. Christ said they shut up the Kingdom of Heaven against men, not going in themselves nor allowing others to go in (Woe 2) and they travelled land and sea to make one convert and then made him twice the son of Hell that they were themselves (Woe 3). They frowned upon men repenting under John's ministry or Christ's because John and Christ did not belong to their sects. Then, their religion stood condemned by the fact that it was so repulsive to any ordinary human being that they had to travel land and sea to find one poor gullible soul willing to join them. Yet their enthusiasm for their 'evangelism' never flagged. They were the most enthusiastic of soul-winners. Beware of any religion that requires enormous efforts to make one gullible convert.

The fourth and fifth woes were about their priorities. They counted gifts of gold offered to the temple more sacred to swear by than the temple itself and they considered gifts on the altar more precious than the altar itself. They were more particular about paying their tithe of the smallest herbs like mint, anise and cummin – dicing them into tenths – than they were about the weightier matters of the law – justice, mercy and faith. They made mountains out of molehills. They swallowed camels while they sieved out insects. We need to be sure we are not living our Christian lives through the lens of a microscope. We need to let Christ's Word dwell in us richly so we see things in proper proportion.

The sixth and seventh woes were about the superficiality of their religion. It consisted only in outward appearance, not in inward reality. They made the outside of the cup clean but the inside was still dirty. They were like whitewashed tombs that appeared beautiful outwardly but inside were full of dead men's bones and all uncleanness. They put on their Sabbath clothes and tried to look as religious as possible in synagogue – but it was all show. Many unbelievers try this – behaving as a morally respectable person to impress their fellow-men. What is worse is when Christians live this kind of sham life. We need to deal with our inner man – not our outer man. We need to be cleansed of internal corruption. God wants to see those hidden beauties of a godly life, not the external appearance and act which only impresses our fellow men.

Chapter 12 - Christ and the Future: 24:1 - 25:46

1. Christ's Prophecy & Disciples' Question about the Temple's Destruction, etc (24:1 – 24:3)

2. Warning about False-signs of the End (24:4 – 24:14)

3. The Great Tribulation (24:15 – 24:28)

4. The Coming of Christ (24:29 – 24:31)

5. The Fig Tree (24:32 – 24:36)

6. As in the Days of Noah (24:37 – 24:39)

7. The Two in the Field and at the Mill (24:40 – 24:42)

8. The Thief in the Night (24:43 – 24:44)

9. The Faithful and Wise Servant (24:45 – 24:51)

10. The Parable of the Ten Virgins (25:1 – 25:13)

11. The Parable of the Talents (25:14 – 25:30)

*M*atthew's main purpose in his Gospel has been to show us that Jesus is the Messiah. In so doing, he has had to explain carefully that Jesus was not exactly the sort of Messiah the people had hoped for or expected. Christ has even had to tell His disciples repeatedly that He was going to Jerusalem to suffer and to die. This was so foreign to the disciples' thinking that they just repeatedly refused to accept it. They were sure that their Bibles said that the Messiah would reign as King. However, as Christ had already hinted to His disciples, His reign would not be until the age to come (13:39-43) when He would come back again in the glory of His Father with His angels (16:27). Matthew therefore in this section interrupts the rising tension of the great climax of Christ's final visit to Jerusalem to tell us more about the eventual coming of Christ and His great Kingdom.

Different Ways of Looking at Matthew 24 - 25

There is probably no subject that causes greater difference of opinion, to put it mildly, amongst Bible students than the subject of future events. The reason for this is pretty simple: we do not know the future – only God does. Ordinary readers might find it funny but there will be some people who will look at this chapter before they read anything else in this book, or perhaps before they decide not to read any more of the book. It is a chapter where it will be nearly impossible to stop readers switching off. The reason for this is because the standard ways of looking at Matthew Chapters 24 and 25 are so different to each other that whatever way we look at it somebody will disagree. Now, the first step that we are going to take here is to see the three standard ways of looking at these two chapters. This is not because we are interested in slavishly following what are only men's models of future events. It will be a way of introducing those unfamiliar with future events to this passage. We are going to overview some of the points in favour of these views and allow the opponents of these views to point out the obvious problems with them, too. Having seen some of the problems with all of these views, we are going to see that Matthew himself provides the key to unlock this difficult section of his Gospel, and we shall see what Christ is teaching here about future events and particularly His Coming.

The AD 70 View

The first common way of looking at Matthew Chapters 24 and 25 is to say that a good part of it is not prophecy at all, it is past history, in that Christ here was prophesying the destruction of the Temple in AD 70. Now, Christ does without doubt refer to the Temple's destruction in Matthew 24. Everybody accepts that Christ's prophecy in the first two verses that not one stone would be left upon another refers to AD 70. Furthermore, following straight on from this, the question of the disciples on the Mount of Olives as they overlooked the Temple in verse 3, 'when will these things be?', also definitely refers to when the Temple was to be destroyed. We would therefore expect the Lord to reply to this question in the rest of the Chapter.

Perhaps the strongest argument that Matthew 24 is speaking about

AD 70 comes from Luke's account of the same speech by the Lord. In Luke 21:20-24, Christ replies to the disciples' question about when the Temple would be destroyed by saying, 'But when you see Jerusalem surrounded by armies, then know that its desolation is near.' Then in verse 24 we read 'And they will fall by the edge of the sword and be led away captive into all nations. And Jerusalem will be trampled by Gentiles until the times of the Gentiles are fulfilled'. This is undeniably speaking about the destruction of Jerusalem in AD 70 and its aftermath. So, if we assume that the Lord was giving the same speech in Luke 21 as He gave in Matthew 24, it seems like we have good evidence that Matthew 24, particularly in verses 15 to 28 (the 'great tribulation' passage), is really a prediction by Christ of the destruction of Jerusalem in AD 70.

However, there are a number of problems with this view. Firstly, in Matthew 24:29 Christ taught that '*immediately after* the tribulation of those days' (of 24:15-26), He Himself was to come again. If Matthew 24 verses 15 to 28 and the 'great tribulation' therefore refer to AD 70, Christ should have come back *immediately after* AD 70. That He has not done so seems to suggest that Matthew 24:15-26 does not refer to AD 70. Matthew 24 must refer to a future tribulation period.

This would, however, be making Matthew and Luke give differing accounts of what Christ said on the Mount of Olives. Most of Luke 21:5-33 is very similar to Matthew 24:1-35. However, the passage about the 'great tribulation' in Matthew 24:15-28 is very different in its wording to Luke 21:20-24. Matthew writes: 'Therefore when you see the abomination of desolation, spoken of by Daniel the prophet, standing in the holy place (whoever reads, let him understand), then let those who are in Judea flee to the mountains'. This is the great end-time sign. It signals the beginning of the period Matthew says will involve 'great tribulation'. Luke is very different to Matthew here. Luke replaces the ten verses in Matthew 24 about the 'Abomination of Desolation' with five verses about AD 70. Of these five verses, about four of these verses are entirely unique to Luke's Gospel. Luke says, 'But when you see Jerusalem surrounded by armies, then know that its desolation is near…for these are the days of vengeance, that all things which are written may be fulfilled…

and they will fall by the edge of the sword and be led away captive into all nations. And Jerusalem will be trampled by the Gentiles until the times of the Gentiles are fulfilled'.

Even more importantly, there are serious differences between Matthew and Luke in the chronology of events related. Matthew describes the 'great tribulation' as being immediately followed by Christ's coming. Luke, on the other hand, describes Jerusalem's destruction in AD 70 and then describes a lengthy period of time in which the Jews were to be dispersed among the nations before Christ would return. Luke 21:24 says that the Jews will 'fall by the edge of the sword and be led captive into all nations. And Jerusalem will be trampled by the Gentiles until the times of the Gentiles are fulfilled'. Then he tells about Christ's coming.

Try as the Harmonists might to squeeze these two accounts into one, it seems a case of trying to reconcile different things. It seems that Luke has dropped out the ten verses about the time of 'great tribulation' just before Christ's coming (Matthew 24:15-24 and Mark 13:14-23) and inserted five verses about the destruction of Jerusalem in AD 70 instead. It is not exactly clear why Luke's Gospel is different here, but perhaps Luke has inserted what Christ said on another occasion, unrecorded elsewhere in the Gospels, into the Olivet Discourse to directly answer the disciples' enquiry about the destruction of the Temple. In any case, the fact that Christ said He would come again immediately after the period of 'great tribulation' seems to be a serious problem for the AD 70 approach to Matthew 24.

A second problem with equating the 'great tribulation' with AD 70 involves the way Christ described the 'great tribulation' in Matthew 24:21. Christ said: 'For then there will be great tribulation, such as has not been since the beginning of the world until this time, no, nor ever shall be.' As terrible as AD 70 was, we have now lived long enough to witness much worse human tragedies than what befell Jerusalem in AD 70. For example, there were five times more Jews killed in the Nazi Holocaust than the number that died in the Jewish War of AD 67-70, leaving alone some of the even worse wars and genocides of the Twentieth Century. How then is AD 70 the greatest tribulation of all time? It seems that there is still to come a time of trouble that will surpass all that has gone before it.

A third problem with the view that Matthew 24 is primarily referring to AD 70 has to do with the sign that Christ said should introduce that time of 'great tribulation' – the 'abomination of desolation' (Matthew 24:15). Those proposing the AD 70 view have suggested a number of different possible 'abomination of desolation' signs in the events just before AD 70. For example, some believe that the eagles on the Roman Army's flags outside the city in AD 68 were the abomination of desolation. However, this seems trivial, particularly bearing in mind the way Christ offhandedly dismissed Caesar's image on a coin as unimportant in Matthew 22. It hardly seems to merit the description *'abomination'*. Others suggest it involved faction fighting in the Temple during the siege. There have been other occasional fresh contestants suggested too. The big problem with them all is that they ignore what Christ Himself said about it in Matthew 24:15. Christ there, in explanation of the 'abomination of desolation', referred back to Daniel 11:31 and 12:11, which clearly teach that it is an idol *'set up'* inside the Temple. 2 Thessalonians 2:4 and Revelation 13:14-15 also teach of an image to be set up in a Temple in Jerusalem. There is nothing matching this description before AD 70. Ignoring Christ's own explanation and Daniel's prophecy and instead combing the writings of Josephus (a non-Christian historian) for a historical 'abomination of desolation' before the AD 70 siege has produced only uncertainty. The 'abomination of desolation' seems to therefore still be in the future.

Finally, Christ's words in Matthew 24:34 ('this generation will by no means pass away till all these things take place') are also taken by some to prove that Matthew 24 refers simply and solely to AD 70, the foregoing problems notwithstanding. Various other interpretations have been attached to these words, too. Some argue that 'this generation' refers to those living during a still-future tribulation period. That is, Christ said 'this generation' but really meant 'that (future) generation'. We would normally take 'this generation' to refer to the Lord's own generation rather than a generation still centuries in the future. Others offer the interpretation that 'this generation' refs to the moral characteristics that colour the entire age. But this rather platitudinous interpretation does not end up telling us very much.

Perhaps the correct interpretation is that 'generation' is here being used in one of its OT senses – that of a 'history, record or account'. The Hebrew word 'toledoth', meaning 'families, descendants, generations', blurred to include a 'family genealogy, register or history' and then 'a history of any kind' (e.g. Gen. 2:4, 37:2, etc). Mt. 1:1 seems to use the word 'generation' in this sense of 'record' and perhaps the 'genealogies' prohibited in 1 Tim. 1:4 and Titus 3:9 also refer to unprofitable *storytelling* in the church. I suggest this is the sense that the word 'generation' is used in Mt. 24:34 too. Thus in Matthew 24:34-35, what Christ is saying is: 'Truly, I say to you, this generation (i.e. *this account* – this Olivet Discourse) shall by no means pass away till all these things take place. Heaven and earth will pass away, but *My words* will by no means pass away'. In other words, Christ is saying that His words recorded here in the Olivet Prophecy will last as long as Heaven and Earth. He is confirming their reliability and endurability. There are difficulties with this view, however, particularly in attributing this meaning to the Greek word 'generation' used in Mt. 24:34. On the other hand, the Greek word 'genea' used here has (like the Hebrew word 'toledoth') a rather wide range of meanings: 'a race of people', 'the contemporary members of a race in a given period', 'a period of time or age', even possibly 'offspring' (Acts 8:33). Thus, in view of the Jewish cultural background of Christ's words and the rather blurred meaning of the word 'generation', it remains an extremely neat possibility.

The Jewish Future View

A second major viewpoint sees Matthew 24 as referring to future events at the end of this age, particularly as they relate to the Jewish people. These Chapters, say the proponents of this view, have nothing whatever to do with the Church. The verses about the 'great tribulation' concern the Jewish nation. The Church is said to be absent from Matthew Chapters 24 and 25 as already having been taken to Heaven to escape the 'great tribulation'. As in the case of the AD 70 view, there are certain features of this view that we have good ground for accepting. A good case can be made for this view from the Jewish tone in the verses referring to the 'great tribulation'.

There are seven features that highlight the Jewish setting of Matthew 24, particularly in the 'great tribulation' section in verses 15-31:

1.   The Audience: The Disciples: Matthew 24 commenced with the disciples' national pride in their Temple. Verse 1 tells us that as Christ departed from the Temple, His disciples came up to show Him the buildings of the Temple. Christ's prophecy of its destruction in response filled them with amazed horror. Christ's disciples were fervently hoping Jesus had come up to Jerusalem to take the throne. The two on the road to Emmaus said, 'We were hoping that it was He who was going to redeem Israel' (Luke 24:21). Even after Christ's resurrection the disciples were still asking if Christ would restore the Kingdom to Israel (Acts 1:6). Those of us who are Gentiles have to remember that these disciples at this point in time had little thought or care for the idea of a Church. *The disciples' interest in Matthew 24:3 was solely in Israel's future*. Christ had never even mentioned the gospel being taken to Gentile nations anywhere up until later in this chapter in 24:14. The only direct references to the gospel going to the Gentile nations in Matthew are 24:14, 26:13 and 28:19.

2.   The Setting: the Mount of Olives: Notice too the setting of these two chapters. The passage was spoken on the Mount of Olives. As Jesus spoke the words in Matthew 24 He and His disciples were overlooking the city of Jerusalem and particularly its Temple. It would be no great wonder then if much of what Christ said concerned the future of the Nation of Israel, its capital Jerusalem and its Temple.

3.   The Holy Place: In verse 15 Christ gave the first of a few signs of His coming. He said, 'when you see the abomination of desolation ... standing in the holy place.' This sign of the end – the image of the Man of Sin – was to be placed in 'the holy place'. The holy place means the holy place in the Temple. The first sign of the end is found in a future *Jewish* Temple. Therefore, at the very beginning of verses 15-31, we have reference to Jerusalem.

4.   Those in Judea: Notice that when this sign is seen, Christ says in verse 16, 'let those who are in Judea flee to the mountains.' The 'great tribulation' particularly affects, at least here in this passage, the land of Israel. Those in the land are to get out of the land, presumably because it would be safer outside of it. Matthew 24:16 is not world-wide in its scope. So in this passage we have a *Jewish geographical* limitation.

5.   The Housetop: Likewise, the reference to 'him who is on the housetop' not going down to take anything out of his house before fleeing (verse 17) refers to Palestinian conditions. The Jews in Israel used their housetops, particularly for sleeping on. Here we have a *Jewish cultural* limitation on this passage.

6.   The Sabbath: Christ also said in verse 20, 'and pray that your flight may not be in winter or on the Sabbath.' Here we have reference to praying and, more importantly, to the Sabbath. This verse applies only to Jews. Only they (apart from untaught Christians) observe the Sabbath. Here we have a *Jewish religious* limitation. Notice that this excludes Christians. Christians are not taught to keep the Sabbath.

7.   The Sign of the Sun, Moon and Stars: In verse 29 we read that 'immediately after the tribulation of those days the sun will be darkened, and the moon will not give its light; the stars will fall from heaven and the powers of the heavens will be shaken'. Then we read in the next verse of Christ coming. This sign of the Sun, Moon and Stars is one of the great events of Bible prophecy. It is mentioned in Isaiah 13:10 and 24:23, Ezekiel 32:7-8, Joel 2:10, 31 and 3:15, Amos 5:18 and 20, Zechariah 14:6, Matthew 24:29, Mark 13:24-25, Luke 21:25, Acts 2:19-20 and Revelation 6:12-13. What does the sign of the sun's darkening, the moon's dimming and the fall of the stars of heaven refer to? If we read Joel's prophecy we see that these signs occur at the Battle of Armageddon. This is what Joel 3 is all about, particularly in verses 9-16. Likewise we are told in Zechariah 14:6&7 that 'the lights (plural) will diminish'. Zechariah 14 is one of the great chapters in the Old Testament about the Battle of Armageddon. Therefore, the primary emphasis of Matthew 24:29 is the sign of Christ coming to war at the Battle of Armageddon. Now bear in mind that Armageddon is a place. It literally means 'Mount Megiddo'.

Megiddo was a strategic town in northern Israel. Armageddon is a war fought in Israel for Israel's salvation (see Zechariah 12-14 and Joel 3). Matthew 24 is therefore concerned with Christ coming back to war with Israel's enemies gathered to battle *in the land of Israel*.

However, there are some problems facing this viewpoint. Firstly, its opponents point out that on this way of looking at these chapters Christ never bothers to answer the disciples' question about when the Temple would be destroyed. Christ completely ignores the disciples' question about the Temple and immediately starts talking about end times. This seems either strange or rude. Christ must respond in some way to the disciples' question about the Temple's destruction somewhere in Matthew 24 or 25.

Another serious problem with this viewpoint is that many of the parables in Matthew Chapters 24 and 25 seem to apply to Christians. For example, the Parable of the Talents in Chapter 25 is applied to Christians, not Jews, by virtually every commentator – and for good reasons. In the parable, the man goes away to a far country and gives his goods to his servants, who traded with them until *'after a long time'*, the man returned home again. Now, the man in the parable is obviously Christ, and Christ obviously went away at the beginning of the Church era in His ascension. The *'long* time' of His absence seems obviously to relate to this whole Church era of nearly twenty centuries – not the 'great tribulation', which we are told in Matthew 24:22 is going to be of relatively *short* duration (see also Revelation 12:12). The parable teaches how Christians should exercise their gifts in view of Christ's coming again. A similar expression is used in the parable of the 10 virgins where we are told 'while the bridegroom was *delayed*' (25:5). Literally the word here means to 'take (one's) *time*'. It is also used in the parable of the faithful and wise servant. The evil servant said, 'My lord is *delaying* His coming' (24:48). The drawn-out delay of Christ's coming in these parables most naturally refers to the present Church period.

Likewise, the Parable of the Faithful and Wise Servant in Matthew 24:45-51, whom the Master appointed to feed the other servants, shares a number of obvious similarities with the Parable of the

Talents. It pictures the responsibility that Christ has entrusted certain believers with to 'feed the flock' in this Church age. Upon the Lord's return the Faithful and Wise Servant is appointed over all the Lord's property, just as we find in the rewards for faithfulness in the Parable of the Talents. These two parables obviously teach us lessons about our service for Christ in this period of His absence, in the Church (24:45-51) and in the world (25:14-30).

Some who hold to this Jewish Future View would try to apply these parables to the 'great tribulation' period. The big problem they run up against is that we do not find any mention of any tribulation or persecution in these parables. Unless there is some direct reference to features of the future tribulation period in a parable, we should be very hesitant to try to read this into the parable. For example, once we try to make the three servants in the Parable of the Talents into three Jews during the Tribulation the whole parable becomes pedantic.

It would seem almost incredible for Christ, having turned His back on Israel in their unbelief in Chapters 13 and 23 and having devoted almost twenty chapters of Matthew's Gospel to training His disciples, to now say absolutely nothing about their future in relation to His Coming and instead solely speak about Israel's future. It seems wrong to assume that these New Testament Chapters have nothing for New Testament Christians. Christ is described using the title 'Lord' some 17 times and as 'Bridegroom' 3 times in the verses from 24:42 to 25:26. These are titles that usually apply to Christ in relation to His Church.

Some will plead that the context must determine what a text means and therefore reference to the 'great tribulation' in the earlier part of Matthew 24 must shape our view of the parables later on. However, context is not the No.1 rule of Biblical interpretation. 'Text' – what the actual words in a passage say – comes before 'context'! We must not interpret a passage in a way that allows us to ignore the actual 'text' on the basis of appeals to 'context'. If a 'text' seems to be at variance with a claimed 'context', then sometimes we need to re-examine the context. The context can, and often does, change.

The Christian Future View

A third viewpoint on these chapters is largely based on the perceived problems of the previous viewpoints. It holds that these chapters foretell the future – not AD 70 – and that these verses concern what will happen in the end times to Christians rather than Jews. Christ is viewed as speaking to the disciples as representatives of His Church. Christ is therefore foretelling the future of Christianity during this age and more particularly, the events at its end when Christ Himself will return.

One of the main arguments used to try to show that the Church will go through the 'great tribulation' in Matthew 24:15-28 is the similarity between Christ's Coming here in Matthew 24 and Christ's Coming for His Church in 1 Thessalonians 4:13-17. Matthew 24:30-31 reads 'Then the sign of the Son of Man will appear in heaven and then all the tribes of the earth will mourn, and they will see the Son of Man coming on the clouds of heaven with power and great glory. And He will send His angels with a great sound of a trumpet and they will gather together His elect from the four winds, from one end of heaven to the other'.

'The Rapture' is a term used to describe Christ taking the Church to be with Him and it is described most fully in 1 Thessalonians 4:13-17. We read that when Christ comes again He will descend from Heaven with a shout, with the voice of an archangel and with the trumpet of God. The dead in Christ shall rise again and those Christians who are alive will be caught up together with them in the clouds to meet the Lord in the air.

Now notice some similarities between these two passages. Both passages speak about the ***Lord's coming***, both speak about ***clouds***, both mention ***angels*** and a ***trumpet*** sound and both speak of the ***gathering*** of God's people. Therefore, if we equate these two passages with the same event, Matthew 24:30-31 seems to refer to the Church being gathered to Christ at His coming. Therefore the verses previous to this must speak about the Church going through the 'great tribulation'.

However, there are two major problems with this argument that Matthew 24:15-31 relates to the Church going through the 'great tribulation' and then being 'Raptured' at Christ's coming after it.

Problem 1: The Case of the Missed Quotation

The most serious problem with identifying Matthew 24:31 with the Rapture of the Church in 1 Thessalonians 4:13-17 is that Matthew 24:31 involves a crucial quotation from the Old Testament. This quotation has either been *missed* or ignored by those advocating a connection between Matthew 24:31 and the Rapture.

The words *'from one end of heaven to the other'* in Matthew 24:31 are a quotation from Deuteronomy 30:4 and Nehemiah 1:9. In Deuteronomy 28:64 Moses had declared to the children of Israel that if they did not keep God's covenant the Lord would 'scatter you among all peoples, from one end of the earth to the other'. However, in Deuteronomy 30:3-4 Moses told them that if the children of Israel then repented and returned to the Lord, He would 'bring you back from captivity ... and gather you again from all the nations where the Lord your God has scattered you. If any of you are driven out to *the farthest parts under heaven,* from there the Lord your God will gather you and from there He will bring you'. Nehemiah quoted Moses' words in Nehemiah 1:9 when he prayed 'but if you return to me, and keep my commandments and do them, though some of you were cast out to *the farthest part of the heavens*, yet I will gather them to the place which I have chosen as a dwelling place for my name'. Isaiah 13:5 and Deuteronomy 4:32 both further prove that 'the end of heaven' is simply a Hebraic way of saying 'the ends of the earth'. Look them up!

Matthew 24:31 is therefore a hark-back to God's promise to eventually re-gather *Israel* from its Dispersion among the nations. Notice the following other missed allusions in Matthew 24:31 that show it refers to Israel's re-gathering to its ancient land – not Christians being caught up into the air:

The Great Trumpet: Isaiah 27:12-13 shows that there is a trumpet to be blown for the future re-gathering of *Israel*. Isaiah 24 foretells the great judgements God will bring on the earth at the end of the age. We have reference to the sun, moon and stars being darkened in v23. Chapters 25-26 describe the blessings of the Kingdom. But in Chapter 27, God re-gathers His people *Israel*. Verses 12 and 13 read, 'And it shall come to pass in that day that the LORD will thresh from the channel of the River to the Brook of Egypt; and you will be gathered one by one, *O you children of Israel*. So it shall be in that day: *the great trumpet* will be blown; They will come, who are about to perish in the land of Assyria, and they who are outcasts in the land of Egypt and shall worship the LORD in the holy mount at *Jerusalem*'.

The Four Winds: Isaiah Chapter 11 proves that the reference to being gathered from the four winds (meaning the four points of the compass) in Matthew 24:31 relates to *Israel*. Isaiah Chapter 11 tells about Christ's Kingdom. It speaks of the harmony of all creation in verses 6-9 – the wolf shall dwell with the lamb, etc. Then in verses 11 and 12 it speaks about the future re-gathering of *Israel*. It says, 'It shall come to pass in that day that the Lord shall set His hand again the second time to recover the remnant of His people who are left, from Assyria and Egypt, from Pathros and Cush, from Elam and Shinar, from Hamath and the islands of the sea. He will set up a banner for the nations and will assemble the outcasts of *Israel*, and gather together the dispersed of *Judah* from the *four corners (lit. wings)* of the earth'. Notice the four points of the compass in the places mentioned. Jeremiah 49:32 and particularly 49:36 also prove that 'the four winds' means the four compass points.

Luke's Gospel: Luke 21 also proves that the gathering spoken of in Matthew 24:31 relates to *Israel*. Luke does not mention the abomination of desolation. Instead he writes about AD 70 and the Jews being taken captive into all nations until Christ's coming (Luke 21:27). Then in 21:28 we read, 'Now when these things (the signs of the future great tribulation) begin to happen, look up and lift up your heads, because your *redemption* draws near'. The word 'redemption' here means 'the release of *captives*' and refers to *Israel's* return from their *captivity* (spoken of just a few verses previously in v24) following AD 70[11].

---

[11] The words 'redeem' and 'redemption' occur four times in Luke. We have already seen that the last reference in 24:21 ('we were hoping that it was he who was going to redeem Israel') refers to the redemption of *Israel nationally*. Zacharias' words in Luke 1:68 do so too: 'Blessed is the Lord God of *Israel* for he has visited and redeemed His people ... that we should be saved from our enemies and from the hand of all who hate us' (v71). 1:74 likewise mentions 'being delivered from the hand of our enemies'. The reference in Luke 2:38, where we read of Anna that she 'spoke of him to all those who looked for redemption in Jerusalem', following on so close from Zacharias' words in the previous chapter, seems to refers to national redemption too.

Problem 2: The Great Tribulation is Jewish

A second problem with the idea that the Church will go through the 'great tribulation' mentioned in Matthew 24:15-28 is that everywhere else we read of the 'great tribulation', especially in the Old Testament, it is directly linked with Israel.

• In Jeremiah 30:7 it is called 'the time of *Jacob's* trouble'. Jeremiah 30:6-9 reads 'Ask now and see, whether a man is ever in labour with child. So why do I see every man with his hands on his loins like a woman in labour and all faces turned pale? Alas! For that day is great, so that *none is like it*; and it is *the time of Jacob's trouble*, but he shall be saved out of it. For it shall come to pass in that day, says the LORD of Hosts that I will break his yoke from your neck, and will burst your bonds; foreigners shall no more enslave them. But they shall serve the LORD their God and *David their King*, whom I will raise up for them'. Notice the connection with Matthew 24 in the words 'none is like it' – just like Christ's words in Matthew 24:21 describing 'great tribulation, such as has not been since the beginning of the world until this time, no, nor ever shall be'. Notice that here in Jeremiah this time of Jacob's trouble is followed by David reigning over Israel – a reference to the reign of the Messiah. This passage therefore can only relate to the future 'great tribulation', followed by Christ reigning.

• In Daniel 12:1-2 we read 'At that time Michael will stand up, the great prince who stands watch over the sons of *your people*; And there shall be a time of trouble such as never was since there was a nation, even to that time. And at that time *your people* shall be delivered, every one who is found written in the book. And many of those who sleep in the dust of the earth shall awake, some to everlasting life, some to everlasting contempt'. Again we notice that this must refer to the 'great tribulation' – only it is followed by resurrection. Again too, it refers to Daniel's people, the Jews.

• A number of New Testament passages teach that the Church will not go through either the great tribulation or God's wrath. 1 Thessalonians 1:10 literally reads, 'and to wait for His Son from Heaven, the One delivering us from the wrath to come'. 1 Thessalonians 5:9 reads, 'For God did not appoint us to wrath, but to obtain salvation through our Lord Jesus Christ'. Some might object that these references to wrath refer to eternal punishment. Now, it is perfectly true in itself that those of us who are saved shall not come under God's wrath in eternity, however, the context of these passages in 1 Thessalonians suggests God's judgement coming upon the world at the end of the age. In any case, the bottom line is that we who are God's children shall not come under *any* wrath from God. And that means that we shall not go through any of the experiences described in Chapters 6 through to Chapter 19 of the Book of Revelation, where there are twelve references to God's wrath being poured out upon the inhabitants of the world. The Church will not be there! In fact, we read in Revelation 3:10, 'I will keep you from *the hour* of trial which shall come upon the whole world, to test those who dwell on the earth'. We shall be kept from that time period altogether.

Thus not only is there a heavy Jewish flavour in the 'great tribulation' passage, but there are no absolutely distinctive references in the 'great tribulation' passage to the Church or Christians. We cannot simply *assume* that the Church is in view here in the absence of such internal evidence.

Time for a Break to Catch our Breath!
Well, so much for an easy introduction to the subject of Christ's coming in Matthew 24! It seems that the whole matter becomes more confusing the more we listen to the various sides arguing out their cases. There definitely seem to be points in favour of each case and yet problems with each case.

The AD 70 View	The Jewish Future View	The Christian Future View
For • Disciples' Question • Luke 21 = AD 70	For • Jewish features in 'tribulation' section	For • Matt 24:31 similar to Rapture, 1 Thess 4
Against • Christ must return straight after 'great tribulation' (Matt 24) • No suitable Abom'n of Desolation	Against • Christ must answer disciples' AD70 question • Christian parables	Against • Missed quote in Matt 24:31 shows gathering is Jewish • 'great tribulation' is for Jews (elsewhere)

To summarise, one case says that Christ must speak somewhere in Matthew 24 about the events of AD 70 because that was what the disciples asked about. The second case says that Christ speaks only about the future of the nation of Israel here. The third case says that Christ speaks only about the future of the Church. Or, to summarise it even more simply, one case argues that Christ speaks to His disciples as Christians, representing His Church. Another case argues that Christ speaks to His disciples as Jews, representing the nation of Israel. The third case says that Christ speaks to His disciples as 1st Century Jews whose generation was largely still going to be around to go through the events of AD 70.

Which Answer is Right?

Which view is right? We are doing our best to keep everybody happy here. We are going to say that *all three* views are right – up to a point. The fact is that Christ was speaking to men who were Jews *and* Christians *and* members of the generation that would see AD 70. The disciples were not simply Jews any more. They were now Christians and Christ spoke to them as such. But they had not ceased to be Jews now that they were Christians, either. We are going to see that Christ in Matthew 24-25 dealt with all three matters. He dealt with the disciples' first question about AD 70 in 24:4-14. He did not rudely ignore it. He also dealt with the Jewish nation's future time of tribulation and the question about the coming of Christ's Kingdom in 24:15-36. But Christ also told the first Christians about their future as believers in relation to all these events in 24:36 – 25:30[12] .

Just as the disciples asked Christ three questions in Matthew 24:3, we shall conclude our study of Matthew 24-25 with three questions of our own:

1.   How did Christ answer the question about the Temple's destruction?

2.   Is there a 'Jewish section' and a 'Christian section' in Matthew 24-25? In what verses does Christ speak about the 'great tribulation' for the Jewish nation and where does He switch to talking about future events in relation to His disciples as Christians?

3.   Where does the Church figure in all of this? What message does Christ have for His disciples in relation to future events in these Chapters?

---

[12] This is no new idea. Over a century ago, J.N. Darby (Synopsis) and C.H. Mackintosh (Miscellaneous Writings - The Lord's Coming) both suggested that Matthew 24-25 deals with the future of Christians *and* the Jewish nation *and* the Gentile nations, arguing their case primarily from the Lord's parables here.

Question 1: How did Christ respond to the Question about the Destruction of the Temple?

To see the answer that Christ gave to the disciples' first question about when the destruction of the Temple would take place, we have to study the first words Christ said in reply to the question: Matthew 24:4-14.

In reply to the disciples' troubled question about when the Temple was going to be destroyed Christ listed a whole lot more mostly unpleasant things that were going to happen in the future. Christ spoke of:

* *false-Messiahs* (vs 4, 5) and *false-prophets* (v11) deceiving many

* *wars* and rumours of wars (v6)

* *famines, pestilences* and *earthquakes* (v7)

* *persecution* for faith's sake (vs 9-10)

* *lawlessness* resulting in many whose *love would grow cold* (v12)

* the *gospel being preached* in all the world (v14).

What was Christ referring to here? Are all these things – particularly earthquakes, famines and pestilences – signs that Christ will soon return? Some take the increased frequency of these catastrophes as a sign of the Lord's soon Coming. Others use Christ's expression in verse 8, 'the beginning of sorrows' to describe a period of time just before the 'great tribulation'. They attach special significance to the mention of the preaching of the 'gospel of the Kingdom' – that is, the preaching of the imminent arrival of the Kingdom (v14). They thus see these verses describing a period of catastrophic conditions immediately preceding the period of 'great tribulation'.

What is Christ referring to in verses 4-14, then? Again, I suggest Luke's version of the Olivet discourse gives us the answer. Luke 21's account of the Olivet Discourse goes like this:

1. In verses 7-19, Christ uses virtually *exactly* the same words as in these verses in Matthew to describe the same catastrophes.

2. Then in verses 20-23 Luke, omitting any reference to the future 'abomination of desolation' describes instead the events in *AD 70*.

3. Then in verse 24, Luke speaks of the Jews being led away captive into all the nations and Jerusalem being trampled by Gentiles until the times of the Gentiles are fulfilled. In these verses he is describing this *present* time period.

4. Then Luke speaks of the signs of the sun, moon and stars being darkened and of *Christ's coming*.

Notice that point 1 above means that Luke uses exactly the same words as Matthew 24:4-14 to describe the period *before* the fall of Jerusalem in AD 70. This means that Matthew 24:4-14 must be referring to *present* conditions under which we live. All of these human and natural catastrophes occur today. We have wars, famines, pestilences and earthquakes. As well, the Church has not been exempt from fierce persecution like that described in these verses.

There are two other proofs that Matthew 24:4-14 is not referring to some still-future day:

(a) The expression 'the beginning of sorrows' in Matthew 24:8 literally means the beginning of 'birth pangs'. It is referring to the calamities, disasters and natural catastrophes mentioned in these verses. Paul writes in Romans 8:22 of these same birth pangs when he writes 'for we know that the whole creation groans and labours with birth pangs together *until now*'. The natural catastrophes and troubles of life that Paul is referring to are the very same things that Christ spoke of – and they were occurring even in Paul's day. The emphasis must be placed upon 'the *beginning* of birth-pains'. That is, Christ was saying that the present-day natural catastrophes are only the early warning signals of much worse calamities to come in the end-time period. Things are going to get much worse in the 'tribulation' period. The Book of Revelation describes some of the full-blown horrors of that future period. We at the moment, however, only experience the *beginning* of sorrows. The natural disasters and human tragedies of our present day are nothing to what this world is heading for.

(b) Acts 20:24-25, as we have shown before, clears up the other matter of the 'preaching the gospel of the Kingdom'. These verses show that 'preaching the Kingdom of God' is exactly the same thing as 'testifying to the gospel of the grace of God'. Paul used the two terms synonymously in the space of two verses. The gospel of the Kingdom is simply another description of the gospel message (see pp 81-83).

Matthew 24:4-14 refers to conditions we live in now. Matthew 24:4-14 teaches that natural catastrophes and times of persecution or spiritual decline and coldness are NOT signs of Christ's coming. 'You will hear of wars and rumours of wars, see that you are not troubled; for all these things must come to pass, but *the end is not yet*' (24:6). There is a seemingly natural tendency among humans generally to see signs of the end of the world in natural catastrophes, wars and famines, or, on the other hand, amongst Christians, to see signs of Christ's Coming in spiritual decline or persecution. But Christ specifically warns us against this here. Why?

Beware of False-Messiahs!

Christ's first words in response to the disciples' questions – even before He mentioned anything about wars in verse 6 – were a warning in verses 4 and 5 about the danger of false-Messiahs. Christ was particularly warning His disciples that in extremely stressful times in history (like the times around AD 70, for example) false-Messiahs might offer some glimmer of hope to troubled believers. The Jewish Wars at the time of AD 70 certainly did throw up a few potential military heroes who were seen by many as Messiahs who had come to overthrow the Roman overlord and establish a Kingdom for God on the earth again. Christ warned His disciples not to fall for such false-Messiahs during times of distress.

The Number One message of Matthew Chapter 24 is that we should not abandon our faith in Jesus as the Messiah in the face of world calamities, persecution and, particularly false-messiahs during times of extreme distress. Three times in Matthew 24 Christ warns strongly against false-prophets – in verses 4-5, 11 and 23-26. And so we see that even here, in a section of Matthew's gospel devoted to future events, Jesus must have the pre-eminent position as the true Messiah. The disciples were keen to know the answers to sensational questions like when the Temple would fall and when Christ would return. Christ was more concerned that they should still believe in Him, whatever calamities came.

Christ's Answer to the Question about AD 70

Christ, having first of all warned against false-Messiahs in vs4-5, then turns to deal more specifically with the disciples' question. He mentions **wars and rumours of wars** in verse 6. Christ said, 'you will hear of wars and rumours of wars. See that you are not troubled; for all these things must come to pass, **but the end is not yet**'.

Christ warned His disciples not to be troubled by wars. Wars would NOT be a sign that His coming was near and the end of the age had come. The end is not yet. Christ did not ignore the disciples' question about when the Temple was to be destroyed. Christ instead pointed His disciples beyond it. It was not the major issue they were making of it. AD 70 would come and go. More important for them would be their Lord's return. The real signs of the end of the age and of Christ's coming would commence with the abomination of desolation, the great tribulation and the darkening of the sun, moon and stars – not with wars or other natural calamities.

Thus Christ's reply to the disciples' question about AD 70 was that wars and other catastrophes were not signs of the end, and that His disciples should be more worried of attendant spiritual dangers – like false-Messiahs.

Question 2: Where does Christ speak to the Jewish nation and where does He speak to Christians?

We have already seen that Matthew 24:15-28 refers to a future period called the 'great tribulation'. We have seen that the focus in those verses is upon the Jewish nation and that the Church is nowhere mentioned there. Christ is talking about the signs that herald the coming of His Kingdom. On the other hand, we have also seen that there are certain parables later in Matthew 24 and also in Chapter 25 which have no references to Jews or tribulation, but which seem to apply to Christians of this Church age. This leaves us with a question: Where does Christ switch over from talking about the future 'great tribulation' for the Jews to speaking about Christians and their attitudes and responsibilities in relation to future events? Some perhaps are still sceptical about trying any 'switches' here and prefer to stick to the entirely-Jewish view of these chapters or the entirely-Christian view of these chapters. So, let us face the issue: what validity is there in suggesting that there are Jewish and Christian parts to Matthew 24-25? I want now to draw your attention to the following table.

It compares Matthew's account of the Lord's teachings about future events with Mark's and Luke's accounts:

Prophecies	Matthew	Mark	Luke
1 Christ's prophecy of the Temple's Destruction	24:1-3	13:1-4	21:5-7
2 Disciples' questions and Christ's reply about false-signs of the end	24:4-14	13:5-13	21:8-19
3 Abomination of Desolation & Great Tribulation	24:15-22	13:14-20	– (AD70)
False-Christs	24:23-26	13:21-23	(17:23?)
(Coming like lightning, Eagles gathering)	24:27,28	———	17:24,37
4 The Coming of Christ	24:29-31	13:24-27	21:25-27
5 Parable of the Fig Tree	24:32-35	13:28-31	21:29-33
(No man knows the day)	24:36	13:32	———
6 As in the days of Noah	24:37-39	———	17:26,27
7 2 in field, 2 at the mill - one taken, one left	24:40-42	———	17:36,35
8 The Thief in the Night	24:43-44	———	12:39,40
9 The Faithful and Wise Servant	24:45-51	———	12:42-46
10 The Ten Virgins	25:1-13	———	———
11 The Talents	25:14-30	———	(19:11-27?)
12 The Sheep and the Goats	25:31-46	———	———

If you study the table closely you will notice two particular features. Firstly, notice the boxes in the Table that have blanks (–). This indicates that the particular saying or parable of the Lord in Matthew 24 or 25 is not included in either Mark's Gospel or Luke's Gospel. The majority of these are found in Mark's Gospel's column although there are a few in Luke's column. There is also the paragraph in Luke where he writes about AD 70 rather than the great tribulation. Then secondly, notice the references that have been written in **bold typeface**. These occur in Luke's Gospel's column and indicate that a saying or parable of Christ's in Matthew 24-25 is recorded in Luke's Gospel but *not* as having been delivered during the Olivet Discourse. Luke tells us that these sayings or parables were delivered in a different place and at a different time (in Luke Chapters 12 and 17).

Now the first observation we must make from this table is that *Matthew's account of Christ's Olivet Discourse is more than twice as long as Mark's and Luke's*. Both Mark 13 and Luke 21 conclude Christ's Olivet Discourse before Matthew has even finished Ch.24. Notice that *Mark's column has dashes in the last seven boxes*, showing that Mark does not include any of the material from Matthew 24:36 onwards. Likewise, *Luke's column only has dashes and references from Luke 12 and Luke 17 next to these blanks in Mark's column – but no references whatsoever in Luke 21!* Thus, Mark's and Luke's accounts of Christ's Olivet prophecy both stop two-thirds of the way down the material in Matthew 24 (about 24:36).

Why The Difference?

The answer to why Matthew is so different to Mark and Luke seems to be that Matthew has slotted in other sayings of Christ about future events spoken on other occasions at appropriate points in Matthew 24 and 25. The proof of this is seen from the table in that *in every case where Mark has blanks, Luke either has blanks too or has references in Chapters 12 and 17 – not 21!* Luke's Gospel shows us that the sayings that Mark omits were not spoken on the Mount of Olives at all – they were spoken elsewhere! Notice particularly the two verses stuck in the middle of Matthew's Olivet Discourse about Christ's coming being like the lightning (Matthew 24:27) and 'wherever the carcass is, there the eagles will be gathered together' (Matthew 24:28). Mark does not have either of these verses even though Mark's account is following Matthew's very closely at this point – and Luke again also omits both of these verses from Luke 21, instead recording them in Luke 17! This is solid proof that Matthew has combined different sayings of Christ from a number of occasions into one section of his Gospel.

This is what we have seen Matthew doing the whole way through his Gospel. Just as we saw that Christ's teachings in the Sermon on the Mount in Matthew 5-7 were recorded by Luke in different places in his gospel (Luke 6, 11 and 12 - in very different settings), so too Christ's teachings about the future in Matthew 24-25 are found recorded by Luke in different chapters: 12, 17 and 21 – again, in quite different settings.

The Dividing Point in Matthew 24 - 25

From here it is quite an easy matter to spot the dividing point between the Jewish section and what we shall call for now the 'Christian section'. It occurs at about Matthew 24:36 where we have Christ's statement about no one knowing the day or hour of His coming. Up until this point both Mark and Luke follow Matthew quite closely. After this point, both Mark 13 and Luke 21 do not include any more of the material in their respective Olivet Discourses. From that point on, Matthew seems to have slotted in various sayings of Christ's on the subject of future events from other speeches that Luke records in their original settings in Luke 12:39-48 and 17:24-37.

Thus, it would seem that the natural division of Matthew's material on future events is found here at the point where the Olivet Discourse ends and the other material is slotted in. This division also corresponds precisely with the division between the Jewish section and the 'Christian section' – as we shall call it for now.

Matthew is a compiler. This explains why the questions that the disciples asked in Matthew 24 are different to the questions asked in Mark 13 and Luke 21. The disciples' questions in Mark and Luke do not mention anything about Christ's coming. However, Matthew's Gospel's second question is enlarged so that Matthew can add more material about Christ's coming spoken about on other occasions. Matthew has zoomed out to enlarge our view of future events. Matthew, I suggest, has deliberately included more material than what was spoken by the Lord on the Mount of Olives. He is giving us the Lord's entire teaching on future events in one body, whereas Luke gives it to us in its separate parts.

Question 3: What is the Church's Relation to Christ's Coming?

Let us now proceed to answer the final question we have set ourselves and see what Christ wants to tell us as believers in the latter third of Matthew 24 and into Matthew 25.

A Strange Change!

In Matthew 24:15-35 we noticed a number of *signs* that pinpoint when 'the end of the age' will be and Christ will come to reign. We were told of:

- the sign of the abomination of desolation,

- the fearful suffering of the period of 'great tribulation' and

- the signs in the sun, moon and stars – the immediate harbingers of Christ's arrival.

- We are told in the parable of the fig tree that just as the appearance of the leaves indicates summer is near, so these signs will indicate that the coming of Christ is near – at the doors (24:33).[13]

In these verses Christ displayed a profound knowledge of what things are going to happen in the future – from the abomination of desolation in the temple right through to His coming on the clouds. He assures us of the trustworthiness of what He has foretold in the words in verse 35, 'Heaven and earth will pass away, but My words will by no means pass away'.

Surprise instead of Signs

However, in Matthew 24:36 to 25:13, we find a strange change takes place. The next five sections of Matthew 24 and 25 seem to be telling us the exact opposite. Instead of finding signs of Christ's coming here, we find that Christ's coming is a *surprise* without any premonitions or signs. Let us look more closely at the five paragraphs dealing with:

---

[13] The verses in Matthew 24:32-33 about the fig tree putting forth its leaves as a sign of the nearness of summer, when read in context, teach that the signs seen *during the Great Tribulation period* are the immediate heralds of Christ's coming and the approaching Kingdom (see the parallel verse in Luke 21:31). Thus, the parable of the fig tree here is not a cryptic or symbolic reference to the establishment of the state of Israel in 1948, as significant (in both senses of the word) as that event no doubt was.

a)   Christ's coming being like the flood of Noah's day (24:37-39),

b)   the two in the field and at the mill (24:40-42),

c)   Christ's coming being like a thief in the night (24:43-44),

d)   the return of the master of the House (24:45-51), and

e)   the return of the Bridegroom (25:1-13).

Let us firstly notice how each paragraph shows that Christ's coming will be a surprise:

a)   In the case of Noah's flood, we read that the people of Noah's day '*did not know* until the flood came and took them all away.'

b)   After the verses about the two in the field and the two at the mill, Christ's comment in v42 is, 'Watch therefore, for *you do not know* what hour your Lord is coming.'

c)   Christ proceeded to speak of His coming being like a thief in the night, unannounced and unexpected, 'Know this, that *if the master of the house had known what hour* the thief would come, he would have watched and not allowed his house to be broken into. Therefore you also be ready, for the Son of Man is coming at an hour *you do not expect.*'

d)   Then again, in the parable of the Faithful and Wise servant we read, 'the master of that servant will come on a day *when he is not looking for Him and at an hour that he is not aware of.*'

e)   Then, finally, in the parable of the Ten Virgins, the Bridegroom's coming is so sudden and such a surprise that there is no time for preparation for those foolish virgins who had not filled their vessels with oil beforehand. Christ's coming is so sudden that *both* the wise and foolish are taken by surprise. The whole point of the Parable is summarised in 25:13: 'Watch therefore, for *you know neither the day nor the hour in which the Son of Man is coming.*'

Notice further that these five paragraphs commence with Christ's words in verse 36, 'of that day and hour *no one knows*, not even the angels of heaven, but my Father only.'

Now, this feature is strange and hard to explain. Why is there so much emphasis placed upon no one knowing when Christ will come if Christ has just listed a whole lot of signs during the great tribulation period that will form a 'countdown' to His coming? Notice that it is not just the ungodly here who do not know the day of Christ's coming. Even the true believer does not know when Christ is coming in these verses. We see this in Christ's words in verse 42, 'Watch therefore, for *you* do not know what hour *your Lord* is coming'. This direct address of Christ to His disciples is repeated in verse 44 after the parable of the thief in the night, 'Therefore, *you also* be ready, for the Son of Man is coming at an hour *you* do not expect'. Then it is repeated after the Parable of the Virgins in 25:13, 'Watch, therefore, for *you* know neither the day nor the hour in which the Son of Man is coming'. This is very strange.

Let me put it this way. There is no end of debate and dispute nowadays amongst Christians about what way future events are going to pan out. But we would expect confusion over prophetic matters to diminish greatly once people are forced to have the mark of the Beast to buy and sell or when the Man of Sin proclaims himself to be God requiring universal worship. How could a believer living through the events described in the book of Revelation *not* know that something was afoot and that Christ was about to return? Daniel 12 tells us specifically how many days there are from the setting up of the 'abomination of desolation' till the tribulation ends. How could a believer be taken by surprise by Christ's coming? A believer would be watching sign after sign being fulfilled. He would hardly be in any danger of becoming carefree about spiritual matters or forgetful of Christ's coming. Thus, these verses seem to be quite at odds with the verses about Christ's coming after the 'great tribulation'. But there is another feature that is strange.

Normality instead of Nightmare

Christ in these five paragraphs says that the reason that His coming will be without warning is that His coming will be preceded by conditions of perfect *normality*. This again seems strangely different to the *nightmare* conditions of tribulation and turmoil preceding Christ's coming in the previous section.

We read of the days before Christ's coming here being like:

a)   the days of Noah when they carried on with life – eating and drinking, marrying and giving in marriage – and then the flood came. Weddings imply conditions of peace in which people look forward with a confident hope to a future life together. We would hardly expect weddings to be a characterising feature of the Great Tribulation period when God's great judgements fall on the earth and a good percentage of the population of the world dies. Marriage would be exceptional during the period of the 'great tribulation', not characteristic. Christ is here describing the *normal domestic* conditions of peacetime.

b)   Then we are told in verses 40 and 41 of two in a field and of two grinding at the mill – getting on with their *normal jobs*, completely unsuspecting of anything about to happen and then suddenly, one was taken and the other left. Here we have *business* as usual.

c)   In verses 43 and 44, Christ's coming is compared to the thief in the night – again, the world will be *asleep* when the surprise visitor comes. Sleep is the ultimate state of peace, safety, security and normality.

d)   Then we are told in verses 45-51 that Christ's coming is like the master who returns unexpectedly to find some servants working and another servant who says his master is delaying his coming and starts living it up, eating and drinking to excess. Normal *Church life* is being carried on here. The servants are not barricading up the windows and priming their guns to ward off the agents of Antichrist coming to arrest them. Likewise, in the parable of the Talents we again have normal Church life – no persecution or tribulation of any sort is mentioned.

e)   Again, in the parable of the Virgins, we again find *all* of the Virgins *sleeping*, unaware of the imminent arrival of the Bridegroom.

If these verses were not intended to convey the picture of balmy normality for believer and unbeliever alike, could someone please explain what they were intended to convey? No one – either saved or unsaved – knows when Christ is coming in the verses from 24:36 to 25:13. Christ's coming is without warning or sign. No one – either saved or unsaved – is undergoing any Divine Judgements upon the wicked like those described in the Book of Revelation or any persecution for their faith like Tribulation saints will have to endure.

So here we have another big question to answer. How could Christ's coming be a surprise for believers of the tribulation period once the period of great tribulation with all its suffering and its signs had started? How could anyone be *sleeping* through the tribulation or through the events of the book of Revelation Chapters 6-19? How could *believers* be asleep during this period like the wise virgins in the parable in Matthew 25? How can these wise virgins be tribulation saints? Surely a believer would not be asleep? Surely once a believer had seen the abomination of desolation being set up, the great tribulation and finally the sun, moon and stars darkened he would be on the tip-toe of expectancy for the Lord's coming. The Lord Himself specifically said in verse 33 that when a person saw all these signs he was to know that it was near – at the doors.

In short, how can these paragraphs refer to the tribulation period at all? Where in these five paragraphs is there one single distinctive feature of the tribulation period alluded to? Just as distinctively Christian features were found wanting in the great tribulation passage, so this passage fails the same test of producing even one single mention of any tribulation, distress, catastrophe, persecution or any other feature of the tribulation period. These five paragraphs are Non-Tribulation paragraphs. They describe Non-Tribulation days. And that means, if you think about it, that these paragraphs must be *Pre-Tribulation* paragraphs. (They can only refer to Pre-Tribulation, Tribulation or Millenial conditions – and the last option is clearly not under consideration here).

There is thus a great contrast between 24:15-35 and 24:36 – 25:13. The verses from 24:15-35 show us that Christ's coming will be preceded by unmistakable and unmissable signs. Those signs will be a countdown to His coming. Yet 24:36 – 25:13 presents Christ's coming as an unannounced surprise, without a sign or warning and at some unknown time. How can *both* be true?

What Event is Happening in these Verses?

The answer to why there is this puzzling change between the first half and the second half of Matthew 24 becomes clear when we look more closely at Matthew 24:37-44 and see exactly what is happening there. Let us look at the second paragraph first of all (24:40-42). Christ talks about the two in the field and the two at the mill, one of whom is taken and one of whom is left in both cases. Now first of all notice that He does not seem to be telling a parable here. It is too vivid and the event described here is mysterious, not a common, everyday event. Parables instead use everyday events to teach truth. Christ here is describing in vivid detail an actual event as it takes place in the future. What event is it that overtakes these two in the field and at the mill?

• Is this a description of what happens at the **Battle of Armageddon**? It does not seem to be so. These people are farm labourers, not soldiers of Antichrist. Anyway, everyone in the army of Antichrist dies at the battle of Armageddon – not just every second person.

• Neither does this event seem to refer to **death** – either by natural catastrophes, diseases or wars during the tribulation. A catastrophic death would normally kill both of the two people standing next to each other. Death would not always be as instantaneous as this, either. No, it seems that we have something here even more sudden than death – and more discriminating. Christ's description stresses **separation** rather than destruction. So what separation is being referred to?

• Is this the separation of the righteous from the wicked on a worldwide scale when Christ returns at Armageddon to set up His Kingdom? No, because the separation of the wicked from the righteous when Christ returns to reign does not occur on the family farm. It occurs rather before Christ's throne at the beginning of His reign, according to what Christ says about the Sheep and the Goats in 25:31-46[14].

[14] The Sheep and Goats judgement is not the Last Judgement. The sheep and goats are separated at the beginning of the Millennium, not at the end as in Revelation 20:11-15. Notice that Christ tells the 'sheep' that they are now to '*inherit the Kingdom* prepared for you from the foundation of the world' (25:34). This judgement therefore happens before the Kingdom, whereas the Last Judgement in Revelation 20 occurs after the 1000-year reign of Christ (read Revelation 20). Matthew 25:31-32 tells us that 'When *the Son of Man comes in His glory* ... He will sit on the throne of His Glory and all *the nations* will be gathered before Him'. Notice that it will be for *Gentiles* – 'the nations' is the Biblical term for speaking of Gentiles. They will be assessed on how they have treated His brethren. His 'brethren' here seems to refer to believers of some description. Yet they seem to be a different class to the Gentile sheep who stand before Christ. They will be believing Jews of the tribulation who have been persecuted by Satan and his Antichrist. Read Revelation 12:6, 13-16 for a description of the Satanic persecution of the Jews during those days and the way in which 'the earth' – the people of the nations – help them. Those Gentiles who have sided with Christ's brethren will inherit the Millennial Kingdom. Those who have not sided with Christ's brethren will have sided against Christ Himself and will go into everlasting punishment. Thus we learn that *all* the people of the Gentile nations – both the righteous and the wicked – will stand in judgement before the King where they are finally separated. They are not separated while they are hoeing or harvesting on the family farm.

- Finally, neither can the two in the field, etc. refer to *Tribulation Jews* at Christ's coming being separated – some taken off to judgement while others are left. The faithful Jews will be in hiding during the great tribulation. Christ has already specifically told them to leave their *fields* (24:18) – their normal places of work – when they see the 'abomination of desolation' and head for a place of hiding. Revelation 12:6 says that 'the woman' – that is, Israel – will go into hiding in the wilderness for the three and a half years of the great tribulation. There will not be any faithful Jews merrily working away in their *fields* at the end of the great tribulation.

Thus this separation does not happen at Armageddon or when Christ returns to reign at the end of the Tribulation. As we have seen, there is no tribulation described in any of the verses from 24:36 on. The paragraphs from 24:36 to 25:30 describe Pre-Tribulation days.

The Rapture

The separation Christ is referring to here is the Rapture. Notice that Christ describes the event in the words, 'one will be *taken* and the other left' (24:40, 41). The word 'taken' here is a different Greek word from the word 'took' used in v39 to describe the ungodly being taken away by Noah's flood. In verses 40 and 41 the word strictly means to 'take to one's side', or to 'take to oneself'. It is translated as 'receive' fifteen times in the New Testament. It is the word the Lord used in John 14:3 when He said, 'If I go and prepare a place for you I will come again and *receive* you to Myself, that where I am, there you may be also'. Here in Matthew 24:40-41 we have one 'received' and the other left. Being 'received' here refers to the same thing that Christ spoke of in John 14:3, 'I will come again and *receive* you to myself, that where I am, there you may be also'. These verses are referring to the Rapture of the Church. In the twinkling of an eye (1 Corinthians 15:52) believers will be caught up in the air to meet Christ (1 Thessalonians 4:17). Men and women will literally disappear right in front of the eyes of the person they are standing beside.

These verses do not refer to the ungodly being 'taken away' by judgements at Armageddon. These verses refer to the ungodly being *left* for the judgements of the tribulation whilst God's people are 'taken away' so that they do not go through them[15]. Christ's allusion to Noah in verses 37-39 shows this. God's punishment upon Noah's world did not fall 'until the day Noah entered the ark'. The Church likewise will be taken out of this world so that it will not endure God's wrath described in the Book of Revelation falling upon the ungodly.

Proof that this is the Rapture

1 Thessalonians Chapters 4 and 5 prove that these verses refer to the Rapture. Immediately after Christ describes this event in Matthew 24:40-41 and warns His disciples to 'watch, therefore, for you do not know what hour your Lord is coming', Christ tells the parable of *the thief in the night* (24:43-44). This is exactly the same way that Paul writes about the Rapture in 1 Thessalonians Chapters 4 and 5, too. In 4:13-17, he writes about the Rapture of the Church, but then in Chapter 5:1-3, Paul echoes Christ's words when he writes, 'But concerning the times and seasons, brethren, you have no need that I should write to you. For you yourselves know perfectly that the Day of the Lord so comes as *a thief in the night*. For when they shall say, "Peace and safety" then sudden destruction comes upon them, as labour pains upon a pregnant woman. And they shall not escape'.

Notice the similarities we see between Matthew 24 and 1 Thessalonians 4-5. Firstly, the Rapture and Christ's coming as a 'thief in the night' are both placed alongside each other in both passages. They are the same event – except that they describe the effect of the Rapture upon two different classes of people. Believers are 'received' at the Rapture whilst the judgements of the tribulation period come upon the ungodly like 'a thief in the night'. Secondly, notice that the Rapture, the coming of Christ as a thief in the

[15] Some would argue that the corresponding verses in Luke 17 refer to Christ's Return, not the Rapture. However, Luke 17 refers to more than Christ's Return at Armageddon. Luke 17:20-21 refers to this present age, 17:22-24 refers to the Tribulation (compare Luke 17:23-Matt. 24:23) and His Return. Then, after 17:25, 17:26-37 refers to the Rapture and its aftermath. For example, if Luke 17:26-37 referred to Christ's Return, why does the Lord say that a man should leave his house and goods and run away (Luke 17:31)? Why run away *after* Christ's Return? Why seek to save one's life *after* Armageddon (Luke 17:33)? Luke 17:26-37 refers to the Rapture and the conditions after it during the Tribulation period. The verse about the vultures in Luke 17:37 is not a vivid description of Armageddon. It would then read 'bodies' (plural). Nor does it refer to Christ. It should then read 'eagle' (singular). It is a proverb, picturing the way moral corruption – the carcass (in this case the morally corrupt state of the world) attracts the 'vultures' of judgement and destruction (here the thoroughly deserved judgements of the Tribulation period). That the proverb refers to Tribulation days in Matthew 24 is seen in that Matthew has inserted the three verses 24:26-28 into the Olivet Discourse at the end of the section dealing with the Great Tribulation.

night, is sudden, unforeseen and preceded by 'peace and safety' (1 Thess.5:3). The Day of the Lord is a period of God's punishment upon unbelievers that comes without any warning. There are no signs that might indicate the judgement of God is about to fall upon an unbelieving world.

Some will object that the verses from 24:36-25:13 cannot refer to the Rapture because Christ uses the term 'the coming of the Son of Man' four times in these verses (24:37, 39, 44 and 25:13). It is claimed that this title is only used of Christ's coming to reign. This claim is usually based on a passage in Daniel 7, but strangely no reference is usually made to the 93 references to the term 'Son of Man' in the previous book in the Bible, Ezekiel, where it is simply used to denote the humanity of Ezekiel. Nor do verses like Psalm 8:4 or Psalm 146:3 ('Do not put your trust in princes, nor in a son of man in whom there is no help (mg. salvation)') get much of a mention, verses which show that the term 'son of man' simply means 'a human being'. Christ usually referred to Himself by the title 'Son of Man'. It was used by Christ to draw attention to the fact that He was a man – a fact that would have remained unremarkable for any other man. Only He found being a man worth remarking upon – because He, as God, had humbled Himself to **become** a man. Therefore, although teaching His humanity, Christ's constant emphasis upon it subtly implied His Deity also. The term is used 32 times in Matthew's Gospel in all sorts of contexts, mostly in relation to His sufferings and death. It certainly was not just used in relation to His coming-again. In relation to His coming again, however, it teaches the wonderful truth that the One who was humbled so low on earth is going to be glorified one day soon. Even Daniel's vision stresses the amazing fact that there is going to be a *Man* brought before the throne of God to receive universal dominion and glory. Yes, He is going to receive glory when every eye sees Him as He returns to reign. But shall not His own glorify the Son of Man when they see Him when He comes for them?

Also, Christ speaks of Himself as 'Lord' six times in these verses (24:42, 45, 46, 48, 50 and 25:11) so it cannot be denied that these verses must have some relation to the Church.

A Pre-Tribulation Rapture

We have thus seen four reasons why Christ's coming to Reign in Matthew 24:15-35 seems to be a distinct event from the description of Christ's coming to Rapture His people in 24:36 - 25:13:

1) The two parts of Matthew 24-25 dealing with Christ's coming to reign and His coming to Rapture His people were spoken on different occasions and in different settings, not all together. We have seen this from Luke's Gospel's arrangement of this material.

2) In 24:15-35 the emphasis is Jewish, whereas in 24:36 – 25:13 we have repeated references to Christians ('Watch therefore for you do not know what hour *your Lord* is coming').

3) In 24:15-35 Christ's coming to Reign is preceded by a period of great tribulation, whereas in verses 24:36 - 25:13 the Rapture is preceded by perfect normality and non-Tribulation. The 'peace and safety' (1 Thessalonians 5:3) before the Rapture is irreconcilable with Luke's description of the period immediately before Christ comes to reign in Luke 21:25-26: 'distress of nations, with perplexity, the sea and the waves roaring; men's hearts failing them from fear and the expectation of those things which are coming on the earth, for the powers of the heavens will be shaken'.

4) In 24:15-35 Christ's coming to Reign is heralded by unmistakable signs, whereas in 24:36 – 25:13 the Rapture is an unannounced surprise. Even the believer is told that he does not know when Christ is coming to Rapture the Church, whereas if a believer were going through the Tribulation he would know Christ's coming was near because of the signs. It would therefore not be a surprise.

The Rapture does not occur when Christ returns to reign. The Rapture must occur before the 'great tribulation' period altogether. It must occur while the world says 'peace and safety' – before the 'distress' of those tribulation days (Luke 21:25,26). It must occur before God starts to pour out His wrath upon the world as described in the book of Revelation. We do not know when it will happen. It will happen in an instant without any warning. We must make preparation beforehand like the wise virgins for the Coming of the Bridegroom – for Christ's coming will be so sudden that there will be no time to make last minute preparations.

A Final Problem, A Final Proof

One final question: why does Matthew record Christ's teachings about the Rapture immediately *after* he relates Christ's return to reign? This seems the wrong way round. The answer to this is yet again seen when we look over at Mark and Luke. Both Mark's and Luke's accounts of the Olivet Discourse conclude with Christ changing the subject. Christ turns from talking about His return to reign (Mark 13:26-32 and Luke 21:27-33) to briefly allude to His coming to Rapture the Church.

In Mark 13:36, Christ warns His disciples that they must be ready because He is 'coming *suddenly*'. The word 'suddenly' means 'abruptly, unexpectedly and without warning'. This again cannot refer to Christ's coming to reign which will be the culmination of a long period of tribulation and signs. It refers to the separate event of the Rapture. In Luke 21:34-36 we have an even more explicit reference to the Rapture. Notice particularly verse 36: Watch therefore, and pray always that you may be counted worthy to *escape* all these things that will come to pass, and to *stand before the Son of Man*'. 'Escaping' the great tribulation and 'standing before the Son of Man' on their own do not have to refer to the Rapture, but when combined they leave little alternative. Thus the reason Matthew slots in the paragraphs about the Rapture of the Church after Christ's coming to reign is simply because Christ finished the Olivet Discourse this way. Thus, Mark and Luke also both provide independent proof that Christ concluded the Olivet Discourse by referring briefly to the Rapture. Matthew simply expands on this reference with some of Christ's other teachings on the Rapture on other occasions.

The reason why Matthew particularly slots in these teachings about the Rapture after the verse about 'no one knows the day nor hour' (24:36) provides another proof of a pre-tribulation Rapture. Matthew 24:36 tells us that we do not know the day nor hour of *Christ's return to reign*. But why should the date of Christ's return to reign be unknown? Matthew 24:20 throws interesting light on this question. There we find that Christ says that the day that the 'abomination of desolation' is set up is unknown as well. He urges those fleeing from the 'great tribulation' to pray that the 'abomination of desolation' not be set up in the winter or on the Sabbath. The season and the day of the 'abomination of desolation' are completely unknown. It may be winter or the Sabbath or it may not be. The initial event that starts the whole period of the end-times rolling determines when all the other events happen in the programme too – and the date of the initial event is unknown. What then is the initial event of unknown date? Matthew 24:37 – 25:13 has clearly shown that the Rapture of the Church occurs in Non-Tribulation days. It therefore must be *before* the 'great tribulation' period altogether. It must therefore be even before the 'abomination of desolation'. It therefore logically follows that it must be the first great event in the future programme of prophecy.

Judgement and Reward

The final two parts of Matthew 25 are both about judgement and reward. We have already looked at the judgement of the sheep and the goats. Let us conclude this chapter by reminding ourselves of the very solemn lesson of The Parable of the Talents. We who are saved are going to stand before Christ and be judged too. Christ is going to 'settle accounts' with His servants. How well are we using the gifts Christ has entrusted to us? Upon this question hangs our eternal reward and place in His Kingdom. Will it be 'Well done, good and faithful servant' for us?

Chapter 13 - Christ's Betrayal: 26.1 - 26.75

1. Christ Foretells and Council Plots the Betrayal (26:1–5)

2. Bethany (26:6-13)

3. Judas' Pact (26:14-16)

4. Passover Preparations (26:17-19)

5. Betrayal Announced (26:20-25)

6. The Supper Instituted (26:26-30)

7. Disciples' Failure Announced (26:31-35)

8. Gethsemane (26:36-46)

9. Judas' Betrayal (26:47-50)

10. The Disciples' Failure (26:51-58)

11. Christ's Jewish Trial (26:59-68)

12. Peter's Denial (26:69-75)

S ome readers may be surprised or sceptical at the thought of divorcing Christ's betrayal from the concluding chapters of the Gospel dealing with His death and resurrection. It is not normally done this way. Some may object to the idea that there is anything of independent importance in Christ's betrayal to merit separate treatment. Well, if it is of any reassurance to these critics, we shall see that Christ's betrayal is not the main *point* that Matthew wants us to focus on in this section. However, the betrayal is the main *event* around which Matthew builds another extremely significant element into his history of Christ. Matthew wants to draw our attention to another glory of Christ that is specially seen in the events leading up to His betrayal, arrest and trials. It is Christ's incredible foreknowledge of events about to immediately overtake Him – a foreknowledge that is nothing short of Divine. What is the central importance of the betrayal in this section? The fact that a normal betrayal only works because of the element of *surprise* involved in it. Yet here the One on whom the surprise was sprung already knew all about it. He walked into the trap deliberately.

This section resumes the history of Christ's final days after the lengthy digression into future events. Christ seemed to have now outmanoeuvred His enemies. He had come to Jerusalem, taken them on right on their very doorstep and won. His calm boldness, His integrity, His wisdom and His superior knowledge of the Scriptures (supposedly their strong point) showed up their hypocrisy and corruption. Their attempts to discredit Him had backfired badly on themselves. He had skilfully avoided their attempts to trap Him and they had nothing to accuse Him of before a Roman court. If they had once thought that His visit to Jerusalem would be their golden opportunity to take Him, they had by now resigned themselves to defeat. They had retired to plan for the next battle.

Yet, Christ's position of seeming impregnability where we last left Him only makes the dramatic reversal that befell Him over the following three days all the more remarkable. Within three days Christ would be dead. Christ's enemies would be triumphing, having completely defeated Him – or so they thought. However, they did not have any real reason to congratulate themselves for this victory – they were taken by as much surprise as everyone else was at the turn of events.

The twist in events took not only them by surprise, it took everybody by surprise – even the disciples. There is only one person who was not surprised by the turn of events – Christ Himself. And this is primarily what this section of Matthew's Gospel is all about – Christ's surefootedness amidst the tragedy engulfing Him.

This section of the gospel stands out on its own as a separate section because of two features that mark it. Firstly, this section shows Christ's foreknowledge of events. Matthew's main point here is to show how Christ foretold His disciples everything that was about to happen. Secondly, we see here Christ's complete control – even during His betrayal when He appeared to be at His weakest.

Christ Foretells His Suffering

In this section Christ repeatedly foretold the events about to overtake Him, although 'overtake' is hardly the right word. Christ knew exactly what was going to happen. He predicted:

- the timing and method of His death (26:2)

- His imminent burial (26:12)

- that His time was at hand (26:18)

- that one of His disciples would betray Him (26:21)

- that it would be Judas (26:25)

- His death – in symbol form by breaking the bread and pouring out the wine (26:26-29)

- the desertion of His disciples (26:31)

- the denial of Peter (26:34)

- His imminent betrayal in the Garden (26:45).

In so doing, Christ assures us of two things. Firstly, this section serves to confirm the reliability of Christ's prophecies made in the last section. Because His forewarnings of His betrayal and death here are fulfilled to the letter and precisely according to schedule, Christ gives us every reason to trust His far-distant prophecies of the future too. His prophecies concerning the eventual coming of His Kingdom will certainly come to pass. Christ knew exactly what He was talking about in Chapters 24 and 25. Some modern writers try to recast Jesus as just another one of the many end-of-the-world apocalyptic prophets of that era, frightening the superstitious people of His day into following Him with vague and mysterious warnings of the future. Christ was no prophetic fraud. His words came true in His own time. Christ gives us every reason to believe that He was describing exactly what would happen in the future because of the way He foretold the course of the next few days.

But secondly, and even more importantly, by foretelling the events of His death, He showed that He truly was The Prophet – as the Jews said of Him in John 7 – the One Moses promised would come. He was the Messiah. His death was no tragedy. His death did not discredit His claim to be Messiah. Instead, because He foretold it in explicit detail, His death was the very confirmation of His claim to be the Messiah.

Thus, this section forms an important link between the prophetic section in Chapters 24 and 25 we have just surveyed and the all-important last two chapters of the Gospel about His death and resurrection. This section looks backward and looks forward.

Christ's Prophecies

The first five verses of Chapter 26 open this section of the Gospel. They are a bifocal look at Christ's approaching arrest and death, firstly looking at how Christ viewed the coming events and then secondly looking at what Christ's killers thought the next few days would hold. They compare Christ's prediction of what would happen on the one hand with the plans of His killers on the other, showing Who knew what was going to happen and who did not.

Firstly, Christ foretold both the precise time and method of His death – after two days and by crucifixion. Then secondly, contrasted with this we have the Jewish Council meeting to plot Jesus' death in which they ruled out any attempt to put Jesus to death during the feast because they feared His popularity with the great Passover crowds.

Christ thus correctly foretold the circumstances of His arrest and death even whilst those who were ultimately responsible for His death were planning the very opposite. He cannot be accused of uttering a self-fulfilling prophecy either – He did not engineer His death. He had no part to play in putting Himself to death. Nor can His prediction be put down to natural foresight. His prediction came to pass despite the utmost improbability – all those desiring His death had now given up hope of its immediate fulfilment and any attempts to achieve it.

The next part of this section – the anointing in Bethany – again shows us Christ foretelling His death. The point of this incident is Christ's defence of the woman anointing Him. He defended her on the grounds that 'you have the poor with you always, but *Me you do not have always*' and 'she did it for *My burial*' (26:11&12). Christ was making explicit references to His death.

Next in verses 17-19, Christ sent His disciples to prepare the Passover, telling them to say, 'The teacher says, My time is at hand…'(verse 18). Thus Christ again predicted His death. However, the point of this incident centres on how Christ referred to the particular man whose house was to be used for the Passover. Christ said, 'Go into the city to *a certain man* and say to him, The Teacher says, My time is at hand; I will keep the Passover at your house with my disciples.' The Greek word behind this expression 'a certain man' is only used here in the NT – nowhere else. It is the way of referring to someone whose identity cannot be revealed or is deliberately being kept secret. In other words, Christ knew whose house they were going to keep the Passover in but He was not letting the secret out.

Perhaps one reason for Christ's secrecy seems to be that he wanted the location of their final meal kept secret from Judas. Christ already knew of Judas' plan – as He later revealed. He did not want His final meal with His loved disciples to be interfered with by an attempted arrest. That was to come later. And so, again, Christ knew all that was to befall Him.

Then in verse 21, at the Passover meal with His disciples, Christ foretold that one of His own disciples would betray Him. The disciples were shocked and became sorrowful and then each worried that Christ might be referring to him. They each asked 'Lord, is it I?' Judas obviously was so good at pretending to be a real disciple that none of the others suspected him. They worried about themselves! Judas himself asked the question so he did not look out of place. How would we have detected the traitor if we had been there? None of the disciples knew who it was. Only Christ did. In response to Judas' question in verse 25, Christ pinpointed him. Christ alone knew, and not because He had some inside information, but because of who He was.

Then, in the inauguration of the Lord's Supper we have Christ symbolically acting out His death. The symbolism of the Supper lies not in the bread and wine on their own. The symbolism lies in the act of breaking the bread and pouring out the wine. Christ was symbolising His death – His body being broken like the bread in His hands and His blood being poured out like the wine. And just as bread cannot be eaten unless it has been broken or wine drunk unless it has first been poured out, so too, the disciples together eating and drinking of the bread and wine symbolises our participation in the blessings that come from Christ's death – the forgiveness of sins.

Finally, Christ forewarned the disciples of their own failure that night in forsaking Him and of Peter's denial of Him (verses 31-35).

Virtually all of these prophecies came true in this very section. One of His own disciples betrayed Him – Judas, and it happened when Christ said it would – at the Passover. All His disciples forsook Him and the section ends with Peter denying Him. Christ shows Himself to be the Messiah, the Prophet. Everything happened just as He said it would.

Christ's Trial

This section begins with Christ and the Jewish Council in 26:1-5 and it reaches its climax near its end with Christ's trial before the Jewish Council. The Chief Priests, the elders and the Council sought for false witness against Jesus to put Him to death (26:59) but they were only able to produce the two who said, 'This fellow says, "I am able to destroy the Temple of God and to build it in three days." ' (26:61). These two hoped the apparent contempt of Christ's prophecy for the Temple would provide a basis for a charge against Him. They were accusing Him of making blasphemous prophecies. But they neither comprehended what Christ was really referring to nor realised that they were in the very process of fulfilling this most important of all Christ's prophecies – His death and resurrection on the third day.

But then, after they finally condemned Him to death, we come to the most poignant moment of this trial. While they were spitting on Him and beating Him they mocked Him, saying, 'Prophecy to us, Christ! Who is the one who struck you?' Men mocked Him for claiming to be a Prophet! But even while mocking Him they were in the process of fulfilling His prophecies.

Christ's Power

However, there is another feature of this second-last section of the Gospel that Matthew emphasises, particularly in the second half of this section. It is the power of Christ.

The account of Christ's arrest in the Garden of Gethsemane is dominated on its surface by the power of those who seized Him. 'Took' – verse 50, 'seize' – verse 55 and 'laid hold of' – verse 57 are all the same word in the original, meaning 'to seize' from a word meaning 'strength, might, power'. We read of their 'hands' in verses 45 and 50. We read of their swords and clubs twice. Here was human power. A First Century innocent bystander looking on from a distance might have said that a small band of men, virtually unarmed, were overwhelmed by a great multitude with swords and clubs. The crowd with its weapons would have been enough to make an ordinary man run off into the darkness. Most of the ordinary men there did just that.

However, appearances can be deceiving. This section is a showcase of human weakness and cowardice. The men who arrested Christ were cowards. Christ pointed out in verse 55 that if they really had any courage they would have arrested Him in the Temple while He was teaching the crowds. Instead, they resorted to arresting Him at night when there was no one around.

Matthew also highlights the weakness of Jesus' disciples. Jesus could ask them in the garden in verse 40 when He found them sleeping instead of praying, 'What? Were you not (literally) *strong [enough]* to watch with Me one hour'? One of them stretched out his hand in verse 51 in a feeble attempt to defend Jesus from His arrest. But ultimately, in spite of all their brave promises they all 'forsook Him and fled' (v56).

Peter provides the final example of human weakness. When Christ was inside on trial, unbowed by approaching death, Peter was outside, unable to acknowledge his Lord before a servant girl. He denied Christ with an oath.

Contrasted with these other three pictures of human cowardice and weakness we have Christ's moral strength. Foreknowledge of death only heightens the fear of it. Yet, in the Garden, knowing His enemies were approaching to take Him to His death, He did not run or hide. He steeled Himself for it by prayer. Having at His call not simply the clumsy swordsmanship of His disciples or the massed legions of mighty angels but the power of His own word, He quietly submitted to be taken by 'the hands of sinners'. What strength of will and purpose!

Finally we see His courage and power while He stood on trial for His life. He did not open His mouth to defend Himself against the false-charges laid against Him. Any ordinary man could have exposed the flaws in the sort of false-charges laid at Christ's feet. More importantly, any ordinary man faced with death *would* have exploited the opportunity to escape conviction posed by such a flimsy prosecution. But Christ did not defend Himself.

Eventually, the Chief Priest, exasperated by the failure of the prosecution and afraid that Christ might go free, confronted Christ with the command 'Tell us if you are the Christ, the Son of God!' The trial had reached its climax. The tension brought a sudden, strained silence. Christ's answer meant life or death. Would Christ continue to remain silent, defying the High Priest, and possibly avoid all conviction except for contempt? Would He deny He was the Messiah and walk out a free – if humiliated – man, with His claims to being the Christ forever shot through? Would He try to avoid directly answering the question with evasive words? Or would His accusers have the satisfaction of being able to condemn Him to death?

Before most of the Council members had even managed to count His options, Christ broke the silence He had maintained from the start of the Trial, stunning the court with His reply. Christ not only said that He was the Son of God, but going further, He warned that they would see Him sitting on the right hand of Power and coming on the clouds of heaven. The court burst into instant uproar, demanding His death.

In Summary
The biggest difficulty for any Jew in accepting Jesus as the Messiah will always be the fact that His own nation rejected Him and handed Him over to their enemies to be crucified. How could someone ever believe in a Messiah whose own nation did not accept His claims? Matthew here provides the answer. We can believe that Jesus truly was the Messiah because all that happened was foretold by Him and, knowing all that would befall Him, He unflinchingly submitted to it. He showed by His foreknowledge and His strength of character that He was the Son of God.

There lies a lesson in this section for us, too, as His followers and disciples. Christ's disciples displayed four reactions to His rejection here.

• Firstly there was the false-disciple Judas, who showed which side he was really on when the pressure started to get to him. He valued Christ at only thirty pieces of silver.

• In contrast, there was the unnamed woman who showed her appreciation for Christ in sacrificing her costly perfume. Christ was going to sacrifice His very life for her. She in return was prepared to sacrifice the most precious and costliest possession she had for Him. Christ appreciated her sacrifice so much that He promised her deed would never be forgotten. Christ asks us too that His sacrifice be not forgotten. He asked us to remember Him in the breaking of the bread and the drinking of the cup.

• Thirdly, there was the main body of disciples who forsook Him and fled in His hour of trial and temptation. They with Peter – whose denial of

Christ was the fourth reaction here – were not prepared to suffer rejection with Him. Of course, the stakes seemed high, but they had not yet really understood what Christ's death was all about. Later, once they had come to understand and value Christ's death, they were willing to suffer and to die for His sake. Christ calls for us, too, in view of His death, to show our value and appreciation of it by living for Him, unashamed of His name.

Thus, this section of Matthew's Gospel is the perfect bridge between the previous prophetic section in Chapters 24 and 25 and the last section of the Gospel in Chapters 27 and 28. It is a separate section to them both. Christ makes very few prophetic pronouncements in the last section of the Gospel. Instead, His claim to be the Messiah, the Son of God, is put to its final and ultimate test.

Chapter 14 - Christ's Death and Resurrection: 27:1 - 28:20

1. Delivery to Pilate (27:1-2)

2. Judas' Hanging (27:3-10)

3. Christ's Trial before Pilate (27:11-26)

4. The Soldiers' Mockery (27:27-31)

5. The Crucifixion (27:32-44)

6. Christ's Cry (27:45-49)

7. Christ's Death (27:50-56)

8. Christ's Burial (27:57-61)

9. The Guard Set (27:62-66)

10. The Women meet the Risen Lord (28:1-10)

11. The Bribery of the Guards (28:11-15)

12. Christ Great Commission (28:16-20)

*M*atthew's Gospel is not written in the way that a modern writer would tell the life of Christ – by keeping us in suspense right up till the very last page of the book. There would have been no point in doing so. Most readers of Matthew's Gospel down through the ages would have known about Christ's death and resurrection before even starting to read Matthew's Gospel. Moreover, it would have been false reporting on Matthew's part if he had ignored Christ's numerous prophecies throughout the book about what lay ahead. Neither does Matthew's Gospel graphically describe the horror of Christ's sufferings in an attempt to satisfy those anticipating or wanting an emotional ending to the story of Christ's life. All Matthew says is simply, 'then they crucified Him' (27:35).

And so, readers of Matthew's Gospel might come to this last section fearing an anti-climax, not expecting much more than a round up of the events already anticipated. Matthew manages to confound our fears in brilliant fashion. Despite the fact that the events of Christ's death and resurrection come as no surprise, this last section of Matthew's Gospel still manages to outshine any other section of the Gospel. It is the climax of Matthew's Gospel, not in an emotional or dramatic sense, but in the way that Matthew shows us the importance and significance of Christ's death and resurrection. Here we have Matthew's Gospel's most important teachings about Christ's person and mission.

Christ's death and resurrection are the all-important events of His life. As Paul could say in his famous words in 1 Corinthians 15, 'Moreover, brethren, I declare to you the gospel which I preached to you, which also you received ... by which also you are saved, if you hold fast that word I preached to you ... For I delivered to in *the place of first importance* ... that Christ died for our sins according to the Scriptures, and that He was buried, and that He rose again the third day according to the Scriptures and that He was seen'. Our faith and our salvation rest upon the central truths of Christ's death and resurrection.

The great issues and questions concerning the life and death of Christ are brought to a conclusion so simple that the faith of a little child can grasp it, yet so satisfyingly complete that the greatest mind cannot but celebrate it. Matthew's Gospel's conclusion is so elegant in its literary execution that it stirs our heart and soul to glorify God not only for the greatness of the work of Christ but also for the way in which God has recorded it for us in His Word.

The Governor

Matthew commences this last stage of his gospel with a two-verse description of how the chief priests handed Christ over to Pilate. It seems more like a connecting piece than anything significant. However, these verses contain the seed to what is without doubt the most important point Matthew is making here at the finish of the Gospel – in fact, the main point of the entire Gospel.

Matthew refers to Pilate here as Pontius Pilate the Governor (27:2). This seems natural enough – this was his official title. However, as we continue reading through this section, Matthew's continued reference to Pilate as 'the Governor' becomes quite noticeable. All up, he refers to Pilate as 'the

Governor' nine times in the last two chapters (27:2, 11, 11, 14, 15, 21, 23, 27, 28:14). The fact that Mark, Luke and John do not refer to Pilate by the term at all in their parallel narratives helps to highlight the fact that there is quite a liberal use of the term by Matthew here.

The use of the term highlights the first of the two great ironies of this last section of Matthew's Gospel. Pilate, although he was the Governor – the one supposed to be in control – was a weakling. He knew Christ was innocent and he wanted to release Him. But he did not have the courage to do so. He firstly tried to get the crowds to choose to release Christ instead of Barabbas to relieve himself of the decision to release Christ. He did not want to have the Chief Priests accusing him to his superiors. He was not strong enough to stand up to the Jewish leaders and release Christ on his own. Then, when the crowds – persuaded by the Chief Priests – called for Christ to be crucified he was not strong enough to withstand them. Pilate was not much of a 'Governor'.

The final reference to him as 'the Governor' is most revealing. We read after the resurrection that the guards were bribed by the Chief Priests to say that the disciples stole the body away. Then they added, significantly 'And if this comes to the Governor's ears we will appease him and make you secure' (28:14). Pilate was putty in the fingers of the Chief Priests.

The King of the Jews

But for all the irony we see in the Governor Pilate's weakness, Christ in these first two verses appears to present an even more pathetic figure. In verse 2 we read 'and when they had bound Him (Jesus), they led Him away and delivered Him to Pontius Pilate the Governor'. Christ was tied up and marched off to Pilate. What a way for someone who had just claimed to be the Messiah, the King of the Jews, the Son of God, *the Great Governor* to be treated! Where was His power now? How ridiculous and absurd His claim seemed as He was brought bound before Pilate!

Pilate thought the idea that Jesus was claiming to be the Messiah, the King of the Jews, was ridiculous. Pilate smelled a rat when the Jews came to him offering to help get rid of a potential revolutionary deliverer of the nation. Did they not themselves want to be delivered? He could see for himself that Christ posed no military or political threat. He knew the Jews were trying to get rid of Him for envy (27:18). And so he proposed to ask the prisoner the simple question of whether He was indeed claiming to be the King of the Jews. He saw in this a possible way of releasing an innocent man. The Jews had accused Jesus of claiming to be King of the Jews. Pilate could not imagine that the man would continue with the absurd idea when faced with death. He suspected the prisoner had been framed and would immediately deny any intention of becoming King. Christ's reply, affirming that He was the King of the Jews (27:11), stunned Pilate. But just the fact that Pilate asked the question shows how ridiculous Pilate thought the idea of Jesus being the Messiah, the King of the Jews, was.

The soldiers of the governor, having witnessed what seemed to them the perverse and stubborn absurdity of Christ's claim to be the King of the Jews – and in spite of the fact that we might have expected them to feel some sympathy for an innocent man – mocked Jesus mercilessly. What humiliation for a Messiah! They stripped Him and gave Him a scarlet robe, crowned Him with thorns, gave Him a reed for a sceptre, bowed down to Him and hailed Him 'King of the Jews' before spitting on Him and striking Him with the reed.

Even at His crucifixion, Roman exasperation with Christ's non-co-operation in their attempts to save Him – and exasperation with the whole Jewish nation – was vented and revenged in the title 'King of the Jews' put up over His head. No doubt they meant by this that such an intolerable and disagreeable nation as the Jews deserved so pathetic a King and that this 'King' in turn rightly deserved such an inglorious end.

And of course, the Jews, not to be distracted or shamed by Roman criticism of their race, mocked Christ's claim to be Messiah as He hung upon the cross: 'If He is the King of Israel, let Him now come down from the cross and we will believe Him' (27:42).

The Ultimate Test

Christ truly seemed to cut a poor picture of a Messiah. It is therefore in His death that the question of whether Jesus really was the Messiah or not comes into sharpest focus. He was bound, mocked, humiliated, scourged, beaten and led out of the city to die – crucified. A crucified Messiah must have seemed an oxymoron – a contradiction in terms – to a Jew. As Paul put in 1 Corinthians 1:23: 'we preach Christ crucified, to the Jews a stumbling block'.

Yet it is here in Christ's death and resurrection that Christ put the matter beyond doubt. It is here when Christ was put to the ultimate test that He gave the absolute and final answer to the question of who He was. We see the evidence that Jesus was indeed the Messiah, the Son of God, the One in control of all things, the Great King and Universal Governor the whole way through this section.

For example, even at His trial Christ showed such self-control that Pilate marveled as Christ answered nothing to the accusations of the Chief Priests and elders (27:12-14). Here was a man who did not defend Himself against life-threatening charges. Here was One who in His oppression did not open His mouth in protest, even as His very life was taken from Him.

His powerful dying cry was proof, too, of who He was. Men nearing their death upon a cross did not have the strength to make much noise. They hardly had enough strength to breathe. Here was someone with supernatural power. The earthquake that accompanied His death so astonished the Roman Centurion on guard that he said, 'Truly this was the Son of God!'

But these displays of power were just previews of the power that was to be displayed at His resurrection. It was in allowing Himself to be brought into death's strong grip that it was possible for Christ to show how great His strength truly was. It was in overcoming the greatest of natural forces and laws – the irreversibility of death – that Christ showed that He was its Master.

Christ's resurrection is proved here by the convergence of three main lines of evidence:

1. The burial of His body proved the reality of His death. Why would *friends* have buried Him if they still detected signs of life?

2. The precautions that the *Jews* took to secure the tomb proved that it was not later tampered with, either by the disciples or by the Jews themselves.

3. The empty tomb and Christ's appearances proved His bodily resurrection – the women *held* Him by the feet as they worshipped Him.

The bribery of the guards and the attempt to circulate the story that the disciples had stolen the body while the guards slept shows firstly the characteristic corruption and lack of integrity of all those who seek to deny the fact of the Resurrection. Why would Christ's enemies have needed to turn to bribery or later reach for their swords if there was some evidence they could have produced to disprove Christ's resurrection? Secondly, the bribery of the guards and the attempt to circulate the story that the disciples stole the body shows the stubborn irrationality of those who attempt to provide alternative versions of events. How did the guards know what happened if they were sleeping? Skeptics still have not advanced any less stupid alternative explanation of the Resurrection and they willingly prefer to clutch at any such straw arguments rather than accept the fact of the resurrection.

Christ not only showed His power over Death, but also showed His power over His enemies in their attempts to keep His body in the tomb and the news of His resurrection from spreading. He had already sent the women on their way with the first reports of His resurrection before the Council had convened to consider the extraordinary report of the guards and bribed them to go out with their different version of events. In fact, the very actions of Christ's enemies in organising the guard to **protect** the tomb from any human tampering could not have provided more satisfactory proof of the fact that Christ did indeed rise. It is almost as if Christ orchestrated their unbelieving opposition so as to cut off any alternative explanation of grave robbery. Christ was indeed the One controlling events here.

Matthew's Gospel commenced with the prophecy 'But you Bethlehem, in the land of Judah, are not the least among the rulers (literally, 'governors') of Judah, for out of you shall come a Ruler (literally, 'Governor') who shall shepherd my people Israel'. In His resurrection power Christ showed that He was that prophesied Governor who was to come, assuring His disciples 'All authority has been given to Me in Heaven and on earth' (28:18).

Here is the great question of the Gospel settled. Jesus is the Christ, the Messiah, the Son of God. Pilate might have been the Governor here in name, if nothing more, but it was really Christ who, even in the ultimate test of death, showed who Governs.

Christ's Innocence

Matthew threads a second theme through these last two chapters of his Gospel – a theme hardly any less important than the question of who Christ was. It is the moral theme again. Matthew forces us to examine Christ's innocence.

The second part of this final section deals with Judas' hanging in 27:3-10. Matthew deliberately interrupts the narrative of Christ's trial, interposing Judas' hanging in the middle of it. The reason Matthew allows this incident to interrupt the narrative is because it focuses on Christ's innocence, in exactly the same way as the trial narrative does.

Judas brought back his blood-money in 27:3-4 saying, 'I have sinned by betraying *innocent* blood.' The word 'innocent' here is found again at the end of Christ's trial in verse 24, where Pilate, washing his hands, attests Christ's innocence saying, 'I am *innocent* of the blood of this *just* person.' The fact that Christ was innocent and righteous is repeatedly brought out during the trial narrative. Matthew alone of the gospel writers tells us about Pilate's wife's interruption in 27:19 when she sent word to him, 'Have nothing to do with that *just* man, for I have suffered many things today in a dream because of Him.' Again Pilate in verse 23, stunned at the crowds' request for Barabbas to be released and for Christ to be crucified, indignantly asked, 'Why what evil has he done?'

Christ's innocence is the central issue of His trial, and it is also the central issue of His crucifixion. His enemies not only taunted His claim to be the Messiah as He hung upon the cross. They also significantly challenged His innocence. They said, 'He trusted in God; let Him deliver Him now – if He will have Him; for He said, I am the Son of God' (27:43). The challenge they threw at Christ was that if He were sinless and God was well pleased with His life, why would God now allow Him to die? Matthew challenges us as readers to think about this question too. It is the great mystery of the Cross, summed up in Christ's cry in 27:46, 'My God, My God, why have You forsaken me?'

The Great Mystery of the Cross

Here we have the central mystery of the whole Gospel. It is mystery enough for the Messiah to have been rejected by His own people – in spite of His teachings, His miracles and His perfect life and character. But how could it be that God could forsake the Messiah He had long promised and prophesied would come? Surely here is the great and final test of whether He was God's Messiah and Son. Here, said His enemies as He hung from the cross, was the final proof that He was not the Messiah nor the Son of God.

The Jews counted Christ a deceiver, a sinner and a blasphemer and therefore to them it was not surprising that God turned a deaf ear to Christ's cry for salvation. But Matthew has gone to a lot of trouble to prove that Christ was just and holy. Judas hanged himself in remorse for his part in Christ's condemnation and Pilate refused to be associated with such an injustice as His death amounted to. Even here in Christ's great cry from the Cross we see His sinlessness. He was still praying to God after six hours upon the cross. He was quoting Scripture when He cried, 'My God, My God, why have You forsaken Me?' He was no unbeliever. His trust was still in God – He called God 'My God'. He affirmed that He had not forsaken God – rather God had forsaken Him.

Neither is the reason for God's silence to be attributed to God being aloof, as the Deist or agnostic might argue. The supernatural events attending Christ's death scotch this suggestion: three hours of darkness at noonday and an earthquake when Christ died. Had God then forsaken His principles of justice and faithfulness? God forbid! How was it then that God's Son and long-prophesied Messiah who perfectly obeyed, faithfully served and fully pleased God upon earth throughout His life – the only man to ever do so – was forsaken by God in His hour of great need? What a mystery!

Christ in His great cry from the Cross left us with the mystery to ponder. But I suggest that Christ was in no way puzzled by God forsaking Him. He was hurt more deeply by this than anything else. But His cry was not an expression of disappointment in God or a doubting of God. The words themselves show that He still called God 'My God'. Rather, in quoting the first line of Psalm 22 Christ invites us to complete the quotation and comprehend the mystery of His death. Psalm 22 reads 'My God, My God, why have You forsaken Me? Why are You so far from helping Me, and from the words of My groaning? O My God, I cry in the daytime, but You do not hear; and in the night season, and am not silent. But *You are Holy*, enthroned in the praises of Israel'. God's holiness was the reason for God's silence – God's hatred of sin! But how could this be? Matthew has already carefully shown Christ's sinlessness. The answer is that it was *our* sin that kept God from helping His Beloved Son.

Earlier in the Gospel Christ had explained what was going to happen. In Matthew 20:28 He said, 'The Son of Man did not come to be served, but to serve, and to give His life a ransom for many.' He said in 26:28, 'This is My blood of the new covenant which is shed for many for the forgiveness of sins.' The later writings of the New Testament further help to explain it. Perhaps Peter explains it best in 1 Peter 2:24, 'Who Himself bore *our* sins in His own body on the tree' and in 1 Peter 3:18, 'For Christ also suffered once for sins, *the just for the unjust*, that He might bring us to God'.

Perhaps the circumstances surrounding His death here in Matthew's Gospel help to illuminate what happened. Notice firstly that the great dividing veil in the Temple was torn in two when Christ died (27:51). This veil, we are told later in the New Testament, symbolised a barrier between God and man because of human sin (Hebrews 9:6-8). The veil kept men out of the ***Holiest*** Place, the place of God's presence. God, being holy, is separate from us humans in our sinfulness. Yet Christ's death tore this veil from top to bottom. Hebrews 10:19-20 provides the Divine commentary: 'Therefore, brethren, having boldness to enter the Holiest by the blood of Jesus, by a New and Living Way which He has consecrated for us through the veil'. This verse is teaching that Christ's blood, that is, His death, has made a way through the veil into the Holiest. Christ has by His death made a way for us to 'come to God through Him' (Hebrews 7:25). Christ's sinless death was for our salvation.

Christ's resurrection also broke the power of Death. Death is one of our greatest enemies – who does not fear it? Yet Christ has conquered Death for us. God demonstrated this by raising to life many of the Old Testament saints after Christ's resurrection (27:52-53). Christ's resurrection thus prepared the way for our resurrection. Christ's death brings us life.

Conclusion

Matthew's Gospel thus concludes with the great climax of Christ's life, showing who He is in such a way that there is no real room for sincere objection any more. We find out why Christ came and why Christ died.

Matthew's concluding section leaves us with three responsibilities. Firstly, we must believe. If the man on the spot, the Centurion presiding over Christ's crucifixion, could exclaim 'Truly this was the Son of God' in 27:54 after witnessing the supernatural events at Christ's death, what can we do but follow his example? Then secondly, Christ's death and resurrection must call forth our worship, just as it did from the women outside the tomb and the eleven disciples who gathered to Christ in Galilee (28:9&17).

But that is not all. Christ has also left us His Great Commission to fulfil. The whole world must be told. Christ's own words conclude the Gospel. 'All authority has been given to me in Heaven and on earth. Go therefore and make disciples of all the nations, baptising them in the name of the Father and of the Son and of the Holy Spirit, teaching them to observe all things that I have commanded you, and lo, I am with you always, even to the end of the age.'

Appendix: Matthew's Messianic Prophecies

*M*atthew's use of the Old Testament is extremely advanced. We will look at three quotes here (see two other prophecies dealt with on pp. 19, 101).

1. Matthew 2:15 – *'Out of Egypt I called My Son'*
(from Hosea 11:1)

If we look in Hosea 11 we see that God is talking about the nation of Israel when he says, 'Out of Egypt I called my Son.' The next few verses go on to speak about Israel's idolatry and rebellion in spite of God's deliverance of them. How then can Matthew pull these words out of context and apply them to Christ as a prophecy that He too would come out of Egypt? The answer is seen when we observe the many parallels between Christ's life and Israel's history.

Christ and Israel nationally both (1) are called 'My Son', (2) had a miraculous beginning (Christ's birth, Isaac's birth), (3) had an Egyptian sojourn, (4) escaped from slaughter of infants (by Pharaoh, Herod), (5) were baptised (Red Sea, Jordan), (6) had wilderness testing (40 years, 40 days), and (7) shared the giving of Law (Sinai, Sermon on Mount). Some of these parallels are perhaps dubious, but some are striking. It seems that Israel's history was a fore-shadowing of Christ's life. Perhaps this was because it was necessary for Christ, in 'being made like His brethren' (Hebrews 2:17-18) to fully identify with Israel (and humanity in general) by going through their experiences and sufferings. Maybe Hosea's words in context are not strictly a specific prophecy about Christ, but rather a **Prophetic Parallel**. Christ's life pathway was in a sense prophetically marked out beforehand to a degree in Israel's history. Matthew therefore lifts Hosea's words out of their context to highlight this connection.

2. Matthew 2:23 – *'He shall be called a Nazarene'*
(from 'the prophets')

This is one of the most puzzling verses in the Bible. There is no verse in the OT that says that the Messiah had to come from Nazareth. However, again Matthew is not giving us a strict 'prophecy' here. What Matthew is doing here is combining prophecy, a play on words and irony all in one incredible verse. First of all, Matthew uses a brilliant word-play in the Greek, far better than Shakespeare's best pun. 'Nazarene' ('Nazoraios') sounds like the OT word 'Nazirite' ('Naziraios', Judges 16:17, LXXA), someone who separated himself to God. However, the Hebrew word Nazirite ('Nazir') also had a double meaning. It also meant 'Prince' (see Gen. 49:26, Lam. 4:7, NIV). Now whilst there is no prophecy that the Messiah would be a Nazirite, there are numerous prophecies of Messiah as *the Prince*. Admittedly, none use the word 'Nazir', but one of the other common Hebrew words for Prince is the similar sounding 'Nasih' which is perhaps a third word-play here. Ezekiel 34:24 and 37:25 are just two of a number of prophecies of Messiah as the Prince ('Nasih').

What Matthew is doing here is using a heavy dose of irony. 'Nazarene/s' was an early contemptuous nickname of Christ/ians because the town had such a bad reputation (Acts 24:5). If it was ironical that the town Nazareth should sound like the very opposite word Nazirite, then how amazing that God should call His *Holy* Son, Messiah *the Prince*, to live in that dirty, disreputable place! But, how fitting philologically (Matthew answers the name-callers) that it was so!

3. Matthew 27:9-10 – *the thirty pieces of silver being given for the potter's field*
Here Matthew quotes Zechariah but attributes the quote to Jeremiah! What a blunder, say the sceptics. But Matthew has not made a mistake here. Notice firstly that Matthew 27:9-10 is an exceedingly free quote of Zechariah 11:12-13. Matthew has even added a rather important detail to Zechariah's quote: *the field*. Zechariah mentioned nothing about a field. Where did Matthew get that bit? Matthew himself tells us: from what *Jeremiah* spoke. Matthew is alluding to Jeremiah 32. There, when Jeremiah was in prison, knowing Judah was just about

to be conquered by the Babylonians, he bought a field. It seemed a poor decision commercially, but God told him to buy the land as a token of the fact that God would one day bring the Jews back to enjoy their land. Matthew directs us to Jeremiah to see the significance of what happened when the chief priests bought a field with the money that Judas threw back at them.

Notice the parallels with Christ. Not only do we see the fulfilment of the prophecy from Zechariah about Christ being valued at such a low price. The story of the money does not end there. Just as in Jeremiah's day, a field was bought. That field was bought with the price of blood (Mt 27:6), the Messiah's own blood-money. That field, the Messiah's only earthly possession, is a deposit and token of the fact that He will return as King and 'the uttermost parts of the earth' will be His.